PRAISE FOR

RUN
THE
STORM

"A fact-filled, exciting tale of a ship's tragic final voyage."

—*Kirkus Reviews*

"With just the right pedigree to tell this familiar story . . . Foy connects the detail with the domino each represented in causing one of the nation's deadliest maritime disasters."

—*The Florida Times-Union*

"Foy does the best job. He tells the story briskly and confidently while working in helpful asides: how cargo containers are fastened to a ship deck, how forecasts are determined, how huge ships stay upright (and how they don't). *Run the Storm* . . . gracefully covers everything you'd want to know about *El Faro*'s sinking and the thirty-three lives that went with it."

—*Outside*

"There will presumably be dozens of thrillers and horror novels published this year that will not have the sheer and frightening strength of Foy's words. They're Conrad by way of James Lee Burke, Melville through the prism of Márquez."

—*The New London Day*

"*Run the Storm* is a dramatic, thrilling adventure story, as well as a cautionary tale about the dangers of going to sea—even today, in our age of satellite communications and real-time weather forecasting. George Foy uses the surviving audio tapes of the crew's final hours on the doomed ship to chilling effect, and he convincingly shows how a series of seemingly unrelated errors and omissions metastasized into a full-scale disaster. A remarkable book."

—William Geroux, author of *The Mathews Men*

ALSO BY GEORGE MICHELSEN FOY

Finding North: How Navigation Makes Us Human

Zero Decibels: The Quest for Absolute Silence

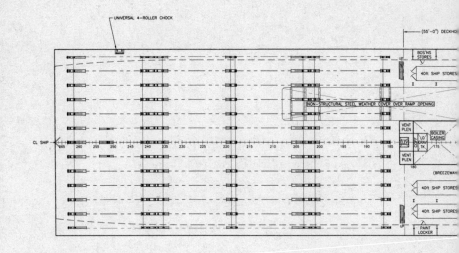

UNIVERSAL 4-ROLLER CHOCK

(55'-0") DECKHO

BOS'NS STORES

40ft SHIP STORES

NON-STRUCTURAL STEEL WEATHER COVER OVER RAMP OPENING

VENT PLEN

LO GRAV TK

BOILER CASING

CL SHIP

ELEV

VENT PLEN

(BREEZEWAY)

40ft SHIP STORES

40ft SHIP STORES

PAINT LOCKER

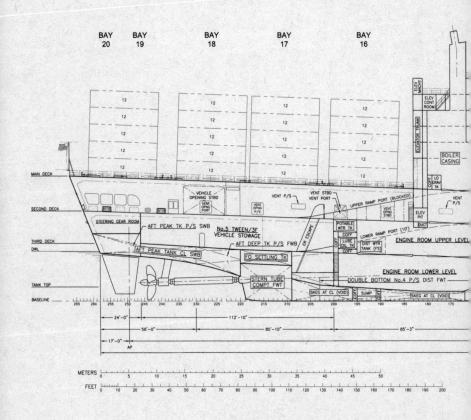

| BAY 20 | BAY 19 | BAY 18 | BAY 17 | BAY 16 |

ELEV MACHY

ELEV CONT ROOM

BOILER CASING

MAIN DECK

12 12 12 12 12

SECOND DECK

VEHICLE OPENING STBD
VENT OPNG PORT

VENT OPNG P/S

VENT P/S

VENT STBD VENT PORT

UPPER RAMP PORT (BLOCKED)

VENT OPNG STBD

ELEV PIT

DUCT

VENT P/S

STEERING GEAR ROOM

AFT PEAK TK P/S SWB

No.5 TWEEN/3F VEHICLE STOWAGE

ER ESCAPE

POTABLE WTR TK

COFF

LOWER RAMP PORT (10')

DIST WTR TANK (F5)

ENGINE ROOM UPPER LEVEL

THIRD DECK

DWL

AFT PEAK TANK CL SWB

AFT DEEP TK P/S FWD

FO SETTLING TK

COFF

LUBE OIL TK

COFF

TANK TOP

STERN TUBE COMPT FWD

ENGINE ROOM LOWER LEVEL

DOUBLE BOTTOM No.4 P/S DIST FWT

BASELINE

SKEG AT CL (VOID)

SUMP

SKEG AT CL (VOID)

24'-0"   112'-10"

56'-0"   80'-10"   85'-3"

17'-0"

AP

METERS 0   5   10   15   20   25   30   35   40   45   50

FEET 0 10 20 30 40 50 60 70 80 90 100 110 120 130 140 150 160 170 180 190 200

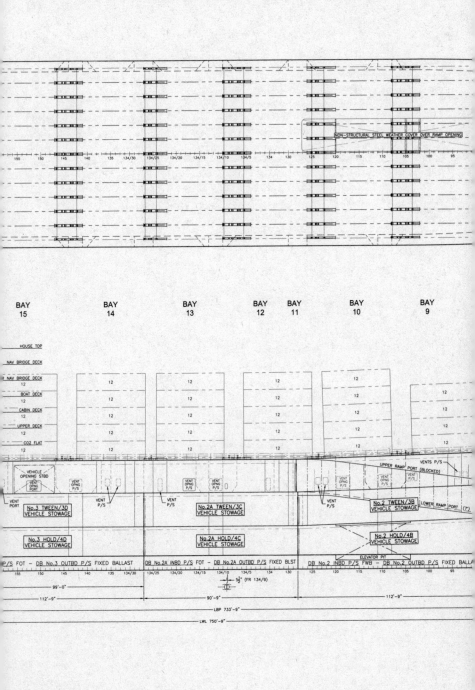

NON-STRUCTURAL STEEL WEATHER COVER OVER RAMP OPENING

155 150 145 140 135 134/30 134/25 134/20 134/15 134/10 134/5 134 130 125 120 115 110 105 100 95

BAY 15   BAY 14   BAY 13   BAY 12   BAY 11   BAY 10   BAY 9

HOUSE TOP

NAV BRIDGE DECK

NAV BRIDGE DECK

BOAT DECK

CABIN DECK

UPPER DECK

CO2 FLAT

12 (across: 12 12 12 12 12 ... 12)

VENTS P/S

UPPER RAMP PORT (BLOCKED)

VEHICLE OPENING STBD

VENT OPNG PORT

VENT OPNG P/S

VENT OPNG P/S

VENT OPNG P/S

VENT OPNG P/S

VENT P/S

VENT PORT

VENT P/S

VENT P/S

VENT P/S

No.3 TWEEN/3D VEHICLE STOWAGE

No.2A TWEEN/3C VEHICLE STOWAGE

No.2 TWEEN/3B VEHICLE STOWAGE

LOWER RAMP PORT (?)

No.3 HOLD/4D VEHICLE STOWAGE

No.2A HOLD/4C VEHICLE STOWAGE

No.2 HOLD/4B VEHICLE STOWAGE

ELEVATOR PIT

P/S FOT – DB No.3 OUTBD P/S FIXED BALLAST

DB No.2A INBD P/S FOT – DB No.2A OUTBD P/S FIXED BLST

DB No.2 INBD P/S FWB – DB No.2 OUTBD P/S FIXED BALL

155 150 145 140 135 134/30 134/25 134/20 134/15 134/10 134 130 125 120 115 110 105 100 95

99'-0" — 90'-9" — 112'-9"

112'-9" — 5½' (FR 134/9)

LBP 733'-9"

LWL 750'-9"

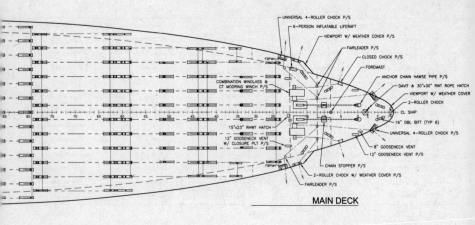

MAIN DECK

Labels (top to bottom, right side):
- UNIVERSAL 4-ROLLER CHOCK P/S
- 6-PERSON INFLATABLE LIFERAFT
- VIEWPORT W/ WEATHER COVER P/S
- FAIRLEADER P/S
- CLOSED CHOCK P/S
- FOREMAST
- ANCHOR CHAIN HAWSE PIPE P/S
- DAVIT & 30"x30" RWT ROPE HATCH
- VIEWPORT W/ WEATHER COVER P/S
- 2-ROLLER CHOCK
- CL SHIP
- 16" DBL BITT (TYP 6)
- UNIVERSAL 4-ROLLER CHOCK P/S
- 8" GOOSENECK VENT
- 12" GOOSENECK VENT P/S

Left labels:
- COMBINATION WINDLASS & CT MOORING WINCH P/S
- 15"x23" RHWT HATCH
- 12" GOOSENECK VENT W/ CLOSURE PLT P/S
- FBPWK
- CHAIN STOPPER P/S
- 2-ROLLER CHOCK W/ WEATHER COVER P/S
- FAIRLEADER P/S

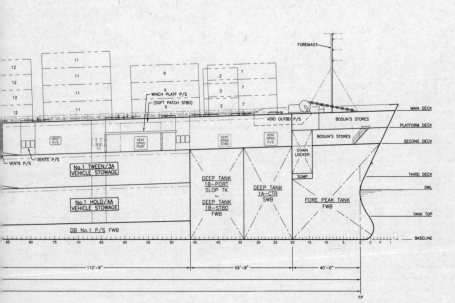

BAY 7	BAY 6	BAY 5	BAY 4	BAY 3	BAY 2	BAY 1

- FOREMAST
- 11
- 12
- 9
- 2
- 7
- WINCH PLATF P/S
- (SOFT PATCH STBD)
- VOID OUTBD P/S
- BOSUN'S STORES
- MAIN DECK
- VENT P/S
- VENT OPNG PORT
- VENT OPNG STBD
- VENT OPNG P/S
- BOSUN'S STORES
- PLATFORM DECK
- SECOND DECK
- VENTS P/S
- CHAIN LOCKER
- THIRD DECK
- No.1 TWEEN/3A VEHICLE STOWAGE
- DEEP TANK 1B-PORT SLOP TK
- DEEP TANK 1A-CTR SWB
- DWL
- SUMP
- No.1 HOLD/4A VEHICLE STOWAGE
- DEEP TANK 1B-STBD FWB
- FORE PEAK TANK FWB
- TANK TOP
- DB No.1 P/S FWB
- BASELINE
- 112'-9"
- 59'-8"
- 40'-0"
- FP

INBOARD PROFILE

RUN
THE
STORM

A SAVAGE HURRICANE, A BRAVE CREW,

AND THE WRECK OF THE SS *EL FARO*

GEORGE
MICHELSEN
FOY

SCRIBNER
NEW YORK LONDON TORONTO SYDNEY NEW DELHI

Scribner
An Imprint of Simon & Schuster, Inc.
1230 Avenue of the Americas
New York, NY 10020

First Scribner trade paperback edition August 2019

SCRIBNER and design are registered trademarks of The Gale Group, Inc.,
used under license by Simon & Schuster, Inc., the publisher of this work.

For information about special discounts for bulk purchases,
please contact Simon & Schuster Special Sales at 1-866-506-1949
or business@simonandschuster.com.

The Simon & Schuster Speakers Bureau can bring authors to your live event.
For more information or to book an event, contact the Simon & Schuster Speakers
Bureau at 1-866-248-3049 or visit our website at www.simonspeakers.com.

Interior design by Kyle Kabel

Manufactured in the United States of America

1   3   5   7   9   10   8   6   4   2

Library of Congress Cataloging-in-Publication Data is available.

ISBN 978-1-5011-8489-5
ISBN 978-1-5011-8490-1 (pbk)
ISBN 978-1-5011-8491-8 (ebook)

PHOTO CREDITS
pp. viii–x: United States Coast Guard; p. xiv: NASA/NOAA GOES Project;
p. 2: Tote; pp. xvi, 16, 52, 88, 140, 146, 181, 190, 192, 220, 244, 246:
National Transportation Safety Board

This book is dedicated to the courageous, steadfast, and skilled men and women of *El Faro*, and to the families and friends of *El Faro*'s crew who have honored their memory with grace and fortitude. And to the unsung heroes of the American merchant marine, who work hard, lonely hours, day in, day out—in conditions that are usually unrecognized, often uncomfortable, and sometimes perilous—to supply their country with 90 percent of everything.

Deadly vortex: Hurricane Joaquin on October 1, 2015. The eye is just visible in the middle of the storm's swirl; *El Faro*'s last known position at 7:30 a.m. was almost exactly in the same place.

I came to explore the wreck.
The words are purposes.
The words are maps.
I came to see the damage that was done
and the treasures that prevail.

—Adrienne Rich,
"Diving into the Wreck"

He said to run it. Hold on to your ass, Larry.

—Danielle Randolph,
second mate of the SS *El Faro*

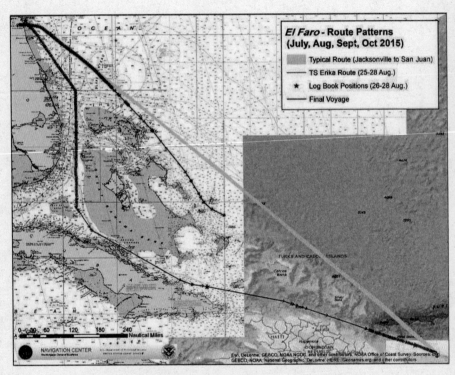

The road not taken: The straight line represents *El Faro*'s usual, direct route from Jacksonville to San Juan. The dotted line below it shows her final journey. The curved line to the west marks the route via Old Bahama Channel that she took to avoid Tropical Storm Erika, in late August 2015.

CONTENTS

CREW OF THE SS *EL FARO*

DECK DEPARTMENT

 Michael C. Davidson, 53, captain: Windham, Maine

 Steven W. Shultz, 54, chief mate: Roan Mountain, Tennessee

 Danielle L. Randolph, 34, second mate: Rockland, Maine

 Jeremie H. Riehm, 46, third mate: Camden, Delaware

 Roan R. Lightfoot, 54, bosun: Jacksonville Beach, Florida

 Roosevelt L. "Bootsy" Clark, 38, deckhand: Jacksonville, Florida

 Larry "Brookie" Davis, 63, able seaman: Jacksonville, Florida

 Frank J. Hamm III, 49, able seaman: Jacksonville, Florida

 Carey J. Hatch, 49, able seaman: Jacksonville, Florida

 Jack E. Jackson, 60, able seaman: Jacksonville, Florida

 Jackie R. "Pop" Jones Jr., 38, able seaman: Jacksonville, Florida

 James P. Porter, 40, deckhand: Jacksonville, Florida

 Mariette Wright, 51, deckhand: Saint Augustine, Florida

ENGINE DEPARTMENT

 Richard J. Pusatere, 34, chief engineer: Virginia Beach, Virginia

 Jeffrey A. Mathias, 42, riding crew supervisor: Kingston, Massachusetts

 Keith W. Griffin, 33, first engineer: Fort Myers, Florida

 Howard J. Schoenly, 51, second engineer: Cape Coral, Florida

 Michael L. Holland, 25, third engineer: North Wilton, Maine

 Mitchell T. Kuflik, 26, third engineer: Brooklyn, New York

 Dylan O. Meklin, 23, third assistant engineer: Rockland, Maine

 Louis M. Champa, 51, electrician: Daytona Beach, Florida

 Joe E. Hargrove, 65, oiler: Orange Park, Florida

 German A. Solar-Cortes, 51, oiler: Orlando, Florida

 Anthony "Shawn" Thomas, 47, oiler: Jacksonville, Florida

 Sylvester C. Crawford Jr., 40, wiper: Lawrenceville, Georgia

STEWARDS DEPARTMENT

Lashawn L. Rivera,
32, chief cook:
Jacksonville, Florida

Theodore E. Quammie,
67, chief steward:
Jacksonville, Florida

Lonnie S. Jordan,
35, assistant steward:
Jacksonville, Florida

RIDING GANG

Piotr M. Krause,
27: Gdynia, Poland

Marcin P. Nita,
34: Poland

Jan P. Podgórski,
43: Poland

Andrzej R. Truszkowski,
51: Poland

Rafal A. Zdobych,
42: Poland

AUTHOR'S NOTE

Run the Storm is a work of nonfiction. The author has drawn on thousands of pages of documentation from three separate hearings and separate working groups conducted by the US Coast Guard and the federal National Transportation Safety Board to solve the mystery of what happened to *El Faro*. The hearings, conducted by maritime experts, called scores of witnesses and were followed by months of painstaking analysis. The author has supplemented the record with dozens of interviews with family members, former officers and crew, search-and-rescue personnel, government officials and spokespersons, independent mariners, meteorologists, and others.

This book also draws heavily on the twenty-six consecutive hours of bridge conversation and other data recovered from the vessel's black box, or voyage data recorder. The drama of hearing the actual voices affords a unique, if emotionally difficult, opportunity to understand firsthand what *El Faro*'s crew were thinking and doing as they sailed into the wrath of Hurricane Joaquin. The conversations used are all direct quotes; they have been edited only for coherence and to avoid repetition, and occasionally to restore some government-redacted salty language used by the crew. In all cases the guiding principle was to remain faithful to meaning and context.

Most important, this fact remains: there are no witnesses to recount exactly what happened to *El Faro* as she went into the storm. The VDR gives us a tremendously useful and accurate tool to track decisions and anxiety levels on the bridge, so when an action is clearly implied by both a conversation and the overall likelihood of its taking place—such as when a navigating officer points out course details, implying that he or she is looking at a chart—that action is described accordingly.

Except in instances when both sides of a phone or radio dialogue could be heard, conversations in the rest of the ship went unrecorded, and so description of what happened in, say, the galley or engine room must be based on guesswork. But any ship relies on solid, recurrent routines to function, and a ship on "liner" service, as *El Faro* was, making exactly the same passage, week in, week out, year in, year out, enjoys more fixed routines than most. The mariners standing an 8:00 a.m. to noon watch, for example, always woke well before eight to eat breakfast; they always reported to the bridge, or the engine-room control flat, fifteen minutes before their watch started, as is the custom on shipboard. The watch rosters and schedules on *El Faro* were well-known and apparently adhered to rigidly on all her voyages. The VDR transcript in almost every instance indicates that crew members and officers stuck by those routines exactly, and while the author is careful to indicate that unrecorded events are presumed, rather than certain, he has faithfully described unrecorded actions of the crew based on what they would normally have done aboard *El Faro* on the southbound leg of her journey.

RUN
THE
STORM

Ready for sea: *El Faro* on a previous voyage. The open ports on 2nd Deck are clearly visible along the hull's side. On her last voyage, containers were stacked four-deep across almost the entire ship.

PART I

THE SILENCE

A ship is safe in harbor, but that is not what ships are built for.

—John Augustus Shedd

Toward the end of the 4:00 a.m. to 8:00 a.m. watch, on the morning of October 1, 2015, the image of his friend Larry came to Kurt Bruer's mind.

Bruer is a five-foot-eleven-inch forty-year-old, of solid build, firm jaw, and an expression, when he's not wearing sunglasses, that reads both confident and wary. That morning, as an able seaman, or AB in the parlance—an experienced deckhand in the American merchant marine—he was standing watch on the bow of the *Texas Enterprise*, making sure no traffic got too near his cargo ship, full of bulk-loaded grain, anchored in the flat early-morning light-field of the Mississippi River.

Bruer's friend Brookie Davis, known as Larry, was much older. That morning he was AB on a different vessel, the SS *El Faro*, a giant cargo ship working a bi-weekly shuttle run between north Florida and Puerto Rico. Despite the difference in age Bruer and Davis were as close as mariners got. Bruer had worked for a year on *El Faro* and on that ship he ate with Davis at mealtimes; sometimes they hung out in the crew's lounge or talked shop when working overtime together. In Jacksonville, where both lived, the two would occasionally meet for a beer, or for a few hands of poker at bestbet, one of the clubs south of the Dames Point Bridge over the Saint Johns River, close to where *El Faro* docked. They had not seen as much of each other recently; Bruer had left *El Faro* the previous year, and his wife and one-year-old son now took up most of his time ashore.

So seeing Davis's image pop into his mind that Thursday morning surprised Bruer. "On watch I don't think about other sailors," he said later, with a frown that might be construed as distaste. "I never thought about Larry. I think about my family, or what I'm going to do next."

This thought of his friend was not only unexpected; it seemed, as an image, unusually strong, vivid. He would have to call Larry when he got off watch, Bruer told himself; just check in, see what was going on.

He never talked to Davis again.

Shortly after 7:39 a.m. on October 1, 2015—toward the end of the four-to-eight watch—*El Faro*, her crew of twenty-eight American mariners, and a five-man Polish engineering gang vanished from the face of the earth.

2

A particular silence forms when you are waiting for a message from a loved one whose whereabouts are unknown, of whose safety you are unsure.

It's a silence that alters the fabric of personal time; a silence in which minutes pass as slowly as hours, when even the unavoidable periods of tending to housekeeping details such as paying bills or picking up kids from school are stretched and wracked by an underlying wait—a wait that feels like a screaming in the very bone.

Such a silence began in the morning of October 1 for the families, coworkers, and friends of *El Faro*'s crew.

The owners and operators of *El Faro*, Sea Star and Tote Services Inc.—both referred to on the waterfront as Tote, part of a spiderweb of interlocking corporations and directorates owned by a single, privately held company in Seattle—were first to learn the ship was in trouble. *El Faro*'s captain, Michael Davidson, had talked to Tote's safety manager, John Lawrence, by satellite phone at 7:07 a.m. on October 1. The captain told Lawrence that the ship, at the time forty-eight miles southeast of San Salvador Island in the Bahamas chain, had taken on water, was tilting fifteen degrees to one side, and had lost power. But his crew were pumping out the water, Davidson said, and he had no intention of abandoning ship.

Davidson's voice was calm, his words measured, and Lawrence hung up feeling that *El Faro* was in no immediate peril, though as a matter of "protocol" he called the US Coast Guard Rescue Coordination Center in Norfolk, Virginia, to notify them of the incident.

At 7:15, however, the Coast Guard received an automated distress message via Inmarsat, an international marine satellite communications service, linked to *El Faro*'s name and identification code. At 7:36, a National Oceanic and Atmospheric Administration satellite picked up a signal from an emergency beacon registered to *El Faro*. NOAA's satellite center in Suitland, Maryland, contacted the Coast Guard in turn.

The signal, which lasted twenty-eight minutes, did not include the ship's position, and the brevity of the transmission, given that such beacons are built to keep signaling for at least twelve hours, worried Petty Officer Matthew Chancery, the officer on duty in Miami at the Coast Guard's search-and-rescue center for the Florida and Bahamas region. Together with the information Tote had relayed and the Inmarsat signal, the aborted message suggested *El Faro* might be in more serious trouble than Lawrence seemed to think. Still, based on Tote's information—the ship was "dewatering," the source of the flooding was secured, the company was hiring tugs—the Coast Guard officer in charge judged the ship was not in immediate danger and it was not yet time to go into "distress phase." Following normal procedure, the SAR center immediately began calling *El Faro* on the Inmarsat satellite communications system and requested that any ships or aircraft in the area do the same.

But from the ship herself, nothing. Not even a Mayday.

That serious trouble might be in the cards for a ship located near the Bahamas on this particular morning should have surprised no one, because of Joaquin. Joaquin was a hurricane, and an unusual one; a meteorological freak that had sidled toward the Americas from an area of the Atlantic far north of the usual breeding ground of such storms. Through the waning days of September this freak had seemed unsure of its identity, appearing to hesitate, in the form, first, of a tropical low-pressure zone, and then as a medium-powered gale, without picking up the intensity and defined shape of the mind-bogglingly powerful and self-sustaining machine that is a full-bore hurricane. As a result, various computerized forecast models, including that of the US National Weather Service, had underestimated its potential strength and to a somewhat lesser extent misread its direction. The consensus view of Joaquin therefore, until the day before *El Faro* sent her messages, was dismissive; like the neighbors' opinion of an erratic, troublesome child nevertheless deemed unlikely to grow up into a vicious criminal.

That was also the prevailing view at Tote. Only a month earlier, on August 27, the company had sent Captain Davidson a heads-up email asking what precautions he was taking to avoid Erika, the previous storm that had threatened to disrupt the company's Jacksonville to San Juan service. Tote's safety office also sent a flurry of emails recommending precautions to take against Danny, the hurricane that had preceded Erika a week earlier. But there had been no messages and apparently little concern about Joaquin before the morning *El Faro* went missing. No one at Tote Services' Jacksonville offices, or Tote Inc.'s corporate seat in Princeton, New Jersey, much less at the holding company's headquarters in Seattle, was carefully tracking Joaquin's route, or noting its proximity to *El Faro*'s. No one among those who knew and cared for *El Faro* realized that the troublesome, wayward delinquent that Joaquin once seemed had grown up, with exceptional speed and horrific energy, into the meteorological equivalent of a monster, a serial killer whose apparent drive to pursue and destroy *El Faro* caused not a few to endow the storm with psychotic intent. Indeed, over the night of September 30, Joaquin had swelled to Category 3 on the Saffir-Simpson scale; a status the National Hurricane Center labels a major storm causing "devastating damage," with thirty-foot waves and winds of up to 129 mph. Around the time *El Faro* disappeared, Joaquin became a Category 4, with sustained winds over 130 mph, gusts approaching 150, and waves closer to fifty feet—the most powerful storm to hit the area in recorded history.

Petty Officer Chancery's worry shot up by several orders of magnitude when he checked the chart and realized, surely with a sickening of the gut, that *El Faro*'s last position, and that of Joaquin, were virtually the same.

3

It is impossible for anyone who has not been in a strong storm at sea to imagine what such conditions feel like, for they are apprehensible mostly in the way physical trauma is read, in eye and ear, muscle and stomach, in the spaced-out limbo of shock. (A NOAA video illustrating the Saffir-Simpson scale doesn't try; it merely shows Categories 3 to 4 utterly obliterating houses and trees on land.) And the thought that something as large and fast as *El Faro* might find herself in danger from mere weather was, for most, just as difficult to imagine. This ship, after all, was as long as an eighty-story skyscraper was tall; she was as high as a twelve-story office block, wide as New York's Fifth Avenue. Her thirty thousand horsepower steam engine, if you tacked all its components together, was bigger than most houses and could drive her at over twenty knots—almost twenty-five miles per hour—which, for a 31,515-gross-ton merchant ship, put her in the category of a racehorse. She was built in 1975 on the outskirts of Philadelphia, lengthened by ninety feet in 1993, and thus was hardly new, but she bore the usual equipment for a modern vessel, all of it up-to-date: satellite navigation systems that pinpointed her position, radar that tracked traffic and even strong weather events thirty miles out, and communication systems that furnished access to the latest satellite forecasts and weather alerts from various expert outfits such as the National Weather Service, its National Hurricane Center, and even a private marine-forecasting service called Advanced Weather Technologies.

Just as important, *El Faro* was US-owned and US-registered, which meant that, unlike ships listed with lightly taxed and poorly regulated registries—Liberia, the Marshall Islands, and landlocked Bolivia, to name a few—she was maintained according to tough standards set by the US Coast Guard. Unlike those of many flag-of-convenience registries her lifesaving gear, life rafts, emergency beacons, and survival suits were checked at preset intervals by either the Coast Guard or an approved inspection service. And her officers were all Coast Guard–licensed personnel, all US nationals, all sea-tested, many of them graduates of some of the finest maritime academies in the world, such as the federal Merchant Marine Academy at Kings Point, New York, as well as Massachusetts Maritime Academy, Maine Maritime, and the State University of New York's maritime school at Fort Schuyler, the Bronx.

The waters near the Bahamas—the so-called Bermuda Triangle—had over the years seen the disappearance and destruction of thousands of ships, many in hurricanes, but almost all of the vessels involved, even in recent times, were small, relatively unsafe, and equipped with navigational gear unchanged in its essentials from the days of Christopher Columbus's flagship, the *Santa Maria*. A ship as huge, fast, and strong as *El Faro* seemed about as likely to vanish without a Mayday as the *Santa Maria* was apt to fly out of a time warp and splash down off twenty-first-century Fort Lauderdale.

Thus, when Tote Services began calling contact numbers on the morning of October 1; as the Coast Guard began planning search-and-rescue operations it would not be able to carry out until the hurricane moved away; while most family members of *El Faro*'s crew were shocked, even afraid for their people, they also expected the crew would soon be found alive.

Rochelle Hamm, the wife of forty-nine-year-old able seaman Frank Hamm, got the call where she worked as a medical data-entry clerk in Jacksonville. She immediately phoned her children and asked them to assemble at her house to pray for Frank's safe return.

Also in Jacksonville, Pastor Robert Green, the stepfather of the ship's cook, Lashawn Rivera, told a reporter, "We still have to maintain hope that our son and the rest of the crew will be found." Rivera's cousin, Schmiora Hill, said, "They haven't even found both lifeboats. . . . I feel somebody, somewhere, somehow, is still surviving."

Glen Jackson heard from his sister, Jill, who saw *El Faro* mentioned on television news; their brother Jack, who was an able seaman on the ship, had given Tote the landline number of Glen's girlfriend as a family contact, but that line had been knocked out when a car ran into one of America's last surviving pay phones outside her house in New Orleans. Glen immediately called the Coast Guard, who put him through to their Miami sector.

Late on October 1, Kurt Bruer heard about *El Faro* from a friend, who'd seen the report on TV news. Bruer at once recalled the image he'd had of Larry Davis on the morning watch. "I thought maybe Larry was trying to tell me something," he said. But Bruer, too, expected to hear that the ship, or her lifeboats at least, had been located; that the crew were safe.

Jenn Mathias took the call at her in-laws' house, where she was staying while her own was renovated, next to the Mathias family's cranberry
bogs in Kingston, Massachusetts. As she recalls it, the Tote representative told her they had just lost contact with *El Faro* but "everything was
fine." Jenn's husband, Jeff Mathias, was a chief engineer in charge of the
"riding gang" of Polish welders and electricians doing conversion work
on the ship. *El Faro* was due to shift to Tote's Tacoma–Anchorage route
at year's end and needed new deicing and other gear vital to Alaskan
conditions. Without letting on what she'd heard to the couple's three
children, aged seven, five, and three, Jenn immediately called a friend
on Cape Cod, a marine engineer who had frequently shipped out with
Jeff. The engineer tried to reassure her, saying that bad weather could
easily have knocked out the ship's radio antennas. The next morning
Jenn was obsessively checking messages, waiting for a report, when
an email from Tote finally popped up in her in-box. "Someone at Tote
misphrased it, I don't know who. It said, 'We are pleased to report . . .' I
screamed for joy when I saw that, thinking they'd found them, [but] all
it was, was a hotline and a website for *El Faro* families." Still, she went to
bed on the night of October 2 thinking, "They'll find them tomorrow."

But her father-in-law sensed something was badly wrong. "I could
hear him bawling all night," Jenn said.

Laurie Randolph Bobillot, too, guessed the truth. An hour before *El
Faro*'s last signals, her daughter, Danielle Randolph, the ship's second
mate, had sent her mom an email over the ship's Inmarsat link: "I don't
know if you've been following the weather, but there's a hurricane out
here and we're heading straight into it. Winds are super bad and waves
not great. Love to everyone."

"She never, ever signed letters or emails with 'Love, Danielle,'" Bobillot said. "Never 'hugs and kisses.' . . . When I read that, I knew she
was gone."

The officers at Coast Guard search and rescue, who knew better than
most what manner of monster Joaquin had become, took all reasonable
action. They requested assistance from the Bahamas Defence Force,
whose officers replied that they themselves were locked down by the
hurricane's shrieking winds and giant waves and could do nothing. The

nearest US Coast Guard cutter, the 270-foot *Northland*, though she was steaming toward the Bahamas, was too distant to be of immediate use. An MH-60 Jayhawk helicopter, the Coast Guard's workhorse of urgent rescue, was stationed at Great Inagua Island in the Bahamas, relatively close by; it, too, could not move because of Joaquin. The USCG asked an Air Force Hurricane Hunter, a C-130 aircraft currently airborne, to overfly the ship's last known position, calling for *El Faro* on the emergency VHF channel. Its calls drew no response.

Only two other merchant ships were in the area. One was a 494-ton coastal freighter named *Emerald Express*; she was being washed by storm waves into a mangrove swamp on Crooked Island in the Bahamas, her crew unable to move or think of much beyond their own survival. But the obligation to help other ships in trouble is drilled into mariners, and her skipper began calling *El Faro* over VHF. He, too, heard only storm static and, behind that, silence.*

Another coastal freighter, the Haitian-owned *Minouche*, was farther away from the storm, between Haiti and Great Inagua. But the *Minouche* was sinking.

Late on October 2, Joaquin, having slowly circled *El Faro*'s last position as if to make sure of the kill, had finally tracked north, moving far enough away that the Coast Guard Jayhawk out of Great Inagua and another out of a Clearwater, Florida, base could fly over *El Faro*'s last position, starting a search pattern to encompass a wider and wider area of sea. They, and Coast Guard and Air Force C-130s also sent out to search, saw nothing.

On Saturday the third, a Jayhawk crew, at a position 120 miles northeast of Crooked Island, spotted and retrieved an orange life ring bearing the words EL FARO—SAN JUAN—PR.

On the fourth, not far from the ship's last reported position roughly forty nautical miles† north of Crooked Island and forty-eight southeast of San Salvador, aircraft discovered a debris field and an oil sheen. On

---

* *Emerald Express*'s crew later claimed to have heard VHF calls from *El Faro*, but those calls were not recorded. It could be that *El Faro*'s officers used handheld VHF sets to make distress calls while abandoning ship; there is no way to verify this.

† One nautical mile, corresponding to one minute of latitude, is equal to 1.15 standard miles.

the same day a salvage tug hired by Tote located a container from the missing ship. On the fifth, aircraft spotted a damaged lifeboat from *El Faro*, and a body floating inside an orange survival suit.

On October 7, the Coast Guard determined that *El Faro* had sunk with no survivors and called off the search. Coast Guard experts assumed the debris field and oil sheen off Crooked Island must mark where the ship had gone down. The area was located on the southwestern edge of the Nares Plain, an undersea plateau stretching from Bermuda to Georgia to the Bahamas Rise, on which the Bahamas Islands sit. At that position the water was fifteen thousand feet deep.

The grave of *El Faro* and her crew, it seemed, was almost three miles down. The hulk of a ship whose name means "lighthouse" in Spanish lay in the abyssal zone of utter darkness, in deep silence and the coldest of waters, at pressures in the vicinity of seven thousand pounds, equivalent to a human body supporting one Lincoln Town Car per square inch of skin; conditions so extreme that only specialized forms of life can survive, often by generating their own light. It was the worst seagoing, nonmilitary disaster involving a US ship since World War II.*

The loss of an American ship and crew drew attention briefly, but in a country so focused on its internal riches and conflicts, the news made front pages only in Jacksonville, San Juan, and the other coastal communities, such as Rockland, Maine, from which many of *El Faro*'s crew came. The Coast Guard and the National Transportation Safety Board planned expeditions to find the wreck, hearings to parse disaster.

For the families and friends of *El Faro*'s people, the silence of waiting was now replaced by a ringing void of absence, of unanswered questions. Why had *El Faro* sunk? Why had she gone in harm's way to begin with? If mistakes had been made, who was responsible? And most of all, why had a ship so large and well equipped, with so experienced and professional a crew, disappeared in Atlantic waters as utterly and abruptly as a tossed stone, without even time to transmit a Mayday?

---

* Two worse or comparable civilian disasters occurred in inland waters: a small car ferry, the *George Prince*, sank in 1976 on the Mississippi, killing seventy-eight; and an ore carrier, the *Carl Bradley*, sank in a 1958 storm on Lake Michigan with the loss of thirty-three crew. Several military ships, including the nuclear submarine USS *Thresher*, sank with significantly greater casualties.

4

A ship, to paraphrase the architect Le Corbusier, is a machine for navigation, and it is in the nature of a machine to work. More precisely, it is in the nature of how we perceive a machine to equate its identity with its functioning. To the driver, a smoothly purring car is escape, motion, sex, speed. But once it breaks down, it's a hunk of useless metal.

Seen from another angle, what we know of a functioning car or aircraft or ship, or indeed their operators, is a list of units, often expressed in acronyms—mpg, rpm, psi, bmi—all of which are quantified and replicable. They move separately and apart in a limited number and along a replicable spectrum of ways.

When the machine starts to break down, however, it does so in forms and volumes we did not predict, in spurts of cracked tolerances we'd not bargained for, in a cascade of off-key interactions far too numerous to track. Function, in the sense of routine operation, is digital and quantifiable, but disaster is analogue. In the analogue cosmos of accident exists an infinity of space, between hordes of still-moving but increasingly skewed subsystems, in which failure breeds and exponentially multiplies.

A giant merchant ship such as *El Faro* is not just a machine, it is a world of systems both mechanical and human: steam boiler and reduction gear, cargo stability and hull design, storm forecasts and navigational computers, psychological stress and metal fatigue, corporate pressure and maritime tradition. Each of those systems seems quantifiable when working but hosts a galaxy of analogue details, of variations in bounce and smash, as it begins to crash.

In that sense, by studying what happened to *El Faro* we are seeking to understand a quantum world, of details that are the smallest possible expression of, say, the molecules of silicon or synthetic rubber in a gasket that fails to seal a manhole in the deck. And this can only be apprehended by a discipline that takes into account not just the complexity of such systems but also a higher level of rules that must apply as breakdown occurs, as a chain reaction of quantum-level events begets a further cascade of accidents; until entities as large as a 40-foot cargo container, a 30,000-horsepower engine, a 790-foot hull, or a human mind are dragged helplessly down in an ever-accelerating rush toward destruction.

The quantum chain reactions that would end in shipwreck began individually and at varied locations, at different hours, sometimes on separate days; but they started to come together most concretely in the afternoon of Tuesday, September 29, 2015, as the SS *El Faro* prepared for sea.

Stability issues: Before she left Jacksonville on September 29, too much cargo was loaded on *El Faro*'s starboard side, causing a four-degree tilt, or list, in that direction. Though the list was corrected before departure, the ship's stability would soon become cause for concern.

PART II

DEPARTURE

Ship and boat diverged: the cold, damp night breeze blew between . . . the two hulls wildly rolled; we gave three heavy-hearted cheers, and blindly plunged like fate into the lone Atlantic.

—Herman Melville, *Moby-Dick*

Lashawn Rivera shows his TWIC, the federal Transportation Worker Identification Credential that allows him into secure harbor areas, to the guards at the Blount Island Marine Terminal checkpoint. He drives down four-lane roadways through flat country quivering with Florida heat; past warning signs and CCTV cams, a totem anchor, cargo areas for different companies, to his company's zone at the island's southwest corner. There he parks in a slot reserved for mariners, between Cyclone fences topped with barbed wire, stacks of white containers marked TOTE, and the company's harbor office.

Rivera is thirty-two, maybe five foot ten, of medium build; he has a trimmed beard and mustache and hair frizzed in dreadlocks to his shoulders. He is chief cook on the SS *El Faro*, and this does not afford him a lot of time ashore, given that he must ensure a lunch of cold cuts, sandwiches, and a salad bar is available for the unloading crew and for shipmates who stay on board for loading.

Maybe, before opening his door to the late-September heat, Rivera takes a minute in the arctic air-conditioning of his Dodge muscle car to look at this ship, docked "starboard-side-to"—the right or starboard flank of her hull snubbed in close against the south-facing wharf. Moored in this way, her sharp bow points upriver, as if reluctant to face the direction in which she is due to sail a few hours from now.

El Faro, seen this close, is a massive flat blue-painted cliff of hull, rising nearly forty feet overhead to the Main Deck. That deck carries a narrow steel balcony all around the hull, the better to support containers. The hull just under the Main Deck is punctuated at intervals by boxy ventilation ducts, as well as by fifteen large rectangular ports through which someone ashore can catch glimpses of work lights and moving truck trailers inside, as of chthonic behemoths restlessly shifting in a cave. The blue cliff is so long it seems to extend, behind a latticework of thick mooring lines, halfway down the island.

To Rivera's right the ship's bow, which has a graceful reverse curve to it—like a clipper's, the top reaching forward much farther than at the waterline as if eager to ride over waves—imparts a feeling of forward motion. The back end, or stern, is flat and vertical, shaped in cross section like the cup of a wineglass. Up two long steel ramps leading to a pair of particularly large openings in the middle and back sections of the starboard side, tractors drag more trailers into the hull.

A stack of seven accommodation decks, usually called the house, painted white, is piled roughly three-quarters of the way down the hull, atop the Main Deck toward the stern; these decks are crowned by a boxy wheelhouse and reach, in a maze of portholes, windows, stairs, and lifeboats, seventy feet over the Main Deck. Atop the wheelhouse an array of radar scanners, satellite receivers, and radio antennas bristle on a tripod mast, almost a hundred feet over the water, near a thirty-foot smokestack rising behind. A chaff of grayish smoke wisps from the red-white-blue-painted stack and is dispersed toward Saint Augustine by a light northerly breeze. SEA STAR is painted in boxy blue letters ten feet high on a steel panel shielding the lower levels of the house. Invisible from where Rivera sits, on the stern, under an American flag flapping listlessly in the near calm, the ship's name is painted: EL FARO, and her home port, SAN JUAN, PR.

The sight of a great ship getting ready for sea, no matter how often a crew member observes it—even if he, or she, is sick to death of the work and the lonely separation from friends and family it entails and would far rather stay home with a brew in one hand and a loved one in the other—nevertheless triggers a kick of excitement, however habitual and mundane, because of the scale, energy, and organization involved; because this ship constitutes a giant, self-contained world that is busily preparing to come into its own, its true reason for being. Because this blue-hulled world is leaving land, and places that are safe and fixed and known, and wandering onto the face of the deep.

The cook has two daughters of grade-school age; a one-year-old son, Yael; and a fiancée, Vana Jules, who is eight months pregnant.

This will be his last round-trip on *El Faro* for a while since he plans to be home for the birth; he and Jules are due to marry shortly thereafter. Rivera, like many of the ship's unlicensed crew—the ordinary seamen, engine-room oilers, stewards, and other nonofficers—grew up in North Jacksonville, a rough, largely poor, mostly African-American part of town. It's a place about which his stepfather, Pastor Robert Green, says, "kids medicate, and someone gets bumped every night." Rivera was good at sports but rambunctious. "As a boy," his stepfather says, "he'd fall, hit his head, be bleeding and still going." In North Jacksonville, clawing clear of the local drugs-crime-prison subculture often goes hand in hand with getting religion, and that was the route Rivera, with the help of his stepfather, ended up taking. In this case, following Jesus also took him to sea. It's more likely than not, while getting out of his car, that Rivera, who is still highly religious, mutters a quick prayer for his family, for his own safe travels, before hoisting his bag and walking to the gangway.

Two men stand guard at the gangway's foot. One is the able seaman on watch; the other is a private security guard. The AB on watch for the noon to 4:00 p.m. shift is Larry Davis, and Rivera perhaps shows surprise since everyone knows Larry, who is sixty-three, was planning to retire after the next trip or maybe the one after that, so a shipmate might wonder, "Why is he still here?" Behind the banter, though, lies a darker awareness of the guard, and why he's checking IDs. Two years ago when *El Faro*'s sister ship *El Morro*, under *El Faro*'s former captain Jack Hearn, docked at Fort Lauderdale, a team of federal Immigration and Customs Enforcement agents swarmed aboard and busted two seamen and a bosun,* along with the forty-three pounds of cocaine they were smuggling into Florida. The smugglers went to prison. Tote fired Hearn, as well as another captain and two mates, though it was clear they had nothing to do with the smuggling and had no suspicion of it. Tote did not sack the current captain, Michael Davidson, who was also aboard but not in command at the time.

---

* Traditionally spelled *boatswain*, pronounced *bo'sun*: the highest-ranking deckhand, essentially foreman for all deck-related work aboard ship.

Most of *El Faro's* crew know each other well and, after months of working smoothly on this "liner" gig back and forth to San Juan, are quietly proud of the discipline and skills that make it possible. The guard is a reminder that discipline and teamwork are not the whole story, and underneath the groomed slope of smooth routines on this ship lie crevasses and fault lines that are no less deep for being, in the main, unacknowledged.

Rivera's routine takes him up the gangway to the Main Deck, to a companionway at the entry level of the house that leads him up two levels to the kitchens, or galley. On Main Deck his route crosses a path obsessively traveled by the ship's chief mate, Steven Shultz, second-in-command to the captain.

If Rivera actually sees Shultz, it's only for a few seconds, a tossed greeting. The chief mate's job in port is to supervise unloading and loading cargo. Now, in midafternoon, with the 8:00 p.m. departure time posted on a bulletin board, called the sailing board, by the gangway head, Shultz probably feels like the demon charged with running the HVAC of hell—a hell wigged out on methamphetamines to boot, for this must be what Hades is like, in this heat on fried steel decks with 391 heavy containers to be hoisted over and stacked four-deep on Main Deck, plus 118 truck trailers, 149 automobiles, 6 tanks each holding eighteen thousand gallons of fructose syrup, and assorted other loads to be rushed, shoved, pumped, and shoehorned into the three enclosed decks below.

El Faro was built as a Ro-Ro: a roll-on, roll-off ship whose cargo largely consisted of the kind of trailers you see dragged in eighteen-wheeled rigs on America's highways, as well as other wheeled vehicles that could be driven aboard and unloaded under their own steam. In 2006 she was modified to carry shipping containers, large rectangular steel boxes full of assorted goods, on the Main Deck, thus increasing her capacity for freight of all kinds.

Now giant gantry cranes that look like light-blue, mutated Meccano vultures with jibs eighty feet high prey on the box-shaped carrion. They roll on rails and steel wheels as they claw up containers of various lengths—twenty, forty-five, fifty-three feet—and lower them, according to a set schedule, on the ship's top deck and atop previously

loaded containers both forward of and behind the house. Longshoremen fasten the top containers to the next ones down with twist locks,
metal mechanisms that insert a thick, half-flanged bolt up and down
into adjacent, horizontal ovals on the two containers; when rotated
the bolts turn the flange across the narrow sections of oval to lock the
boxes together. The lower containers are either locked in the same way
or tied down with steel rods hooked in a cross-breast pattern, upper
left corner of the container to a purchase under its lower right, top
right to bottom left, and tightened with threaded steel tubes the size
of a man's leg, called turnbuckles. The purchases are usually padeyes
or D rings—half circles of steel bolted into a mortise that's welded
onto the deck. The turnbuckles, screwed into opposing threads on the
rods, are twisted—the dockers use metal "cheater" bars to lever them
around—until the lashings are hard and tight as rifle barrels.

As the containers are being stacked and locked, small diesel-powered
tractors, known as yard pigs or hustlers, drag truck trailers to and from
giant scales in Tote's cargo lot. Once the trailers have been weighed, the
hustlers haul them fast up the two starboard loading ramps into the
depths of *El Faro*'s highest covered deck, known as 2nd Deck. Those
assigned to the two lower decks are either shunted down one of four
internal ramps or, for 3rd Deck only, onto a giant, hydraulically powered
elevator similar to the aircraft lifts on a Navy carrier. Inside the holds
they are parked and chocked in the spaces reserved for them.

These trailers are secured differently from the containers, with a
version of the twist-screw known as a Roloc box, essentially a square,
vertical bolt linking the trailer's hitchpin into "buttons," slotted steel
pads welded, like the D-ring mortises, to the deck; that is, if the buttons are not rusted out. If they are corroded, or no button is available,
the trailers are lashed down tight with chains at six different points,
front and back, right and left; these in turn are hooked into D rings or
more distant buttons to prevent rolling. (If the Roloc is functioning,
the trailer is secured with two to four extra lashings.)

The scene, if you substitute steel decks and bulkheads for buildings,
and orange-jacketed, hard-hatted stevedores for tourists, is as busy
as Times Square at rush hour on a Friday evening; everywhere yard
pigs snort and roar, dragging in trailers, circling around each other,

speeding back down the ramp for another trailer. Containers boom, the gantries whine, cars race down ramps, mates and longshoremen yell; in the thick of loading it gets so loud at times that deckhands use earplugs to cut the noise. It all moves "hard and heavy," as the saying goes; a foot left too long in one place, a misjudged move can break a leg, cut off an arm. On deck seagulls screech, exhaust is braided into the superheated breeze; and Chief Mate Steve Shultz keeps an eye on all of it, pacing Main Deck, where the boxes are stacked thirty feet above his head, all the way to the raised "forecastle" (pronounced *fo'c'sle*) at the bow, back to the transom aft; plunging down into the vast echoing neon-shined garage systems of the lower decks, 2nd Deck, then 3rd Deck, to the lowest level of all, known as the Tank Top, set on plates above the ballast and fuel tanks and the steel ribs and shell of the ship's bottom. It's a rough job, especially since Tote last month got rid of the shoreside assistant for cargo work, known as "port mate." Third Mate Jeremie Riehm, who helps out with loading, describes the current process, lacking the extra help, as "a storm of shit."

Now and again Shultz consults with Riehm; with Second Mate Randolph, who is on cargo duty in the afternoon; with the chief engineer, Richard Pusatere; and with Louis Champa, the ship's electrician, whose job it is to hook up every one of the 238 refrigerated trailers and containers to the ship's electrical system and make sure the reefers' compressors and evaporators, blowers and pumps, are all working and at the right temperature. Ice cream's in those freezers, and milk, butter, Halloween candy, frozen waffles; the future happiness of Puerto Rico's kids depends on keeping the contents cold.

At regular intervals Shultz scales the nine flights of stairs to the house's top deck, just under the bridge (or wheelhouse), to his office, to check if emails containing cargo updates have come in from Tote's shoreside operation; to make sure the loading schedule is going according to plan. For everything that comes aboard his ship has to be choreographed and stowed according to a precise map and timetable in order to preserve the ship's stability.

Stability is crucial. This ship took on a tilt, or list, before disappearing; a ship this large and well built should not lean sideways like that, ever—not even, especially not even, in storm.

2

A ship's stability is a function of two components. One is her center of gravity, which makes sense intuitively: a person holding a heavy suitcase at head level will be far more likely to topple over, because of the levering effect of the body's length, than if the suitcase were somehow fastened at ankle level. The same is true of a ship whose cargo is carried too high.

The second component is the center of buoyancy, which in turn depends mostly on hull shape. Generally speaking, since light air is what keeps the ship floating on denser water, buoyancy is determined by how much air is contained in the hull. A wide hull tilting (or listing) to port holds a lot more air in the space between its centerline and its port side than would a narrow hull, and all that air will fight whatever force—waves, wind, shifting cargo—is pressing the hull down on that side.

There's nothing to be done about hull shape, but the center of gravity depends on weight and location of cargo; in loading, the company's port engineer and *El Faro*'s chief mate seek to keep the ship's burden low and evenly spaced, achieving maximum stability for a given freight. The optimum relationship between buoyancy and center of gravity is expressed by a number called the GM margin.*

Computing all this with pen and calculator once required hours of intellectual sweat. A ship's officer nowadays figures out stability by plugging cargo numbers, as well as figures representing the weight of stores, equipment, ballast (water pumped into bottom tanks to further

---

* The lower its center of gravity and the farther away from the centerline its buoyancy center can travel, the more resistant a ship will be to rolling too far or capsizing in rough seas. Stability in merchant ships is therefore reckoned—you can see this as an elegance of graphics, without needing to follow the math—by measuring how far to one side the center of buoyancy shifts at a given angle of tilt. The lower the center of gravity, the farther away from the centerline the buoyancy center can move, the longer will be the "righting arm" that fights to keep the ship upright. The goal is to maintain the minimum length of righting arm necessary to keep the ship from rolling too far or even capsizing in rough seas. Minimum righting arm is called GM, where *G* stands for the center of gravity and *M* for a geometric point defining the center of buoyancy; GM margin is the extra margin of stability mariners require before departure (or the difference between the minimum and actual GM). For *El Faro* the average GM margin at departure is around 0.5, diminishing to 0.25 at arrival due to fuel burn-off. On this trip *El Faro* leaves with a margin of 0.64, which burn-off will reduce to 0.3.

lower the center of gravity),* and fuel, into a custom-made program called CargoMax and pressing the enter key on his workstation. The GM pops out within seconds.†

At this stage the preliminary numbers are tallied and organized in Tote's Blount Island office, where trailers are weighed, bills of lading processed, and loading schedules figured out; not an easy task, as was proved earlier in the day when the ship was loaded too quickly on one side, causing a four-degree list to starboard, which had to be corrected by loading to the opposite side.

Shultz's job now is to make sure that what went into the CargoMax program is accurate, that the six fructose tanks up forward in the lowest levels of 1- and 2-holds have been pumped as full as possible; that the containers containing hazardous materials have been parked in designated areas and locked down. At least on this trip no cattle or horses are aboard; loading livestock would require that an area aft be set aside for their trailers and feed, and a cabin prepped for their wranglers.

Everywhere Shultz double-checks to make sure the twist-locks are engaged, that chains, bolts, and rods holding down the cargo to buttons and D rings are bar tight, that everything is lashed as strongly as it should be. This is hurricane season, and the National Weather Service says a tropical storm is out there somewhere, though it's not supposed to amount to much. The Tote ships on the Puerto Rico run are fast; if a hurricane develops, they can easily outrun it, and therefore they are rarely affected by dangerous weather. But rough seas are always possible,

---

* *El Faro*'s ballasting options were reduced during her 1992 and 2006 conversions, when four of her ballast tanks were permanently filled with iron slurry, which lowered her center of gravity; another effect was to reduce her officers' ability to counteract a list by emptying extra ballast tanks on one side and filling them on the other, a problem that will have a bearing on the ship's ultimate fate.

† CargoMax—which is not required to be and has never been officially approved as a stability-calculating program by the Coast Guard or any other official agency—is the child of a joint venture between Herbert Engineering, a California marine-software company, and the American Bureau of Shipping, or ABS, a nonprofit, New York–based "classification society." A classification society is a company that promulgates marine safety standards and inspects ships according to those standards worldwide. The involvement of ABS in the software Tote uses might not be a coincidence. ABS, which boasts yearly revenues of over $1 billion, is also the outfit that, for a fee, inspects Tote ships for regulatory compliance.

and loose lashings on any one of the stacked containers topside, or the lined-up trailers below, can have a domino effect as the container or trailer works against its lashings, loosening them further, and then the cargo slides harder and faster and in the end breaks what ties it down. "It's only seventy [-gauge] chain," says Olabode "Odd Rod" Borisade, a former longshoreman who used to tie down cargo on *El Faro*. "It's not going to hold a forty-thousand-pound container." Chain of this strength is commonly rated to hold up to sixty-six hundred pounds working load, with a breaking strength of twenty-six thousand pounds, insufficient to restrain a large box. Once adrift the container will start to bang or roll into the cargo beside, the lashings of which will loosen in turn, and so forth.

Tote apparently has printed a short "lashing manual" to ensure consistent tie-down, but several longshoremen say they've never seen it. And no one has ordered extra securing gear, called storm lashings, which would require that more chains, rods, and hooks be brought to the ship and fitted. This would mean a lot more work; with no clear and present threat on the horizon Shultz has gone along with this decision and runs the usual sailor's controlled tumble down the steep companionways to check again the situation on 2nd Deck, where the second mate is working.

3

Shultz, along with everyone else, likes working with the second mate, and not just because Danielle Randolph is cute and female in an industry where, even now, women are rare as snow in Florida; there is one other female aboard *El Faro*, Mariette Wright, an AB. In this environment guys can get sick of the preponderant locker-room maleness, the harsh angles and fart jokes. Danielle Randolph, sometimes called Dany, is "five foot nothin'," her mother's description, of rounded, compact build, hair either light brown or dirty blond depending on how much sun has got to it; a heart-shaped face, slightly aquiline nose, and a wide-open smile that narrows her North Sea–hued eyes into an expression that seems to say, "Mischief? Bring it on!"—or if not mischief exactly, certainly a joke. She likes cracking one-liners as much as she enjoys fielding them and is quick as hell at getting any joke you throw at her.

Randolph, like most, is the balance of her contradictions. She is gregarious, cheerful, easy to get along with; open to everyone, officers and unlicensed mariners alike. But when it comes to her job she is dead serious. Her MO is to define exactly what has to be done and then do it now, all the way and right. Although she was brought up in Rockland, Maine, a town still hungover from the hard-ass cultural brew of coastal schooners and the lobster fishery; though both her parents are ex-military and she was raised in a house where orders were orders and you obeyed first and asked questions later; although, like Captain Davidson and two of the engineers, she graduated from Maine Maritime Academy, which like other US maritime academies is run along military-service lines with half an eye to spawning tame naval officers, which means in turn that discipline is prized as much as or more than other qualities; she is not afraid to speak up when she sees a better way of doing things.

At work she wears a worn jumpsuit, construction boots. Under a hard hat a faded kerchief lashes down her hair. Yet her mother, Laurie Bobillot, describes her as "a real girlie girl," who once painted her cabin pink and collects Barbie dolls; who sells Mary Kay cosmetics in her spare time;[*] who loves dressing up in 1950s skirts, makeup, and heels, and riding around in her dad's 1948 Chevy Fleetside.

A lot of bullshit is spoken and written, mostly by people who don't ship out, about the lure of the sea, the romance of seafaring. Any merchant mariner knows only too well how hard, boring, lonely, and sometimes cruel the trade often is; most everyone on commercial ships would not be out there if the job didn't pay pretty well. But if anyone has a calling for this trade, and a feel for how ships work, it is this thirty-four-year-old woman. "Her first day of kindergarten I took her to school," Laurie Bobillot recalls. "I was crying like a damn fool; she looks up at me and says, 'Mommy, how'm I gonna learn about boats

---

[*] Despite family skepticism as to how she would make money selling makeup on a ship full of men, she once scored her "biggest order ever" with Chief Mate Shultz, who bought almost $500 worth of cosmetics for his wife.

and the sea if I don't go to school?'" Randolph applied to one college only. Ever since graduating from Maine Maritime she has worked on ships happily, enthusiastically. She once consoled her mother, who was worrying about some of the risks her daughter took at work, by saying, "Shipping out is dangerous, life is dangerous. But if something happens to me when I'm at sea, it's where I want to be."

And yet, before she boarded the flight to Jacksonville for this last rotation, Randolph for the first time expressed doubts about going; even thought, or so she told her mother, of asking Tote to find another mate to replace her for this trip. Partly it's because she loves Christmas, all the snow and carols and sugared cookies of it, and this cycle will keep her away from home for the holidays. And partly it's just a funny feeling. Randolph is the opposite of psychic, she is focused on tools and jobs and conscious logic; she knows that everyone gets a weird feeling now and again on the order of "Maybe this will be the plane that crashes and I really should change my ticket." But you don't want to lose your fare and you don't change your reservation, the plane lands safely, and the feeling disappears like a dream you neglected to write down.

In any case, a big ship loading for departure—her navigation, cargo, engine, and steward departments all buzzing, thumping, racing, humming with the urgency of getting a job done now because once you're out there it's too late—tends to swamp doubt and the luxuries of fantasy in a torrent of deadlines. Randolph, who splits a twelve-hour loading watch with Shultz, must also remember to take a break before her bridge duty starts at midnight. Like many watch standers she takes over-the-counter meds, such as ZzzQuil or Tylenol PM, to sleep; like Riehm and Shultz in particular, she has trouble getting enough snooze-time over her standard four-hours-on, eight-hours-off cycle. When she leaves the ship, her mother says, Randolph spends at least a week sleeping ten to twelve hours a night to catch up. In hearings later, the question of watch officers' fatigue will crop up again and again.

Today Randolph has another goal to fulfill, one that has no bearing on ship's business, and to do that she needs to keep an eye out for a new third engineer, Dylan Meklin, who was supposed to report for duty early but did not show up as scheduled.

4

Most of the containers have been loaded by now, almost all the trailers jockeyed into place by dockworkers and lashed down. The Jacksonville stevedores are used to this work and know their jobs, and they know Shultz and Randolph and Jeremie Riehm, the third mate, and in that knowledge of shared competence Shultz and the mates get along with shoreside but still everything has to be double-checked. At forty years of age *El Faro* is an old lady, and old ships rust, and a lot of the buttons and D rings are clogged with rotted metal and, if they're seized up, have to be reamed out with a specialized tool, designed and hammered into a combination crowbar and pick by the previous captain, Hearn. Not all can be rescued, however; no one even knows how many D rings are deficient, since no program is in place to log, test, or replace them; and for this voyage a number of containers and trailers have been secured "off-button," meaning they are not lashed to anything more secure than the next container over, or (in the case of trailers) to a chain stretched to a working D ring. Most of the cars are stored on the lowest deck, Tank-Top, where chains are stretched across the ship's width and the cars then individually lashed to the chains; a method that speeds up the loading process, but contravenes Tote's own guidelines.*

Now the nine watertight gates that section off the vast parking spaces of the lower decks are hydraulically shut and locked, thus defining 1-,

---

* A one-page "guideline," the authorship of which is uncertain, details minimum lashing requirements for *El Faro*; by this document's standards, according to Captain Philip Anderson of the industry group National Cargo Bureau, most of the ship's container stacks would be deemed compliant. But Anderson also will state in testimony that by normal NCB standards some of the cargo stacks and "a significant" number of the trailers carried below would be considered unsatisfactorily lashed down. Inspectors will later determine that anywhere between three and forty of the trailers on 2nd Deck are stowed off-button. The lashing guideline requires that cars be secured individually to D rings, which is not the case on *El Faro*. Anderson later will judge loose cargo to have had a "domino effect" on other cargo, and to have become a problem during the ship's final voyage.

2-, and 3-holds, counting aft.* The closing and bolting—"dogging," in the lingo—of both the massive gates (all are over two hundred square feet) and of smaller watertight access doors within those gates must be carried out, verified, and logged by a mate. One former bosun describes the process as complicated enough that the gates between 2A- and 3-holds are at times not securely locked. Kurt Bruer says two of the nine gates seldom closed completely. In March of 2014 *El Faro*'s gates failed inspection due to significant leakage around the doors' seals and dogs.

On the 2nd Deck, seven scuttles—round hatches ringed by steel lips, or coamings, a couple of feet high and painted yellow—carry covers that are locked by four large movable bolts, cranked home into the coaming lips by wheel-driven gears. Gaskets along the covers' inner edge deter waves, which in heavy seas will break through the thirty big ports (fifteen on each side) opening onto 2nd Deck, from sloshing down into the dry decks below. The integrity of the scuttles is important, for not only is 2nd Deck accessible to the elements, but it is much more open lengthwise than the other cargo decks. Only one bulkhead, or watertight steel wall, bisects this deck, between 2A- and 2-holds, whereas bulkheads break up the lower decks at each end of the five holds. Any water entering 2nd Deck will thus have relatively more space to run and do damage. Moreover, some of the scuttles lie in an angle between ventilation housings and the ship's side, and water tends to collect there when the ship rolls. The scuttles are all supposed to be dogged before sailing; a quick three-quarter turn of the wheel on top is all it takes to secure them. But the wheels look the same open or closed; there is no way to check visually if the bolts have slotted home and, whereas standard procedure with the big gates is to log every time they are touched, the scuttles' status is not recorded. Some of the bolts, too, are worn. And no one checks the gaskets; the consensus is that only a shipyard test, using high-pressure hoses, could assess their continuing integrity.

---

* The engine room (technically 4-hold) lies under the house; 5-hold, where steering and propulsion machinery reside, is all the way aft, against the stern, and does not extend to Tank Top level. Regulations require that all gates be shut before sailing, since they are part of the system of watertight compartments that contributes to the ship's overall safety.

Where daylight is not masked by overcast, it's starting to pull long, ash-colored shadows from the Dames Point Bridge. *El Faro*, already stained by rust in places—in parts of the ship, some deckhands claim, rust has eaten right through the deck—turns more orange still under a beam of shine filtered horizontally through the pollution from downtown Jacksonville to the west.

A flight of pelicans, like flying machines designed by a committee, cross the sky and splash down awkwardly in a creek separating Blount Island from the mainland. The two Moran tugs that will unstick *El Faro* from her dock lie moored on the mainland side of the creek, at Dames Point, deck lights burning, a slight thud of diesel emanating from their stacks.

Around the point to the north—hidden among spavined trailer homes, swamp oaks ghouled with Spanish moss, and rotten pilings—lies a small marina, half-peopled with pleasure boats, a few of which are almost as old as *El Faro*. Just down the creek float a couple of shrimpers, nets splayed for repair. Between the docks and the marina office is Paulie's dockside bar, open on three sides to the light, warm breeze wafting off the river. It's a friendly place, sporting the usual maritime kitsch: a yellow life ring, a stretch of fishnet, a stuffed bonito. Signs read FISH NAKED: SHOW OFF YOUR BOBBERS; NO WORKING DURING DRINKING HOURS; $5 CHARGE FOR WHINING; JELL-O SHOT $3.

One or two of *El Faro*'s crew have been known to slope into Paulie's for a drink before departure since it has the advantage of being both hidden and a five-minute drive from the secure port area. No alcohol is allowed aboard the ship although, ironically, *El Faro* has carrried hundreds of thousands of gallons of rum as freight from Puerto Rico to the mainland. Sitting at the south end of the bar, a guy scoring his last cold one before going to sea can keep an eye on the cranes and tell, from their sustained pace or else a slowing in their rhythm, how close he is to sailing.

5

Joaquin.

It starts as a shift in a goatherd's robes.

Experts in global weather might quibble; they'd claim it really started earlier, at a scale even more minute, such as one stroke of a seagull's wings over Tasmania, a 2 percent hike in the frog population of a Saskatchewan pond: a function of the Lorenz effect, which posits a snowballing of weather consequences from the tiniest of initial causes. But the first recognizable symptom of the meteorological event that will become Hurricane Joaquin is a new, southerly breeze, very light at first but strengthening, that must disturb the cotton robe of some Omoro herder where he watches his flock in the high mountains of Ethiopia, near the east coast of Africa.

The breeze is scout for a stronger, drier wind blowing north through the Turkana Channel between Kenya's upcountry and Ethiopia's highlands. Those mountains flick the breeze upward, where it bumps into a broader rush of warm, wet wind from the summer monsoon, flowing west out of the Indian Ocean. As the two winds touch, a tiny kink happens—a microcosmic roil, a twist of lower pressure in the vast flow of humid, low-pressure monsoon air.

But the roil subsists, becoming its own miniature low-pressure system in the process. Since air always flows from higher pressure to lower, the kink starts to pull in air around it and rides the monsoon's frontal system as an "African wave," westward across the continent.

Many such systems do not survive the journey. This one—albeit weakened occasionally by hot, dry blasts of air from the Sahara, and clogged by sand from the same desert;* its moisture content boosted at other times by wetter air bouncing off highlands in Congo and Cameroon; like a thirst-mad legionnaire dragging himself over sand dunes to water finally makes it to the Atlantic coast, somewhere around southern Morocco, near the Canary Islands.

---

* Sahara sand can weaken the wave by causing a dry haze that screens solar heat, eventually impeding the storm's growth at sea.

Here appears the first sign of Joaquin's freakish nature, since it's highly unusual for a potential hurricane to appear in the waters off Morocco. The low-pressure systems that later become hurricanes tend to reach the Atlantic much farther south, between eight and twenty degrees north of the equator, around the latitude of Senegal and the Cape Verde Islands. That latitude is normally free of the eastward-tending, high-altitude jet stream, which at lower levels induces wind shear. Wind shear—winds blowing from varied directions across a vertical column of atmosphere—will rip a low-pressure system apart, and such conditions are the norm where Joaquin shows up, farther north near the Canary Islands. This year, however, is an El Niño year, when the jet stream has been dragged southward by low pressure off South America, leaving the atmosphere off the Canary Islands relatively calm.

Even at its inception, therefore, this pre-Joaquin is a freak system. Yet much of the basic mechanism of meteorology is visible in its formation, such as the destructive force of crosswinds on a low-pressure zone, the strengthening effect of heat and humidity on that zone. The change of state from warm humidity to vapor, the cooling of vapor back into rain, also mirror how *El Faro*'s steam engine works, and while it's tempting to spot portent in such shared traits, they are only indicative of how basic to planetary physics are the movement from high to low pressure, the relationship of temperature to evaporation, the cyclic flows of a heat pump.

But how this system transforms now—though it functions according to the same laws as continental weather systems—is so powerful, so dramatic, that it feels more like a science-fiction device; like what happens to a young superhero when he is exposed to the radioactive overdose that endows him with freakish powers, after which this normally meek, unathletic dweeb starts to toss locomotives around like Ping-Pong balls for the hell of it.

The waters of the Atlantic off the Canary Islands in this postsummer season are extraordinarily warm, and they add both heat and humidity to wet, warm air at the low-pressure system's core. Jazzed on the extra bolus of humid heat, the core starts to rise faster, drawing in more air, which rushes in as wind, further speeding up evaporation; this sucks in more air and stronger winds from all around in a self-sustaining, self-accelerating chain reaction.

6

Dinner on *El Faro* bears little resemblance to the sumptuous affairs on cruise ships with their creamy linen tablecloths, flower arrangements, haute cuisine, and servile third-world waiters. Two mess halls, one for officers, one for unlicensed personnel, take up the starboard and port sides, respectively, of the mess deck in the house. This is three levels up from the open Main Deck, upon which containers are stacked.*

The galley and pantries lie between the two eating areas; freezers and other food-storage spaces take up separate spaces on mess deck, which is arranged, like the three accommodation decks above, with a connecting passageway in the shape of a squared horseshoe, open side facing aft. The passageway surrounds a steel casing containing the ship's boiler-exhaust system, which extends vertically to the smokestack. Living spaces are lined up on the horseshoe's outer edge, while utility areas—for laundry, linen, and other stores—lie inside, next to the casing.

The galley is the usual food-service warren of stainless-steel ranges, fryolators, cabinets, and harsh neon, with lockers and refrigerators bolted against the bulkhead. Here, safe and protected in his domain, Lashawn Rivera is apt to talk football with Lonnie Jordan as Jordan, the assistant steward, baker, and breakfast chef, pulls a tray of Stouffer's rolls from the oven.

The crew's mess is an equally functional area, little different from the average office canteen except that the tables are bolted down against the ship's motion. As elsewhere on the ship the color scheme is largely industrial, gray-speckled decks, off-white walls. A few safety posters—one of them urges deckhands to lift with the legs, not with the back—and framed

---

* The bottom two levels of the house are narrow compared to the upper four; they mostly consist of the boiler-exhaust casing, plus (off a corridor running port and starboard) the main stairs, a fire-control room, a cargo office, and a toilet. The rest of the area, a semi-open "breezeway" sheltered under the roof of wider upper decks, holds three dedicated containers full of bosun's supplies, paint, and other ship's stores.

images of *El Faro* in Alaska and Kuwait, relieve the walls' monotony. Serving arrangements are curiously formal. Deckhands and oilers pick their choices off a menu, and the cook and stewards load the plates and hand them out through an access hatch between galley area and mess. The two menus for each main meal usually include two of the three staples: beef, chicken, fish. Sometimes Rivera will tweak the dishes in the direction of soul or Latino food to please the unlicensed personnel.

The officers' mess looks no different except that, in deference to the officers' loftier position in the chain of command, the tables are neatly set by the chief steward, Ted Quammie, who combines the positions of waiter, concierge, and stores manager; essentially, with Rivera's help, he runs the ship's housekeeping side.

Quammie is sixty-seven but doesn't look his age. He smiles often, one of those soft smiles that people sometimes rely on without know-ing it to make daylight a bit brighter, in good part because the man behind the smile is nonjudgmental and reliably kind. Though he talks as easily as he grins, he rarely mentions his personal life. His accent, which comes from an English-speaking island in the Caribbean, no one seems to be quite sure which, kneads the vowels till they seem soft and full of colors and adds to the comforting effect.

In one corner of the crew's mess the Polish riding gang sit on their own. "Riding gang" is the mariner's term for workers not part of the normal crew or watch schedules. These men work a full twelve-hour day shift and, when they get off, talk among themselves in what to the rest of the crew is a strange code of *n*'s, *sh*'s, and *y*'s. They are all weld-ers and pipe fitters this trip; two electricians, their projects done, have just been sent home from Jacksonville. Only two of the men, Marcin Nita and Piotr Krause, speak any English, so none of the regular crew knows what they're talking about except sometimes Jeff Mathias, the chief engineer assigned by Tote to supervise their work, who spends a lot of time asking Krause or Nita to translate.

On departure it's common for the captain to host a meal for available officers and the various Tote personnel responsible for arranging cargo and ship's business ashore. On this evening at the butt end of September, Tim Neeson, Tote's port engineer, is finishing up a discussion about payroll with the captain.

Here, too, a landsman's romantic view of the sea falls somewhat short of the truth. Instead of standing eagle-eyed at the helm, the master of a large commercial ship delegates most of the traditional captain's duties to his or her mates,* and in such a system a good part of the skipper's job consists of fielding reports from subordinates and dealing with paperwork: overtime, requests for equipment, company forms. Given that much of the office work must be printed out and physically logged, digitization has not lightened this workload much. Officers who trained to work with salt and steel, charts and weather, often resent the desk-job aspect of a captain's brief.†

But a captain learns not to betray his thoughts, let alone resentments, and Davidson seems at ease and comfortable, lounging at the dinner table on the evening of September 29, cool in the air-conditioned house, while the chief steward stacks plates and the sunset paints peach tones on a bulkhead. In any event he's unlikely to be worrying now about the balance between paperwork and deck duties. Davidson is an athletic man with close-cropped silver hair, an engaging grin, a friendly manner. Though of average height, he is known for his outsize appetite. Usually he orders both menus at dinner.

Some masters, mates even, take refuge in their authority as officers and refrain from talking to deck or engine peons except when giving orders. Davidson harbors no such prejudices. This might in part be due to his down east background; like Danielle Randolph, like Third Engineer Michael Holland, like the new third engineer, Dylan Meklin, Davidson is a native of coastal Maine and a graduate of Maine Mari-

---

* Each mate runs the ship individually, with the assistance of one or two ABs on lookout or general backup duty during his, or her, respective watch. On *El Faro* the eight-to-twelve watch is assigned to Jeremie Riehm, the third mate; the twelve to four is Randolph's; the four to eight belongs to Chief Mate Shultz. In addition, the chief mate is responsible for implementing safety regulations and general inspection; the second mate's remit is navigation and communications systems, supervising the voyage plan, and keeping the wheelhouse (or bridge) in efficient operating order; the third mate usually takes care of hands-on maintenance and inspection duties such as sounding (or measuring the contents of) bilges and ballast and fuel tanks, and checking that emergency supplies on the ship's two lifeboats are up-to-date.

† According to John McPhee, one skipper working for Maersk, the world's biggest shipping line, said he dealt with paperwork by ignoring it as long as he could, letting the printouts pile up in a single stack on his desk until it got so high and top-heavy that the ship's roll caused them to topple over; from this he knew he could not put off paperwork any longer.

time Academy in Castine. The no-bullshit culture of the Maine coast includes a healthy contempt for authority, or at least for authority that is unearned.* Davidson's family had a summer home on Great Diamond Island and he grew up sailing. While in his teens he worked as a deckhand on Maine State ferries running across Casco Bay, an area known for its fogs and nor'easter storms. He earned his coastal captain's license at an early age, and it could be that being promoted "through the hawsepipe" on ships too small to tolerate caste systems had something to do with his egalitarian style.

Those who have shipped with "Captain Mike," as he is often called, know him to be a skilled and professional mariner, someone who worked on tankers in Alaska, where rough seas are run-of-the-mill. On *El Faro* he has surely been keeping a close eye on the weather, which an expert captain will do almost instinctively, especially in Florida during hurricane season. Without a doubt he has repeatedly checked the principal sources of meteorological information on *El Faro* as they are emailed to his office workstation and relayed to a console on the bridge.

7

The forecast a Tote master consults, and which Michael Davidson is using to plan this voyage, consists of maritime predictions created by the federal National Weather Service, part of NOAA. The predictions for tropical cyclones are generated by a weather service subgroup, the National Hurricane Center, based in Miami. These forecasts are grouped under the headings Tropical Analysis and Forecast Branch high seas forecast (TAFB) and SAT-C. They are issued jointly as text messages around five and eleven eastern daylight time, both morning and afternoon (thus 0500, 1100, 1700, and 2300 in

---

* A tale is told in the hills west of Bangor of a native Mainer, a man not unacquainted with strong drink, who was in the habit of taking potshots with his .22 at Air Force jets landing and taking off. When he was finally arrested, the neighbors were astonished—not (they said) because he had taken potshots at the jets, which was considered understandable, if not entirely normal—but because he'd managed to hit one at all.

ship's time), over the Inmarsat system, a satellite-based, privately run text/data-transmission service that has replaced long-distance shortwave radio sets on most commercial ships. The service includes not only communication and weather functions but two discrete distress-transmission modes as well.

Inmarsat also provides satellite telephony and email transmissions, which are *El Faro*'s primary links to shore. The distress function includes GMDSS, for Global Marine Distress and Safety System, capable of transmitting a preformatted, ship-specific distress call with either automated or manually inputted position information in a text to the ship's owner and the Coast Guard; and a more specialized, "covert" function called SSAS (Ship Security Alert System), which does the same thing only without any outward alarms or confirmation of transmission in case of takeover by pirates or other security-related emergencies.

Earlier, when the scheduled NWS bulletin was due, Davidson probably left his stateroom and climbed one level up to the bridge, where he checked the Inmarsat console for the NWS bulletin, to compare Joaquin's projected track to *El Faro*'s route off Florida's eastern coast.

The morning forecast today, September 29, puts Tropical Storm Joaquin at latitude 26.6 north, longitude 70.6 west, over five hundred miles east-southeast of Blount Island; the storm is said to be moving 270 degrees, or due west, and slowly, at four knots. Joaquin will remain a tropical storm, the NWS predicts. Its winds will top out at forty to fifty knots on October 1, weaken thereafter. Not much to worry about, though Davidson must bear in mind, as always with a tropical system, that no forecast is foolproof, that a storm can change direction quickly and with little warning.

Catastrophe starts with small details, such as the cross-flip of wind in the Ethiopian highlands that first triggered the low-pressure zone that would become Joaquin. Davidson and his mates do not spot such small seeds of trouble: they are invisible even to experts at the outset. But it is here, in the forecasts, that what will happen to *El Faro* starts to acquire more visible form; because on September 29 the packages, and the forecast, contain serious, and ominous, mistakes.

At 11:00 a.m. on the day of departure, the predicted position for Joaquin is 180 miles too far northeast. Its wind speed is underestimated by sixty knots. Worst of all, perhaps, this forecast is dismissive of the storm and predicts it will not become a hurricane but will weaken instead and veer, eventually, northward.

Davidson keeps an eye on the Weather Channel on a television in his stateroom—nearly everyone on the ship has a screen mounted on his cabin wall, or bulkhead—but the TV forecasting services, and most forecasters for that matter, are attuned to a land-based clientele, and from what you might glean from the six o'clock news on the twenty-ninth, you'd be forgiven for thinking no storm stewed out there at all.

Before he went to dinner, Davidson would also have checked his office computer for the latest package sent by the bespoke marine-weather service Applied Weather Technology.* AWT's Bon Voyage System, or BVS, sends emails on a schedule roughly concurrent with the National Weather Service's SAT-C transmission. While AWT bases its predictions for waters around the United States entirely on the National Weather Service forecast, the company enhances those data with fancy, easy-to-read graphics, formatted for Microsoft Outlook, that show various weather events in vividly colored maps and graphs: very high winds are displayed in red, less strong in orange and yellow. The package also includes projections of the effect of wind, waves, and currents on an individual ship's course, which the NWS does not.

Each ship subscribing to BVS can elect to receive a more specialized "tropical weather update" simply by clicking on the option. This comes in thirty minutes after the main package and elaborates on the basic information sent earlier. But according to BVS, *El Faro*'s officers never click on the option.

Also, for a further fee and for a specific ship, BVS will plan and recommend tailor-made routes to a given destination that avoid bad weather and maximize fuel efficiency. Tote has not forked over the extra $750 per month, per ship, and no routing advice is included in *El Faro*'s package.

---

* AWT was bought in 2014 by StormGeo, a Norwegian weather-consulting firm created by forecasters at Norway's TV2 television channel, but in 2015 the US group and its services were still operating under their previous names.

Just as the Weather Service did, BVS's email package clearly shows the predicted, westward-trending track of Tropical Storm Joaquin running well to the north of *El Faro*'s course to San Juan: clear graphic images of a spatial buffer protecting the ship from potential peril. Based on this information, a captain keeping to his usual course would expect seas and winds depicted in yellows and maybe orange, stronger than routine but not unusually so, especially compared to what passes for normal wind and sea conditions on the Alaskan route *El Faro* ran for years.

The flawed weather predictions are certainly one big reason Davidson does not consider taking a safer, more southerly route to Puerto Rico. Alternate routes from Florida to Puerto Rico are few because the Bahamas chain, to mariners, reads the way a high barrier fence thick with razor wire reads to a horseman. It's a nightmare of shoals, reefs, and stupidly shallow water. *El Faro*'s usual path keeps her safely north and east of the chain, in the profoundly deep water over the Nares abyssal plain.

But one deepwater path behind the chain exists: the Old Bahama Channel. It lies much farther southwest of *El Faro*'s usual route, and even farther from Joaquin's predicted track on September 29: a line of deep blue running between central Florida and the Bahamas, hugging southern Florida and then—via the Old Bahama Channel proper—the coasts of Cuba, Haiti, and the Dominican Republic. All the way to Puerto Rico. Though it adds 160 miles to the trip, it's not an unusual route: Davidson took it on his way north in mid-August to avoid Tropical Storm Erika, and another Tote captain, Bror Erik Axelsson, is known to have done the same to avoid a different storm. The channel, accessible only from its northern and southern ends and through a handful of winding "holes in the wall," principally the Northeast Providence Channel between Abaco and Eleuthera Islands, and the Crooked Island Passage between San Salvador and Crooked Island farther south, can seem narrow as it threads between Bahamian sandbars and the big islands of Cuba and Hispaniola to the southwest. And its lack of breadth would restrict further evasion if a storm should come that way. But it is so far to the south and west that a captain choosing to take that detour could be reasonably certain he is out of range of a storm raising Cain hundreds of miles offshore, in the Atlantic.

The Old Bahama route—including the holes in the wall—are alternatives that Charles Baird, a former second mate on *El Faro*, urges Davidson to consider in the last of three text messages sent from his home in South Portland, Maine, to Davidson on the twenty-ninth, in which he counsels caution regarding Joaquin; advice that Davidson acknowledges politely, but rejects on the grounds that he is already aware of the storm and factoring it into his plan, which is to "skirt under" the hurricane.

These are the roads not taken.

8

Davidson's equanimity at dinner should surprise no one; why worry, when the ship seems okay and is nearly ready for sea? He knows that a tropical disturbance was officially recognized as having turned into a storm yesterday evening—was even given a name, something hard to pronounce for the Anglo palate, Joaquin, apparently pronounced Wa-*keen*. But the forecasts are reassuring. Though the port engineer remembers Joaquin being mentioned at table, it is without emphasis, as someone discussing the weather in his kitchen might say, "It's supposed to rain." No heavy weather is expected.

This is in marked contrast to the previous month, late August, when Tote's safety manager sent out that email advising masters to prepare for Hurricane Danny by checking weather maps and reviewing cargo procedure with Tote's shoreside personnel. Updates were also requested on preparations for Erika, which followed close on Danny's heels. Both cyclones, of course, looked set to become the season's first bad-ass hurricane and like all firstborns got more attention; by the time the fourth or sixth storm rolls around, what once seemed noteworthy has become run-of-the-mill.

In the mess, loading updates crackle on UHF frequencies from walkie-talkies. The engineers and mates pop in and out to grab a cup of industrial coffee from the urn, or a sandwich, a plate of food. Coffee shows rings in the cup as the turbines are tested. Last cargo is now aboard and the port engineer, Neeson, has delivered a flash drive containing the latest CargoMax stability calculations;* Shultz has taken the drive to his office, where he plugs it into his workstation, downloads the worksheet, and compares it to the finalized cargo manifest. It all checks out, the GM margin stands over the desired 0.5, and Shultz has earned himself a sigh of satisfaction, a stretch, an instant of rest. Even the new third engineer, Dylan Meklin, who was late reporting for duty, has shown up, a fact that seems oddly important to Dany Randolph, now up on the bridge spinning the wheel to test the steering—right ten degrees, twenty degrees, then port ten and twenty—which translates under thirty feet of murky dark green water to a turn of the ship's massive, twenty-foot-high steel rudder.

Someone who knows Randolph might well detect, beneath the second mate's professional concentration, an extra two or three degrees of smile; likely no one's aware that earlier she received a cell phone call from her mother, now living in Denmark, Wisconsin. Laurie had just heard a rumor that a former neighbor's son, another Maine Maritime grad, might be joining Danielle's ship; Laurie phoned to ask her daughter if *El Faro* had just signed up a young third engineer named Dylan.

"Oh my God, how did you know?" Randolph exclaimed.

"Do you remember that kid across the street?"

Silence, then: "Oh my God, it's the *baby*!"

---

* The chief mate's eye seeks out the results of three CargoMax calculations that particularly affect ship safety. One is the bending moment, another term for stress that the cargo will exert on the ship's hold in different directions as she sags from freight loaded in her midsection; or "hogs," her bow and stern dipping in relation to her middle from too much weight on each end. Also, the ship should not be loaded in such a way as to lean to one side, as this would obviously make her more vulnerable to rolls in the same direction—and this calculation on *El Faro* must be tweaked because when she was built, or perhaps when she was lengthened by ninety feet in 1993, her hull ended up with more steel on the port side, which, all other things being equal, would give her a 2.5-degree tilt, or list, to that side. But the CargoMax has been fine-tuned to compensate and the mates, working with the stevedores' foreman, have tweaked the loading in such a way that enough weight is added to starboard (every 130 tons on one side works out to 1 degree of list) to bring her to an even keel; any persisting tilt can be dealt with by adding water to ballast tanks on one side or the other. Although the four main ballast tanks are permanently filled, two "ramp" tanks aft, one to port and one to starboard, can be pumped out or filled to compensate for list.

Twenty-five years earlier, Dylan Meklin's parents had moved into their new house in Rockland with a newborn son. "Danielle was eight, nine, just a little shit herself," her mother recalls. When Danielle was told about the baby, she insisted on going out to buy a toy—a set of building blocks—and presented the gift herself to the infant Dylan.

A quarter century later Randolph, chuckling, told her mom, "I am *so* going to give that kid a hard time. I am so going to have a field day with him, do you know he had the nerve to get to the ship late?"

Laurie protested; Dylan's mother had phoned her out of sheer anxiety, this was the boy's first ship after graduation and she was worried. Dylan's plane was delayed; it was not his fault that he was late. But Randolph will not forgo the chance at a practical joke and presumably has made good on her threat: knocked on the door of Dylan's cabin, given him the tongue-lashing she promised, smiling inwardly all the while.

9

As the air inside Joaquin warms and rises, it expands and is shunted outward as well by a local wind pattern that torques it away from the system's center. But as anyone who has watched the flight-data screen in a commercial airliner knows, the higher you rise, the colder the atmosphere; that's because less air exists high up to be heated by the sun. Therefore, as a hurricane's warm air moves into the next layer up, the stratosphere, it cools. Cooling, still moving outward, the system's vapor begins to condense into clouds, thunderheads, and then into water droplets that fall back to earth as rain. The downward cooling motion adds to what is now a vertically circular pattern: upward rush of warm wet air within, downward flow of cool air and rain without, all braided into more and more powerful winds that are both the result of and contributor to this increasingly rapid cycle.

The effects of the planet's spin, known as Coriolis force, now come into play. As Earth rotates from west to east, it deflects north winds toward the west, and south winds toward the east (in the northern hemisphere; the opposite in the antipodes).* The net effect of these winds is to spin this low-pressure system counterclockwise. Like Apaches circling a wagon train in a fifties western, the entire complex of rising warm vapor at the core and falling cool rain on the outskirts rides an increasingly furious cavalcade of winds that gallop harder and harder counterclockwise. The stronger the wind blows, the more air flows in toward the center; the faster it evaporates on its way up, the more hot, moist air it drags upward, the more rain falls outside the circle, and the faster the winds below.

Until now no one has paid much attention to this particular low-pressure system. But as its mechanism becomes more defined—a "tropical cyclone"—meteorologists start to peer closer at satellite pictures of the eastern, then the central, Atlantic. The doughnut-shaped swirl of clouds at the system's top is distinctive, as is the hole of plummeting atmospheric pressure in the middle. From ship reports, radio buoys, instruments parachuted from weather aircraft, data start to flow in that show a growing difference in pressure between the doughnut hole and its outskirts. While the winds stay below thirty-three knots, or thirty-eight miles per hour, the system counts as a "tropical depression" and is merely numbered. Hurricane watchers at the National Hurricane Center, located on the campus of Florida International University in Miami, give this system the number 11, as the eleventh of its type to spin into the Atlantic this year.

But the system keeps developing: the winds of number 11 move up the scale to 40, 50 mph. Beyond 34 knots, or 39 mph, the system is now officially a tropical storm. Eventually, as the tenth system to achieve

---

* A playground analogy makes what happens to the winds because of Coriolis more intuitively accessible. Imagine a playground merry-go-round (recently banished from many kids' areas by the no-risk-childhood movement). If you stand at the center of the merry-go-round as it spins, you feel much less centrifugal force and cover far less ground than you would standing at the edge. If, while standing at the center as the merry-go-round spins counterclockwise (or west to east, if you imagine the center as north), you take your rubber ball and aim it straight at a given point on the edge, the ball will miss your target and hit the edge at a point slightly to the west (against the direction of movement) of your target, because that target was moving faster than you were at the center. In the same way, winds blowing from the north are deflected slightly westward, while southerly winds are deflected eastward; between them they rub up counterclockwise movement in a developing low-pressure zone.

storm status in 2015, it is given a name, tenth down an alphabetical list compiled at the World Meteorological Organization headquarters in Geneva, Switzerland:

Joaquin.

It might have a name, but to forecasters Joaquin still doesn't look like much, it remains the troublesome kid next door who nine times out of ten grows out of his rebellion, his acting out, and, leaving for college or a job in the city, drops out of locals' ken. The predictive models of the NHC as well as those of other forecasters show little likelihood of significant growth. Joaquin will churn along, increasing only slightly in strength and then, confronted by the fronts perpetually rolling eastward off North America, take the usual path, northeast and out to sea; and there it will die, harmless, ignored, alone.

Unfortunately, the models are flawed.

10

On deck a quiet reigns, it feels strange because of the uninterrupted noise of the day so far. The gantry cranes have stilled, the yard tractors are parked and shut off, the ship's loading ramps winched up and stowed. Most of the longshoremen have by now punched the clock and gone home to families, tuna casseroles, *Wheel of Fortune*. The wind is still light, north-northeast; the air has given up some of the day's heat. Behind the overcast the sun went down fifteen minutes ago, and only a vague smear of flamingo cloud shows over *El Faro*'s bow to the west. Lights glare like a prison on lockdown over Blount Island Marine Terminal. On the trip south, with a full order of goods for Puerto Rico, cargo load is always near capacity and *El Faro*'s spotlights shine metallic, eye-smarting, across the looming containers stacked four-deep on almost every stretch of her deck except the house and the very bow of the ship.

A mate has switched on the ship's running lights, a jewel of bright emerald glowing outward on the starboard bridge wing, sharp ruby on the port. White range lights shine forward on the masts, there's a light astern as well. Warm yellow glows at portholes and windows on the house's sides; shadows lurk everywhere else, but the third mate, or perhaps the bosun, has already checked for stowaways. The shadows are uninhabited, and the chief mate declares the ship secured for departure.

Two pilots show up and, as a skeleton crew of dockworkers drop the gangway, are escorted by an AB to the wheelhouse.*

Jeremie Riehm, the third mate, is in the wheelhouse, along with Jack Jackson, the able seaman on watch, who will be steering. Chief Mate Shultz is now standing by on the bow with the bosun and the two "day" ABs, ready to winch in docking lines and pay out towlines to the tugs when the order comes. Riehm and two seamen stand at the stern. The docking pilot, James Frudaker, has maneuvered this ship in and out of Blount Island on over fifty occasions; for St. Johns Bar pilot Eric Bryson, this will be his fourteenth gig on *El Faro*. Davidson emerges from his cabin on the deck below, and everyone chats easily for a few minutes. The captain, too, has worked with these men before. He is known routinely to show off snapshots of his two daughters, Ariana and Marina, both athletic, attractive teens, both going to college in Maine. At one point in the conversation Bryson asks Davidson what he's planning to do to avoid this new tropical storm, Joaquin.

"I'm just going to—we're just gonna go out and shoot under it," Davidson says.

No one comments. There is no hurricane plan or checklist on board to refer to. Tote's advice on the subject is limited to two sentences in the safety guidelines: captains should take all precautions—and consult the maritime classic, Bowditch's *American Practical Navigator*. The guidelines take care of all heavy weather routines inside two paragraphs.

Davidson and the pilots go over departure conditions. There is

---

* Pilots are shiphandlers expert in local conditions and are required by law to maneuver large ships in and out of a given port; as in this case, usually one pilot is in charge of docking and undocking, while another will specialize in maneuvering the ship out of the harbor proper and to sea. In Jacksonville the pilots—who belong to two independent trade groups called, respectively, the Florida Docking Masters Association and the St. Johns Bar Pilot Association, both of which contract out to shipowners—are hired for individual vessel movements. If the ship is not ready within two hours of the appointed time, the company is billed and the pilots leave. This is sometimes another factor adding to the pressure felt by officers to keep to schedule.

almost no traffic. The *Kingfish*, a 965-foot, Bahamas-flagged container ship owned by the French shipping conglomerate CMA CGM,
is entering the river from the east. They can see her on radar, a yellow
icon; her name, call sign, speed, and course are signaled by transponder
and show up in a tiny text box next to the icon. The wind, still light
and northerly, won't be a factor tonight. Nevertheless, as the ship
will be heading east when she drops her pilots, they'll rig the Jacob's
ladder, down which the pilots will climb upon leaving, on the sheltered,
starboard side. Saint Johns River is tidal, and the tide is coming in,
so it will be a little harder to turn the ship's bow 180 degrees against
the upriver current, but that is what the two Moran tugs standing by
across the inlet are for.

Then captain and pilots sign the "docking card," a form that lists the
vessel's draft and affirms also that all required equipment is running:
radars, radios, engine, steering. If any essential gear is broken, it should
be listed here, and the pilots cannot take the ship out until the gear is
fixed or the Jacksonville port captain signs an exemption. Everything
works, with the exception of the ship's anemometer, a device for measuring wind speed and direction.

The anemometer is not on the list.

With departure plan discussed and pilot form signed, Davidson
telephones the engine room; his usual style is to loudly call, "Put some
heat on 'er," to which the chief replies they have sufficient steam on the
boilers and the engine is ready to go. Davidson then gives the okay to
the docking pilot, now standing on the port bridge wing, who radios
the tug masters on his portable VHF. The pilot orders let go forward
lines, let go aft, let go spring lines. There are splashes as the mooring
lines and wire hawsers drop into the harbor; *El Faro* is free of land.
The tugs take up slack on the towing lines, and the three-inch-diameter
ropes straighten into nylon bars, hard as iron, water spraying from
their compressed fibers. Roils of churned white water appear under
the tugboats' back ends as, with painful slowness, they start to pull
the huge ship sideways.

Someone on the bridge pulls the foghorn lanyard, and the wail, both
earsplitting and mournful, of a great ship departing echoes through
the depots and gantries, the Spanish moss and saw grass. At Paulie's

the drinkers at the counter turn to watch, and for a few seconds their chatter wanes.

On the fo'c'sle and in the covered section aft on 2nd Deck, where mooring lines are handled, the ABs finish winching in the ropes and wires. They lash their ends with lighter cordage to the bits, the twin vertical steel posts around which lines are looped to hold the ship in harbor; in rough seas, if a four-hundred-foot, three-inch line of nylon or wire goes overboard, it can wind itself around the prop and slow or stop the ship. For big storms the lines are fed off their winch reels into storage boxes below. But no such storms are expected and the lines are not stowed.

When *El Faro* is several hundred feet off the dock, Frudaker tells the tugs to stop pulling. He orders slow ahead and left full rudder, and Jack Jackson, at the helm, repeats the order, spins the wheel all the way left, counterclockwise—not an easy task, as the wheel is set low on the console and even for a man of average height requires bending the knees to operate; but the joystick that would turn the rudder mechanically, through the ship's autopilot, is too slow and clumsy for practical use. The deck begins to tremble as the turbine rolls. Seventy feet beneath the bridge a delta of crushed water emerges from *El Faro*'s stern. The ship, though carried upriver by the current, slowly turns leftward. The captain who knew her best, the one fired after the Lauderdale incident, claims that because the ship was not built for containers, a full deckload of freight will cause her to tilt centrifugally, which would mean to starboard now, when turning; but if that's the case, the pilot doesn't notice.*

In less than five minutes *El Faro*'s bow is pointing downriver. The tugs drop their lines. The river pilot now has control, and Riehm escorts

---

* Despite the ship's apparent "stiffness" (her lack of propensity to tilt) as she turns in the river—which might be because the turn is slow and gentle, given the ship's length and the river's narrowness here—it turns out, after *El Faro*'s accident, that the GM margin has been miscalculated, and the ship has sailed with slightly less of a margin than Shultz and Neeson figured; still within accepted safety limits, however. Yet the GM margin, which is a numerical representation of how willingly or reluctantly a ship will list, might have been flawed to begin with. The Coast Guard, with twenty-twenty hindsight, will later calculate that the standard GM margin *El Faro* sails with is too low for safe operation of this type of ship. Specifically, with only one compartment of one hold flooded, and assuming wind speeds of over seventy knots, the GM margin shrinks to zero, and the ship's ability to right herself dwindles with it.

Frudaker to the Main Deck, the ship's topmost exposed level. One of the tugs has crept up and rides next to the ship, keeping pace, her port side to *El Faro*'s starboard; the dock pilot climbs carefully down to step aboard the tug, which now, with a roar of engines and a farewell peep of her whistle, peels off, back to quayside.

On *El Faro*'s bridge the VHF squawks. Bryson, the bar and river pilot, talks to the pilot on the *Kingfish*. Quite soon the two ships cross paths, huge dark shapes blanking the suburban glow, port to port. One deck down, the windows in Shultz's stateroom shine brightly where the mate double-checks the cargo manifest against CargoMax figures; this is their last chance to turn back and reload if something is off. But he finds no discrepancies.

Mile Point Turn, Mayport Cut; finally *El Faro* moves down a line of buoys and two long breakwaters marking the end of the Saint Johns River. Now the ship, which has been gliding, stable as an apartment building, down the placid river, begins to feel the ocean; starts an almost imperceptible pitch forward to aft as her bow rises and falls, and a tiny roll, left and right, from the echoed waves bouncing off the rocks. A crew member, standing, doesn't even have to shift his weight, the movement is so small. At the red-and-white sea buoy marking the channel's end, Bryson radios the pilot boat to pick him up. He shakes hands with the bridge crew and makes his way to the pilot ladder.

The direct course to San Juan is 132 degrees. That number, along with the ship's speed, is written in greasy felt tip on the course board, which hangs between wheelhouse windows directly ahead of the helm. Riehm programs the course into the autopilot and checks radars, but the only seagoing traffic this evening is the dot, between breakwaters, of the pilot boat speeding back to Jacksonville.

The engine room has been called again and the boilers are pumping more steam, turbines accelerating to roughly 120 rpm, which translates to a little over 20 knots, or 23 mph. Riehm settles himself at the watch keeper's usual station, on the bridge's port side, his electronic eyes—two of the three radar screens—within easy reach. The ship rolls a bit more to the northerly swell. Mayport, Manhattan Beach, glow orange, shift rightward as *El Faro* adopts her southeasterly course for San Juan; to the left, to port, the sky is veiled and there are few stars, only the black, limitless presence of the Atlantic.

It is 10:30 p.m., September 29, 2015. *El Faro* and her crew have just over thirty-three hours to live.

Theater of navigation: The ship's command center, known as the bridge or wheelhouse. The windows face forward, over the stacked containers. The mate on watch typically stands on the left (port) side, by the twin radar screens. The ship's wheel is set low in the console's center.

PART III

THE SAILING

You do not ask of a tame seagull why once in a while it feels the need to disappear toward the wide ocean. It goes there, that's all, and it's simple as a ray of sun, as normal as the blue of sky.

—Bernard Moitessier

To a mariner, even if a storm is out there, and a storm is always out there somewhere, it feels good to cross at last into the zone of deep ocean.

Sailors like to blow a landlubber's mind with the counterintuitive statement that, to a ship, "the land is more dangerous than the sea," but this is only partially true. It's the interface between sea and land, where the ship faces both the sick danger of rocks, reefs, and combers twisted and amplified by shore, and the oceanic perils of wave and wind, that multiplies risk.

In deep ocean those foes do not team up.

Crossing into the deep is not the only reason for feeling good here. Many of her crew take pleasure in the way *El Faro* moves, they say she shows grace in a seaway. Her "scantlings"—the graceful slope of her stem (the hull's leading edge), the arc known as "turn of bilge" where bottom curves into sides, the flow of her "buttocks line," where, underwater, broad hull sweeps into thin stern—all feel like how a man might describe a lover's curves. All do their bit to make her lift easily to waves coming from ahead or behind, roll gracefully but not too much when they come from the side; steer true. Her hull is long in relation to her breadth, which partly accounts for her relative fleetness. Her sharp bow and relatively low house look better to a sailor's eye than the floating boxes that are modern container ships, or the obscenely decorated, top-heavy wedding cakes that cruise liners resemble.

Even the skipper who knows her best, who finds her "tender," or apt to roll too far when maneuvering fully loaded, appreciates her sea-kindly qualities. And Joe Letang, an electrician who worked on this ship till three weeks ago, says he would even now feel ten times safer on *El Faro* than on the slab-sided, state-of-the-art vessels powered by diesel and natural gas that Tote is building on the West Coast.

Some of the crew are familiar with her history in the rough winter waters of Tote's Tacoma–Anchorage run. They know that between 2003 and 2005, under contract to the government's Military Sealift Command, she ferried war gear to Kuwait for the invasion and occupation of Iraq; there she was drafted into service as a bomb shelter for infantry, came under attack from Scud missiles fired by Iraqi forces, and earned a Navy decoration.

Besides the history, apart from how she feels when moving, there's a built-in bias that sets a mariner to caring for any oceangoing craft. It is based on a commonality of interests, because from thirty-foot sloop to supertanker she was made to cross wild waters with no outside help and for the duration of the voyage must furnish both community and life purpose for her passengers and crew. The sense of those complex systems, not only machinery and navigation but hull structure and ballast, man-overboard and fire drills, cabin and laundry and food services, all churning and working together 24-7, adds up to a whole greater than the sum of its parts, a unified expression of living that has much to do with why ships, in English, are given a human pronoun; why mariners will call the ship "her" and love her, sometimes, as if she were alive, or at times hate her guts for being wayward, for being "wet" (because she punches through waves rather than going over them), for being jerky or unbalanced in her movements, for making them seasick—for not taking care of her people.

Some of *El Faro*'s crew call her a rust bucket, the mariner's term for an old, beaten-up, rotten-steel ship. But many of those same crew members feel affection for her and stay aboard anyway, year after year.

At night, as land disappears, as the ship relaxes into the longer-wavelength swells of deep ocean, the crew also relax into familiar input. The decks tremble in resonance with the engines' spin, a cabin's joinery creaks from the hull's gentle roll. The ship's smell: of porthole grease, salt, and detergent; of coffee, fuel oil, and chafing dish; takes on a supplementary waft of iodine and wind. On deck you can smell steam and bunker exhaust, hear a breath of boiler pressure, but the loudest sound is the deep, rhythmic crunch and hiss of sea as the great hull drives through four-foot waves southeast.

Course 132 degrees true,* direct for San Juan, eleven hundred miles away. Speed 21 knots, 24 mph. Wind light from the north. The sky is still overcast. The wheelhouse is quiet; an occasional crackle from the VHF; sometimes, near the coast, the mates will turn on the FM radio and pick up yee-haw country or gospel music from Florida stations; or else a Sirius satellite channel. The only illumination on the bridge is the glow of radar and GPS screens, the dials of gyroscope, gauges, and radios, the red-tinted lights that allow watch standers to work without utterly losing night vision. On the mast above the wheelhouse roof, radar scanners turn steadily, obsessively, providing the mate in charge with short- and long-range images of the sea around, from three to thirty miles off.

El Faro's bridge is small, roughly thirty feet by twenty-five, a tight theater for the drama of navigation. Seven square windows face forward; a door on each side leads to open air, to the long "wings" like fenced steel observation terraces running to the ship's edge, from which an officer can see up and down the hull's length. This is particularly useful when carrying a full load of containers, which block the view for several hundred yards dead ahead.

Under the windows a console holding instruments spans the bridge's width. The two radar sets the mate uses, one of them calibrated for short range, stand on the port side. The small steel wheel is set in the middle of the console, along with controls for "Iron Mike," the ship's automatic steering system or autopilot, and the gyroscope and compass dials. A third radar screen, set on thirty-mile range, stands near the captain's chair, by the starboard side-door. A settee and a row of cabinets, and then the Inmarsat terminal, line the port side; the back end of the wheelhouse contains a chartroom, where a navigator can plot courses on an extrawide desk. Bookshelves full of nautical manuals, wooden cabinets holding charts, and various electrical panels and switches are

---

* All courses are listed as "true," which means cardinal points based on the actual geographical position of Earth's north-south poles, as opposed to "magnetic," based on the planet's magnetic pole, which not only is hundreds of miles distant from the geographical pole but varies yearly. Old-fashioned ships, reliant on magnetic compasses, primarily used bearings based on magnetic north, sometimes converted to true. Modern ships mostly use gyroscopes or flux-state compasses that show true north.

built into the chartroom bulkhead. A curtain screens the area's lights from the rest of the bridge. Access to the bridge is provided by a companionway, or set of stairs, behind the chartroom.

2

The normal third engineer's watch is twelve to four, but for greenhorns it's split six on, six off for training purposes. Anyway it's likely that Dylan Meklin visits his new world, the engine room, much earlier than any assigned watch. Probably he was told to observe closely the process of firing up the boilers, getting the ship under way; kept safely to one side while the pros deal with different "bells," the commands rung down from bridge to engine-room telegraph for various speeds, the forward and reverse commands of maneuvering. This means Meklin, a large twenty-three-year-old ex–football player with a thick brown beard, is in double culture shock, wondering why the pretty second mate with the weirdly familiar accent has it in for him; trying to absorb, as well, this universe of machinery that seems half-familiar, because he learned of it in school; half-alien also because it's a big ship, an old plant, and every ship, every engine room, and especially this one has its own culture, idiosyncrasies, and character dynamics that have to be figured out fast before they get a newbie in trouble.

If cargo loading felt like a hell of heat and frenzied activity for the mates, the engine room takes the prize for all-time Big League Inferno. First, it's deep—the eighth and ninth circles of this ship, if we're talking Dante. To get there you open a watertight door on Main Deck and drop down a couple of levels of metal steps into a darkness only partially alleviated by banks of neon lights. An elevator exists, but it's as old as the ship and judged unserviceable, and anyway it only goes down to 2nd Deck.

Also, it's hot as the usual nightmare of Hades, well over 100°F in spots in spite of big steel vent openings on Main Deck that funnel air into fans blowing hard and loud in multiple corners of the engine room; despite the watertight door in the forward bulkhead on 3rd Deck, which is almost always hooked open to provide a draft.

Finally it's unpleasantly, in places even harmfully, loud, from the blast of ventilators as well as the whoosh of steam, the rumble of turbine and gears, the continuous hum of generators and pumps—though modern engine rooms built around giant thudding diesels can be even louder. Young Meklin, as he nervously negotiates the last steps of the companionway to the engine room's upper level, would be met there by yelled greetings: from the chief engineer, Richard Pusatere; from one of the two more experienced third engineers, Mitch Kuflik, assigned to train the new kid; possibly from the senior third, Michael Holland, another Mainer and a Maine Maritime grad as well.

This upper level of the engine room includes long corridors, nicknamed bowling alleys, on each side, the starboard lane holding a rank of electricity panels plus two two-thousand kilowatt generators, the port a machine shop (including lathe, drill press, welding equipment) and office; but its focus is the main control panel. This functions like the wheelhouse console does for navigation officers. It's a metal bank of electronics, over ten feet long and six high, holding many dozens of gauges, switches, levers, buttons, and valve controls, with a soundproof booth at one end for telephone conversations with the bridge. Standing at this panel an engineer would face aft, toward the ship's rear end, the two massive boilers rising at his back and right up through the house toward the smokestack. Though he cannot see them over the banked dials in front of him, the tops of two turbines and then the reduction-gear housing rise like the gray backs of sea monsters into the fraught penumbra. A "gravity-fed" lubricating-oil tank sits well above, in the casing through which the boiler exhaust runs, at Main Deck level; a second, reserve tank containing an extra ten-ton supply of oil lies behind and to port of the turbines.* Every other nook and corner is stuffed full of junction boxes, wire conduits, firefighting equipment, pipes, dials, and valves; everything is painted gray and cream or else color-coded; all is wiped down and shiny.

As Kuflik guides Meklin to the level below, they'd descend into another crowded space containing the cozily insulated lower bulk of

---

* The gravity-fed tank, which is looped into the lubricating system, is topped up automatically by the oil pump as the engine runs. It is there to provide temporary lubrication should the pumps fail.

the boilers at the engine room's forward end. Arrayed across the steel plates above, thick, insulated steam pipes hang from spring-loaded brackets. Several of the brackets are rusted, a few broken outright. The main condensers rise toward the ship's stern; giant pumps and associated controls rise in front of them; more pumps are on the port side, with cooling gear and the two lubricating-oil pumps farther aft. In the rear and middle portion of this level stands the reduction gears' lower housing. Behind those lie two more workshops, and an emergency escape stairway to 3rd Deck; and finally the propeller shaft, cradled by massive bearings and a watertight housing that leads through the ship's aft end to the vast propeller, churning away at the dark, warm Atlantic water.

To Meklin this would all seem both strange and familiar: strange because his school's training ship, the *State of Maine*, runs a diesel engine instead of the more complex steam plant—in this she reflects a contemporary reality, for modern ships are almost exclusively powered by giant diesels, fueled by oil or liquid natural gas, and Tote itself is phasing out its steamships in favor of new, environmentally friendly, hybrid LNG-diesel-powered vessels. But it would also seem familiar because steam remains part of the academy curriculum, and Meklin would have had to memorize every aspect of this type of plant to pass his Coast Guard license. It's not unusual for new third engineers to seek assignment on a steam-powered vessel, just for the experience. If this is the case, Meklin is lucky in the officers he will be working under because the chief, Rich Pusatere, and Third Engineer Kuflik— not to mention Jeff Mathias, the chief engineer responsible for the riding gang—are near-fanatical devotees of steam, of the elegance and power of its systems. The chief and his first and second engineers all have over ten years' experience on steam plants. "It was a steam culture," a former first engineer on *El Faro* says of the ship's engine room. "If you want to be an automobile mechanic," Pusatere is fond of quipping, "sail diesel. If you want to be an engineer, sail steam." Ironically perhaps, the chief has been selected to sail on one of the new Tote ships but needs more time on diesels to qualify; that is one reason he's still on *El Faro* today. To these three men the interlocking cycles of a marine steam system evoke, if in more prosaic form, the divinity Rudyard Kipling wrote of in "McAndrew's Hymn," his paean to marine engineers:

> Lord, Thou hast made this world below the shadow of a dream,
> An', taught by time, I tak' it so—exceptin' always Steam.
> From coupler-flange to spindle-guide I see Thy Hand, O God—
> Predestination in the stride o' yon connectin'-rod.

The poetry is not hard to identify with because a certain beauty does exist in the way these thousands of components, changing from one chemical state to another then back again, bursting with fire and pressure, function in even balance—*El Faro*'s propulsion system is called, in the trade, a balanced system—as they pull together to turn a bronze prop taller than many town halls at over 100 rpm, driving a ship big as four city blocks at 24 mph through the indifferent ocean.

The other side of a balanced system is that if one part of it goes down the rest, suddenly unbalanced, goes with it. To train for such breakdown, Pusatere, who is known as Mr. Policy for his love of un-bending routine, regularly schedules pop drills, watching his crew go through the various steps necessary to get propulsion back in case of, for example, sudden electrical failure, a breakdown in the lubricating system, or a shutdown in pumps feeding water to the boilers.

So Meklin knows the theory: that the guiding principle behind *El Faro*'s propulsion plant comes down to a closed, two-phase cycle. The first phase, evaporation, consists of taking purified water, heating it up in two boilers, and then superheating it till the H_2O has totally evaporated into high-pressure steam, thus vaporizing even the tiniest drops, which at high pressure would fly hard and sharp as shrapnel. Then the steam is blasted through the delicately ranked propellers of a turbine that spin shafts, which, after passing through a series of gears, rotate the ship's massive propeller shaft.

The second phase is the condensation cycle, in which used steam drains from the turbine, as well as from the ship's main generators, which also run on steam. The vapor passes through a seawater-cooled condenser and reverts to water. The recycled water is then pumped back into the boilers to start the steam cycle again.* From this perspective also, the similarities with a hurricane's cycle are not hard to spot.

The lubrication system runs on the same dynamically self-sustaining principle. Even outside the boilers, pipes, and turbines, the components of a steam cycle—including the valves and gears that control it—generate tremendous heat, and it's the job of the lubrication cycle to lower that heat, reducing the friction of turning parts. This cycle is not much different from a car engine's. Thick, viscous lubricating oil is pumped over every square inch of madly spinning steel, the turbines, gears, and bearings especially; and after cooling, buffering, and greasing the machinery, the used oil is collected in a sump underneath the machines, then chilled, filtered, and pumped back over the system.

While the lubrication cycle might seem secondary to the main event, its importance in the overall engine-room scheme is hard to exaggerate. If the cycle fails—if the oil pumps, for example, stop running—the soaring heat of the turbine will quickly cause it to seize up and stop, and the ship will lose propulsion. If this happens in high waves the ship will be helpless to evade them. If both the on-line and backup pumps fail, to prevent destruction of the turbine an automatic shutoff stops the turbine cold when oil pressure drops below redline level; this happened last July when an inexperienced oiler, mistaking an oil for a seawater valve, shut off supply to the oil pumps. The pumps went off-line, causing the engine to stop, and left *El Faro* drifting, helpless, in the middle of San Juan Harbor.

The mishap was reported to the company and to the Coast Guard. Better training was recommended, and the lube-oil valves were tied

---

* The turbine blades work as all propellers work, steam pushing against the leading edge and exhausting toward the trailing edge, creating a pressure differential between the two that translates into lift; here, too, they replicate in microcosm a process that will affect, on a larger scale, *El Faro*'s fate. The pressure and speeds in this system are extremely high— although the plant, due to age-related wear, cannot produce the power it did forty years ago, the superheated steam still roars from boilers to turbines at 850 pounds per square inch, at 900°F, and it is one of the top nightmares of a marine engineer to be standing anywhere near a steam pipe when it ruptures, since the vapor would within seconds both scald and flay the flesh from his or her bones, which by any standards ranks low on the list of desirable ways to die. Ship's electricity is a stepchild of the steam cycle, a one-way conversion of kinetic energy to electromagnetic tension, as the twin two-thousand-kilowatt Terry/GE turbo-generators are turned by steam hived off the main system. The cargo's multiple refrigeration units work off these, plus, in case of emergency, a circuit powered by a Detroit Diesel engine on Main Deck.

off and painted in different colors. The incident became part of a "risk matrix" that Coast Guard inspectors maintain on every US-flag commercial ship, a file that includes injuries and breakdowns as well as other particularities of the vessel.

No one on this ship, no one even at Tote, is aware that *El Faro*'s record, while by no means abysmal for a vessel of this age, has recently moved the ship into a new category in the matrix. On October 1, 2015, she is to be added to a "target list" of vessels that are deemed at particular risk of dysfunction, requiring additional oversight.

3

El Faro is an hour out from the Jacksonville sea buoy by 11:30 that night. The third mate, Jeremie Riehm, is on watch till midnight. He is forty-six, a quiet man with an easy grin, thick brush-cut hair. Riehm, the only navigation officer who did not graduate from a merchant marine academy, is by definition a "hawsepiper," and his experience at all levels of deep-sea work is held in some respect: one of the ship's bosuns claims Riehm is the best seaman aboard. He has been at sea since he was twenty-four.

The deckhand on duty is Jack Jackson. At age sixty Jackson is in good shape—tall, reasonably fit, unlike a lot of the crew on this relaxed and regional schedule, who run to fat. Like Riehm, he is one of the most experienced hands on board. Jackson became curious about sailing as a teen in the seventies, watching freighters amble up and down the Mississippi from where he worked as a waiter at Café Du Monde, a restaurant on the levee in New Orleans. At that time, American shipowners were busy trading their US-made and -registered ships for "foreign-flag" vessels built in Korea, registered in Liberia, manned by poorly paid crews from Indonesia or the Philippines, and thus much cheaper to operate. But enough Yankee freighters remained that Jackson had no trouble finding work on runs that turned him on. He is attracted to excitement; his younger brother remembers riding pillion, both aghast and thrilled as, late at night, Jack tore at mad speed through the French Quarter on his Norton 850 Commando motorcycle; and exotic ports were exciting

then. Unlike now, when ships are turned around within hours in su-
permechanized, isolated, massively protected container or bulk-cargo
terminals—as in Rotterdam, Singapore, Blount Island—in those days
ships going to Angola or Senegal or up the Congo River, or to various
out-of-the-way harbors in Asia, allowed a sailor time to experience
the country. It was the old "merch," ancient mariners will tell you. In
such ports the cargo was unloaded slowly, using the ship's derrick, and
sometimes on the backs of local stevedores, in a process Conrad would
have recognized. The harbors were often hot, clogged with bumboats,
native sailing craft, and smells of spice, woodsmoke, sewage; plagued
with delay. This meant Jackson could take days off to explore.*

The former bosun on *El Faro* says Jackson is the only AB on the
ship who is proficient at traditional sailor's rope work, such as making
a monkey's fist, an intricate ball of Manila used to weight heaving lines
so they can be thrown to shore. "Officers learn seamanship from the
sailors," the bosun says, and Jackson is one of the teachers. He learned
navigation early and might have become a mate decades ago. Once,
while he was working on a Navy-contracted ship charged with secretly
testing Soviet submarines' defenses off Kamchatka, in Russia's Far East,
the company offered him a free ride at maritime school to earn his third
mate's license. Jackson refused; he prefers a job without the hassles of
paperwork or the drag responsibilities of leadership, work that allows time
off during which he can read or draw—he is seldom seen without paper
and a Rapidograph pen. Perhaps for similar reasons he has stayed single,
though there have been women aplenty, in different parts of the world.

But Jackson, like Danielle Randolph, had doubts about this trip.
Probably it's just a sleight of autumn, a coincidence of wavelengths in a
thirtysomething and a sixty-year-old who are both, at different points
in their lives' cycles, verging on a new phase.

"Usually he called when he was in Jacksonville, we talked for three,

---

* Jackson was proud that he steered a ship up the Congo River, into Conrad's "heart of
darkness." And once, hiking deep into Thailand's Chiang Mai Province, he wounded his
foot, contracted blood poisoning, and, far from the nearest medical facility, might have died
had not a group of Buddhist priests showed up and over the course of several days nursed
him back to health. The experience presumably lies near the heart of an enormous chicken-
wire-and-concrete Buddha figure he is building in the backyard of his home in Jacksonville.

four minutes," Jack's brother, Glen Jackson, says. "This time [September 8, 2015] I was in Lowe's, or Home Depot, and we talked for forty-five, fifty minutes. For the first time he said, 'Man, I think I'm gonna get off [the ship].' He never broke a contract before, but he was seriously concerned." Jack thought *El Faro* was a rust bucket, but that wasn't the problem; he had sailed on rust buckets before without worrying overmuch about it. Still, the last time Glen and his brother talked was the usual three-minute check-in, the day *El Faro* left on this trip, and Jack didn't mention leaving then.

Tonight, perhaps, he and Riehm talk gearhead: the mate owns a classic Ford, and Jack is still into motorbikes, a passion he also shares with the electrician, Champa. Jackson and Riehm both check the radars, which on longest range show only the thin orange line of Florida receding, thirty-odd miles to starboard.

Other merchant ships should show up as orange wedges with their automatic identification system transponder* info flagged on-screen, but now there are zero, none at all; it turns out later they have either stayed in port or scooted back to shelter because of Joaquin. *El Faro* is going against the flow, against wisdom in a way, but she and her crew are old hands at this route. They know Tote's profits depend on providing regular and uninterrupted service, as far as possible, to the island.

Many sailors and especially islanders are conscious that Puerto Rico, which produces few household items besides some coffee, sugarcane, fruits, and rum, depends for life support on the goods *El Faro* and her sister ship *El Yunque* bring to the island: everything from cereal to TVs, lightbulbs to Popsicles, steaks to car parts to tampons. The dependency is decades old and has only grown starker over the last twenty years as the island's economy has crumbled. Unemployment in Puerto Rico in 2015 stands at 12 percent, more than double the US average. Tourism still brings in cash, but other local businesses fail daily, in good part because the monsters of mainland retail, chiefly Walmart and Walgreens, drive hard their usual business model, using economies of scale in orders, advertising, and transport to offer products cheaper than elsewhere. This

---

* AIS is an identification beacon that transmits a ship's name, course, and speed to the radar screens of all nearby vessels and port authorities. It's required on most ships over three hundred tons sailing internationally.

is a smart move in Puerto Rico, where nearly half the population lives at or below the poverty line, and where 10 or 20 percent off the weekly food budget is therefore a big deal; but it guts the bodegas and main streets.*

Walmart is known to include delay clauses in its transportation contracts, essentially penalizing shippers if goods aren't delivered before a specified deadline,† and this might exacerbate a natural tendency, at Tote headquarters, to insist everything must be done to get the ship to its destination on time, with due deference to safety concerns of course.

Riehm, a cigar aficionado, tends to take breaks on the bridge wings, where he can light up and watch the horizon and feel the wind on his face, something a good navigator needs to do once in a while to sense in his gut what is going on. Just as a competent engineer will not sit exclusively by his dials but will walk around his machines, his servo-mechanisms, touching and tweaking and smelling them sometimes, a navigator needs to get a feel, unmediated by gauge and software, for the elements through which the ship is moving. This is more important than usual given the offline status of the ship's anemometer, the instrument that measures wind speed, which is crucial in heavy weather at night when the effects of high winds on waves are invisible. The anemometer has not worked properly for at least three months, and Davidson has filed

---

* It is no coincidence that Puerto Rico in 2015 holds the distinction of containing the greatest number of Walmart stores (including its subsidiaries) per square mile and per inhabitant in the United States. It's the biggest employer on the island, with over fourteen thousand people working in its stores, warehouses, and offices. In 2014 Walmart and its subsidiaries owned 65 stores in Puerto Rico; by way of contrast, Massachusetts, with double the population, had 50. Walgreens ran 127 outlets on the island. In 2015 Walmart is in the process of suing the commonwealth's government to oppose a coming sales tax increase from 2 to 6.5 percent. The company has threatened to leave the island if the increase, known as Act 72, is passed. Walmart will later win the suit, based on evidence that diverting some of the Walmart stores' profits to public projects was a specific aim of the proposal and thus discriminatory. Overall, Puerto Rico's economy in 2015 suffers from a failed policy of tax breaks, called Section 936, that brought in a slew of big manufacturers, many of them pharmaceutical, which mostly spent their money off-island. Section 936 was phased out in 2006, and the manufacturing sector has steadily declined since; the commonwealth will file for bankruptcy relief in May 2017, the first time a US state or territory has ever done so. In September 2017, Hurricane Maria will compound the island's problems, causing multiple fatalities and largely wrecking Puerto Rico's infrastructure.

† Neither Walmart nor Tote replied to the author's requests for information on that score. Jim Fisker-Andersen, Tote's ship-management director, when asked during hearings whether he was aware of penalties for delays incurred by Tote, will respond that he didn't know.

an online request for repairs through the company's AMOS spreadsheet (the acronym standing for Asset Management Operating System), but nothing has been done so far. Tote is known, among some of *El Faro*'s people at least, for being slow, if not downright reluctant, to replace gear, and both officers and crew have complained about it.

Another good reason to get a gut feel for the night is to judge the "sail" effect of wind on the forty-foot-high container stacks, which can affect the vessel's stability; this effect, for some reason, is not included in CargoMax stability numbers.

Jackson instinctively keeps an eye on "distance made good," how far the ship has traveled on the chart. Basic navigation on modern ships is carried out on an ECDIS, or Electronic Chart Display and Information System, essentially a computer that graphically melds a digital chart with the ship's GPS position; more recent versions will overlay radar images, including other traffic, plus tide and weather data, so that a navigator can read almost everything he or she needs to know by eyeballing one screen. But *El Faro* doesn't have an ECDIS; its GPS workstation merely fixes the ship's position, including distance, speed, and time from waypoint to waypoint. The person navigating has to keep visual track of where he or she is on a paper chart.

Still, the GPS position is ridiculously accurate, to within a few yards. In any case both Riehm and Jackson have no problem navigating the old way, multiplying speed and time to see how far they've come, how much time remains till the next waypoint, a calculation known as dead reckoning; estimating how many degrees off a planned course wind or current will push them, and how to change course to compensate. There are no currents to speak of, this far off the Florida coast, no ships whose vectors they have to plot.

The evening passes without incident. A few minutes before midnight Danielle Randolph and Larry Davis appear in the wheelhouse for their regular twelve-to-four shift. Given that both Jackson and Riehm will be on watch again in eight hours, and Riehm will probably get up earlier to check lifesaving equipment, including life rafts on deck and survival suits in individual cabins, it's near-certain that the off-duty watch standers now retire to their cabins to sleep: Riehm to his stateroom in the navigating officers' quarters on the next level below, and Jackson to the crew's quarters three decks down, one deck up from mess deck.

A little before 4:00 a.m. Chief Mate Shultz appears in the wheel-house, along with Able Seaman Frank Hamm. The routine of watch change is like a rite in the church of navigation, a ritual of call and response. There is even a missal of sorts: it's the overall voyage plan that the captain and second mate worked up before departure, Jacksonville to San Juan; plus the captain's "night notes," which describe his instructions for this particular period of darkness, including when and if the captain should be woken up.

The officer on duty shows the relieving officer their current position—roughly seventy miles east of Cape Canaveral when Shultz comes on watch—and course and speed. He lists any planned course changes, and the relieving officer repeats the information. Traffic, if any, is described, along with any other relevant data, such as engine problems, cargo state, and weather.

4

Sometime before 6:00 a.m. on October 30, Captain Davidson leaves his stateroom and takes the companionway to the bridge. It is still dark out, still overcast. Chief Mate Shultz is probably at the usual watch-standing officer's position on the forward port side, next to the two radar screens.

If relations between Davidson and Chief Engineer Pusatere are sometimes strained, the captain and his first officer get along well. Both are social by nature and appreciate each other's qualities. In a tight society like a ship's, that also means knowing some of each other's darkness, and the darkness, especially the captain's, is relevant here.

One former engineer on *El Faro* says Davidson is considered by some to be "weird," idiosyncratic in his habits and tastes. Randolph has told a Coast Guard officer she's friendly with that she is wary of what she considers to be Davidson's mind games. The captain can be irritable—his flare-ups with the chief engineer are a case in point—though that is hardly a comment worth making on a ship that sometimes feels like a floating pressure cooker, thirty-three people locked together on the same run week after week, some of them you get on with and some you don't, some are diligent and some, in your opinion, fuck off. Jeff Mathias has been described as an "undiplomatic New Englander"; Dany Randolph, too, has been known to erupt. The alternate third engineer, Mitch Kuflik, who at almost six and a half feet is imposing enough physically, is not exactly sunshine and daylilies when he sees someone slacking—can even be a tad scary when he spots a job he considers botched.

Davidson is well liked in some respects, and people appreciate his easiness with unlicensed personnel, but this doesn't necessarily facilitate command in the tight autocracy that is a ship, and it can prove a downright handicap in a corporate situation. Davidson's openness, for example, might have worked against him last August, when a crewman showed up drunk after shore leave in San Juan. Davidson, once summoned by the duty officer, not only allowed the crewman back on board but did not immediately report him to Tote, which violated what corporate officers term their "zero tolerance" policy toward drinking alcohol.

More seriously perhaps, there have been comments from crew as well as from officers to the effect that Davidson's style leans toward that of a "stateroom captain," someone happy with the increasingly bureaucratic, job-delegating role of the modern ship's master. Davidson is "doing bridge paperwork all the time," an ex-bosun on *El Faro* says. Another ex-crewman notes that Davidson spends an inordinate amount of energy enforcing clear handwriting in the ship's log. Certainly, having been brought up by a father who is a certified public accountant might imply an ease with desks and computers, spreadsheets and paperwork, and a concomitant acceptance of this more abstract nature of modern command. By way of contrast, such ease is not shared by another Tote captain, Bror Erik Axelsson, a former commercial fisherman and master on *El Faro*, who is known to be an old-style, even stubbornly old-fashioned, skipper; for roaming around the ship at all hours, checking lines and lashings, getting his hands dirty—a hard-nosed and intrusive routine not always appreciated by the crew.

Tote's staff have heard the reports about Davidson's style. Corporate evaluations, while noting he has an excellent record and is "able to handle a diversified and unpredictable crew quite well," also mention his reputation as a stateroom captain.

Jim Fisker-Andersen, the director of ship management at Tote Services, has stated in internal communications that Davidson is "the least engaged in crew management" of all Tote skippers. Another captain, Earl Lawfield, will report that Tote sees Davidson as someone who's "not going in the direction Tote is going in."*

Not all of the crew would agree with the owners' assessment. Some of them have spotted Davidson checking containers, weather, and the Main Deck generally, in the early hours. Kurt Bruer notes that when on the bridge Davidson is not reluctant to take over watch standing for a while, to allow the mate or AB on duty break-time, enough at least to grab a cup of coffee or fix a sandwich of cold cuts from the "night lunch" buffet the cook has prepared, or to write an email home from a terminal in the ship's office on the next deck down. Davidson is concerned with crew safety, known for telling crew members to wear hard hats, to "come back with all your fingers and toes." And this captain is courteous: one bosun notes that Davidson is the only Tote captain he has worked with who routinely thanks him for "doing a good job."

Davidson, as well as being egalitarian, is respected as a good family man. This is no small compliment on a run that includes a lot of Florida or Puerto Rico people who waited weeks, even months, in the Jacksonville or Lauderdale union halls for a Tote job to light up on the digital "job board" specifically so they could stay close to their families; for *El Faro* will be in Jacksonville, or San Juan, every other week, regular as clockwork, which affords those who live nearby time to go home and hug the kids, or have dinner with the wife or husband, get laid maybe. And when their tour of duty ends—typically they work sixty days on, thirty off—they won't have to fly from Singapore or Rotterdam or Oakland to get home.

Davidson's usual rotation would have taken him off the ship for this trip, but that would have meant, during his next tour, he would have missed his twenty-fifth wedding anniversary. As a result he requested

---

* Perhaps to help Davidson improve his management style, Tote sent him to the STAR Center in Dania Beach, Florida, a professional training school run by the officers' trade union (AMO, or American Maritime Officers). There he attended a "leadership and management" course that included subjects such as "personnel management and administration," "effective communications," and "safety and environmental leadership in the maritime industry." He also completed a radar refresher course. Davidson took no classes in heavy-weather tactics, emergency shiphandling, stability, or cargo management, although such courses were also on offer.

an extension to his current tour so that he could be home later for the celebration. This is the main reason he is running *El Faro* tonight.

None of this matters, though, when the ship is sailing; when all of a mariner's training, all his experience, incessantly din his brain with protocols to run through, problems to foresee, data to check, because it's only through unending observation—the Navy catchphrase is "situational awareness"—that one can ensure the myriad systems that make up a ship keep running and working safely. This morning, given the presence of that tropical storm somewhere off to port, the key routines to observe concern the weather.

5

Here is the weather as observed from a ship. First, there's what you actually see with your own eyes; at night, under overcast skies, the stars are few or nonexistent, and not much is visible of the sea but the recurrent, kaleidoscopic shimmer of wake, sometimes backlit by phosphorescence, spreading blue-white from the sides and stern over a half-seen undulation of waves. On this night the actual wind is still from the north and remains light. If you knew this was a tropical system and could measure the wind accurately, with an anemometer for instance, you would know that if you stood facing the wind in the northern hemisphere, given that the system's wind rotates counterclockwise, the zone of low pressure would lie to your right.* Presumably, with a northerly breeze, as you face the wind blowing at the ship's stern, this puts Tropical Storm Joaquin to your right-hand side (the ship's port side), to the east. But you can't consult the anemometer, and anyway the wind's southward progression tonight is slower than the ship's; therefore what breeze exists is relative, it comes from *El Faro*'s movement, from dead ahead.

The overcast means little in itself. So you turn to the latest marine forecasts.

The previous SAT-C forecast, at 11:00 p.m., showed Joaquin altering

---

* This is known as Buys Ballot's law.

course slightly to the south, to 240 degrees or west-southwest, with winds rising as high as sixty knots but no higher. It is still predicted to remain a tropical storm, and its projected path continues to run well above the ship's planned route. It transpires later that this forecast places the storm 104 miles farther to the northeast than will be the case and underestimates its strength by thirty-five knots.

Davidson turns to the next forecast, the SAT-C transmission that comes in at 5:00 a.m. This one is the most misleading of all. It predicts that Joaquin will remain a tropical storm, moving slowly west-southwest, with winds just below hurricane force and declining. The mariners on the bridge mark the storm's first symptoms (and from here on, the conversation on the bridge is reproduced verbatim).*

"First wall of water," Shultz remarks, presumably watching the fuzzy line on his screen that indicates precipitation, "gonna get a whole line of rain squalls . . . got the swell."†

"Oh, yeah," Davidson replies. "Probably gonna get worse. . . . Look." They study the SAT-C bulletin together. "Remember how we saw this the other day. Festering. And we talked about these [slow-moving storms] are the worst."

"I'm anxious to see the newest BVS," Shultz says. ". . . Guessin' we're just skirtin' the yellow [weather graphic] here. . . . We'll see."

"We'll see how it goes," the captain says. ". . . This is forecasted to go north . . . and that takes your option out to top it."

"Even so, the worst weather's up here."

"Correct."

---

* *El Faro* carried a black box, a digital voyage data recorder or VDR that was programmed to store the latest twelve hours of conversation on the bridge, and in fact recorded twenty-six hours' worth. Subsequent to *El Faro*'s loss, the VDR was successfully recovered and, following eleven hundred hours of painstaking work by National Transportation Safety Board audio engineers, its contents retrieved. From this point in the text relevant portions of conversation on the bridge are transcribed directly from the record. (See the Author's Note for further details of this process.) Occasional brackets mark phrases NTSB's audio engineers had to tease out of the surrounding noise.

† A swell is a wave of relatively long wavelength, which can sometimes run in a different direction to shallower waves, and reflect more distant or long-lasting weather events. In the case of Joaquin, based on bridge conversation, waves and swells rarely appeared to differ markedly in direction or quality, and except where specifically described as one or the other, the terms are used interchangeably.

"So we'll just have to tough this one out," Shultz continues, "come down south of the track line."

And at this point the captain and his chief mate agree to alter course slightly westward, to 134 degrees, to steer the ship farther away from the storm's anticipated position. However they will not take one of the "holes in the wall" to the Old Bahama Channel, or rather, they'll put off any decision to divert till they are farther south.

"Either that or it's merging," Shultz says. ". . . Old Bahama Channel when we get there. I would wait. Get more information. . . . This doesn't look bad. . . ."

Davidson comments that even on this new course the waves will be twelve to fifteen feet high.

"The ship can handle it," the chief mate says.

At around 6:10 a.m. Davidson goes below, saying he will send up the BVS weather package, which is emailed exclusively to a workstation in the captain's office and reaches the bridge workstation only if forwarded by the skipper via the ship's intranet.

When he comes back, the two men examine the Bon Voyage graph.

"We're south and west of it," Davidson comments.

"Uh-huh," the mate agrees.

"So let's open that up." The captain points with one finger. ". . . Come down here a little bit, you know what I'm sayin'? Yeah, you can steer a little bit more away . . . from the center." The two men plug the new course and waypoints into the GPS set. ". . . What's helpin' us right now is our speed."

"It's twenty—twenty additional miles," Shultz says.

"And then if the storm doesn't come this deep to the southwest as anticipated," the captain replies, "we can just come around it."

"Yeah, and what we'll do is," Davidson continues shortly thereafter, "once we know what this storm is clearin' up outta here, we'll be more assertive toward getting back to the, uh, optimum track line. . . ."

"Yeah," Shultz agrees.

"I think that's a good little plan, Chief Mate. At least I think we got a little distance from the center."

"And that's more like fifty miles out."

"Much better."

A little later, the ship rolls more heavily than usual. "Startin' to get the seas," the captain comments, and for the first time pronounces, or rather mispronounces, the enemy's name: "Joe, wa-kin."

"That's some name, huh?" Shultz says.

"They're twins."

Still entering names of waypoints into the GPS, Shultz laughs. "You know they couldn't give us Jimmy—James or Erika. Equal-opportunity storm-naming."

The sun comes up. Davidson yawns hugely. "Oh, look at that red sky over there. Red in the mornin', sailors take warning. That is bright." As if looking for reassurance, Davidson reiterates to Shultz, "It's a good little diversion. Are you feelin' comfortable with that, Chief Mate?"

"Better, yes, sir. . . . The other option* is drastic."

"Yeah, it doesn't warrant it. . . . You can't run . . . every single weather pattern."

"Not for a forty-knot wind."

Davidson (feigning panic in his voice): "Oh my God, oh my God! . . . We'll just sit on the bank and fish for trout."

Both captain and mate are living out a paradox here. While it's a given for mariners that the Bahamas chain constitutes a near-impenetrable barrier of reefs and shallows, especially for a big, deep-draft freighter (heavily loaded as she is, *El Faro*'s keel reaches almost fifty feet below the waterline), and particularly in storm; while fifty years ago even skilled navigators would have blanched at the thought of trying to thread their way through one of the few deepwater channels between the islands in high winds and poor visibility; the near-pinpoint accuracy of modern, satellite-based navigation technology has rendered such fancy navigation much more feasible. Now even a moderately skilled skipper, knowing his position in real time to within a few meters, can take his ship safely through reefs and rocks, shoals and islands, in zero visibility, while his radars give him a visual to back up the GPS track.

The paradox, however, lies in the overconfidence such technology can instill in its users. Fifty years ago a captain would consider a dodge behind the Bahamas, through the one or two "holes in the wall"

---

* Presumably, taking the Old Bahama Channel.

available in the chain, too dangerous given that he could only find his way by celestial navigation, in weather that might make it unfeasible, and by dead reckoning. So he would likely have avoided the area entirely—would have "given it a wider berth," as maritime historian James Delgado says—either by staying in port or by taking a route such as the Florida Strait and Old Bahama Channel, well to the southwest of the storm. "Tickling the dragon's tail" is what Delgado terms the habit of relying on the fantastic precision of GPS to evade maritime perils at the last minute. The confidence Davidson seems to feel in his slight westerly diversion certainly seems to fall within that definition. And this dragon is far more ticklish than most.

The wind is still on the ship's port quarter. Clouds are moving in to hide the newly risen sun. The ship's course is now almost due southeast. It is a little after 7:00 a.m. on Wednesday, September 30.

6

And so you wake up in your cabin on a Wednesday morning in the warm early-autumn of a tropical Atlantic, with the sky restless and the sea out your porthole like a living thing, not unfriendly but vast as the sky, vaster maybe, a complex fractal repetition of chevrons and crests, green-blue except where the ship's passage throws light spray: it's not rough but there's a swell, you can feel it slowly roll the ship back and forth, enough so that your inner ear has slid back into the rhythm and habit of measuring roll and pitch and shifting your center of gravity, back and forth, back and forth, to compensate; every minute, every second, you counterbalance so thoroughly that when eventually you go ashore your body continues to adjust, trimming itself to a roll that isn't there, a phantom swell, a sea that lasts in the deepest, darkest chambers of the brain, forcing you to think twice about where to put your feet though you're walking down a solid concrete sidewalk all the while. A phantom sea that can last hours, days even, after you've left the ship . . .

And you roll out of your bunk, barely taking in your stateroom: the speckled tiles, white-painted steel walls, tiny metal dresser, the flat-screen TV you're allowed to hang off the bulkhead, the porthole with its single channel of sea and clouds (or containers if you have the misfortune to be facing forward or aft),* the door to the diminutive bathroom; and you shower, dress, prepare for the duties and routines of shipboard; thinking, as Kurt Bruer, the former shipmate now crewing a bulk carrier on the Mississippi, does, as almost everyone does, of what the people most important to you are up to: the kids waking, rubbing sleep gum from the corners of their eyes, smell of charred Eggos in the toaster—or your wife, or sweetheart, boyfriend, still dreaming, warm and untensed beneath the sheet, the floor immobile under bedposts or feet, and nothing more exciting or risky than the drive to work, a fast-food enchilada for lunch, to look forward to—missing them hard, all of a sudden, though maybe you saw them as recently as yesterday or last week, so that you wonder sometimes why the hell you do what you do, spending days, months sometimes away from home (even if you can get back for a few hours every fortnight) in an occupation that, while not as physically dangerous as commercial fishing or lumberjack work, still pops up now and again on the list of the ten riskiest jobs in America.

Why *do* they do it? For Larry Davis, working on ships is a job that, compared to being in the Marine Corps, in which he served for a while, compared to commercial fishing, which he did for too long, is relatively safe and well paid. Mariette Wright, a fifty-one-year-old AB, finds in shipping out a mixture of stuff she likes: seeing different countries (she's been to every continent but Africa and Antarctica), being part of a tight company of people with whom you always have something in common, even if they are almost always men . . . she went to sea at eighteen and has never looked back.

James Porter, a forty-year-old "goodie"—a job title derived from "general utility deck engine," or basic deckhand and wiper—has, like Wright, always wanted to see different places, to get outta Dodge. Now that he has two young boys who have become the center of his life, the

---

* Ironically, since *El Faro*'s accommodations were laid out before she was refitted to carry containers, some of the senior crew's staterooms lie in the forward part of the house, which on a Ro-Ro ship would afford a clear view of the sea in front; their windows are now partially blocked by steel containers, whereas the smaller cabins of the junior sailors ("general utility" deckhands, wipers, and third engineers) tend to line up on the port and starboard sides, with unobstructed views.

Puerto Rico run is a good compromise, it allows him to travel to the islands and still get home frequently enough.

Porter is first cousin to AB Jackie Jones, thirty-eight years old, another African-American from the rougher areas of North Jacksonville. Jones grew up in the same neighborhood as Lashawn Rivera and told him about the "merch," which resulted in Rivera's going to Piney Point, Maryland, to the training school run by their union, the Seafarers International Union (SIU), and then to sea. Both Jones and Rivera had got into trouble as younger men, Rivera for evading arrest, Jones with a check-kiting jacket, both of them in court frequently for the kind of minor roadside offenses known to African-Americans as DWB, or driving while black.* For Jones as well as for Rivera, shipping out has offered an escape, a chance at the good life as well as enough money to support a family. Jones, known as Pop to his pals, has six kids, most of them still at home, and he keeps them well fed; matter of fact, he likes good food so much he once set up a restaurant in North Jacksonville called Wing Palace and now brings his own bespoke barbecued chicken wings aboard and sometimes sets up a Crock-Pot to cook red beans in his cabin.

At breakfast these men and one woman show up in the "unlicensed" mess, to port of the galley, sitting together or apart, breaking away according to their watches and duties, except for Rivera and the two stewards who are always present, accessible through the wide hatch in the mess hall's starboard side. Though the assistant steward, Lonnie Jordan, is in overall charge of breakfast, Rivera will be in the galley as well, getting lunch together. Quite possibly the cook, only partly in jest, vents agony at his crewmates shuffling by as they pick up eggs, bacon, pancakes, Rivera complaining of the record of the San Francisco 49ers, a team he has supported since he was a kid, when he hero-worshipped Joe Montana. San Francisco is letting Rivera down badly this season: in their last game against the Arizona Cardinals, just three days ago, they lost 47–7; a week before that, the Steelers beat them 43–18. Football is king in North Florida, and *El Faro* is a Southern ship, at least in

---

* Racial profiling in Jacksonville will be spotlighted in 2017 by a *Florida-Times Union/*ProPublica investigation focused on "walking while black," which finds that for the previous five years African-Americans were three times more likely to be stopped for minor, sometimes arbitrary, pedestrian offenses than were whites.

her unlicensed roster. *El Yunque*, her sister ship, running the opposite schedule, in San Juan when *El Faro* is in Jacksonville and vice versa, is known to be an Islands ship, much of the talk in her mess being in Spanish, and most of her unlicensed personnel from Puerto Rico.

Speaking of football, the last thing Carey Hatch, a forty-nine-year-old able seaman on *El Faro*'s day schedule, said to his dad before leaving was "Make sure Florida State keeps winning." Jackie Jones reads the Bible every morning before he reports to work, but he is also a hard-ass Gators fan and hugely proud of his football-playing son. A lot of the men spend their time off watching pigskin, live on TV if they are within range, which is usually for the first twenty-four hours southbound; or else on DVDs on the crew's-lounge screen, or on the screen-plus-DVD-player nearly everyone has rigged up in his or her cabin. Jones has discs of his son playing on a championship football team in a statewide junior league. Randolph, too, gets into the football banter, but as a Mainer she's naturally a New England fan, and her Patriots T-shirt draws good-natured abuse from the Southern faction.

Mostly, whether it be cable or films or TV series on tape, during the long hours of boredom or sleeplessness off-watch people hang out in their cabins watching screens, with the exception of Jack Jackson, who prefers to draw or paint. This is different from what mariners call the "old merch," when video amenities were rarely available, with perhaps the exception of a screen and cassette player in the lounge, and there was more interaction between crew members; more brawls, too. Back in the day, older mariners will tell you, seamen were a wilder bunch, booze and drugs found their way aboard more commonly; crewmen had more time, as Jackson once did, to go ashore and party their asses off, and get into trouble often enough. But that was before an American-flag cargo ship, a dead-to-rights rust bucket called *Marine Electric*, went down in a storm off the Virginia coast in 1983 with thirty-four people aboard, and only three rescued; a disaster that caused the Coast Guard to crack down hard, though maybe not hard enough, on rules and regulations governing both equipment and personnel.

As a result they're a different breed, this crew, from the pre-nineties merchant marine; less used to the variety of seagoing demands, since a fair number of them have known nothing but this placid run for years;

older, on average, more staid, though former crewmates suspect there's still some covert drinking aboard, and a little drugging, maybe some amateur smuggling, all of this seriously discreet because discovery will mean automatic loss of a cushy job, and the Coast Guard demands drug tests for all license renewals. Many of these people sail at a lower rating and salary than they're entitled to just to get work on the Puerto Rico run. Yet all are recognizable still as mariners, by what they have in common with seamen everywhere, the art of holding fast away from land, knowing the grinding boredom and loneliness and occasional risk, and balancing that against shipboard camaraderie and the skills of basic seamanship and rope work; sometimes, a secret joy in the play of light on water, a deepwater sunrise, the dwindling of land. These qualities are as old as Odysseus, they set such men and women apart and hold them together.

Not that social time doesn't exist aboard *El Faro*, some kind of seagoing society on this family-oriented ship, and that usually happens around meals. Beyond ship noises, one gets used to the rapid tap-tap of the black guys playing dominoes in the crew's lounge, slapping their counters in hard, fast sequence on the metal tables; sometimes, muffled and largely unmeant insults around a game of cards; the occasional laugh, people teasing or joking as they score a cup from the coffee machine. Humor is the oil that cools this social engine, often enough. Bitching, too, often enough, about not getting sufficient overtime. Overtime from Tote often pads out the month's-end budget, helps make a car payment. Chief Mate Shultz is liked because he is an enthusiastic teacher, willing to cheerfully explain details of ship- or cargo-handling to crew members; but he's also the target of a fair amount of resentment on the part of the crew for not allowing them more hours. They know it's not really Shultz's fault, since Corporate caps the amount of money that can be spent on OT. Still, on a ship at sea, there's no one to blame but the messenger.

A Seafarers International Union meeting was held this morning on the unlicensed deck, before breakfast, run by the bosun and Mariette Wright; voices were raised as union members got worked up, most likely over the overtime issue. The ruckus pissed off ABs trying to get in their last hour of rest before watch.

Generally speaking the unlicensed crew, who are two-thirds black, two-thirds from the Jacksonville area, feel a low-level but chronic irritation at what they see as the caste system underpinning *El Faro*'s sociology. The all-white, largely Yankee, fairly Republican officer class, with a few exceptions such as Randolph and Davidson, are perceived as acting somewhat superior to the deckhands, oilers, engine-room wipers; the officers being treated and paid better than hoi polloi. "The Southern blacks are different from Northern, they've been through a lot, they have some prejudice [against whites]," one former *El Faro* deckhand says, but in truth the unlicensed crew members feel far more united against their officers than separated by their ethnicity. The crew are a family of sorts, linking arms against the arbitrary diktats of the brass.

Resentment against the officer class was honed last July when Marvin Hearman III, an able seaman and oiler, coming upon a chief mate asleep on watch, took a cell phone picture of the dozing officer and sent it anonymously to Tote's safety manager, John Lawrence. The mate was demoted and reassigned, but the company spent a fair amount of energy trying to figure out who had sent the image. When Immigration and Customs Enforcement officers boarded the ship afterward and searched Hearman's cabin with a drug dog, finding nothing, some of the men on board assumed this was a form of retribution instigated by a Tote official; they noted, as well, that the crewman targeted happened to be black.

Generally there's a feeling that it's not a good idea to lodge complaints, even about safety issues, with Tote reps ashore, because doing so can lead to retaliation against the complainer.* "You could get fired if you call the DP [Designated Person], that's on any ship in the fleet," Hearman will say later. Even the company's human-relations officer, Melissa Clark, will admit in subsequent testimony that crew members are reluctant to stick their neck out to raise issues. The only way to report violations anonymously is on land, on a secure phone, to Tote's safety hotline. Emails and sat-phone calls from the ship are under the master's control.

The company denies targeting whistle-blowers. While Tote is aware of the crew-officer tensions, the in-house title of its recent policy aimed at defusing strain between officers and crew, "Divide and Conquer," is not such as to inspire confidence in HR's goodwill. And this localized

---

* It should be said that Tote Services' safety record, for on-the-job injuries anyway, is good; the subdivision has won several awards from the industry group CSA (Chamber of Shipping of America) for keeping injury time at low levels.

tension rides piggyback on a light but pervasive sense among American merchant mariners of being ignored or even disrespected by the general population, despite the vital importance of their work.

7

The United States as a whole, like Puerto Rico, relies on the world trade in household goods and commodities, 90 percent of which are shipped by sea; but the nation traditionally is inward-looking, both fattened and stoned on the shoreside riches of the continent it dominates, hooked on the increasingly illusory ideal of economic self-reliance. "Go West, young man," Horace Greeley thundered in print, not "Go to sea." Every man and woman on *El Faro* has got used to explicating her or his job description because everyone, *everyone* not in the trade—everyone in America it seems—assumes that if you work in the "merchant marine," then you are in the "Marines," the Marine Corps, and the next phrase uttered will be the facile and automatic "Thank you for your service." When ships docked in downtown Manhattan or San Francisco they used to be a presence, the mournful lowing of a foghorn part and parcel of the urban experience, but now they are by and large quarantined like lepers in those faraway automated docklands, and the landsmen's ignorance of merchant mariners is on a par with their indifference.

This attitude, or ignorance, pervades Washington, too, and has solid consequences: from 1951 to 2011 the fleet of US-registered and crewed ships, which at its zenith totaled almost 1,300 vessels, declined by 82 percent to 166 ships, less than 1 percent of the world's total.* The decline is due to a strict safety environment and high labor costs in both shipbuilding and crewing in the United States, compared to places such as China and Indonesia. In 2015 the average daily cost of running a flag-of-convenience ship is $9,600, compared to $21,200 for a ship flying the Stars and Stripes. But the decline is also a function of deregulation and neglect: while domestic airlines and trucking

---

* The number of US-*owned* foreign-flagged ships is still high, but this is irrelevant to the American mariner.

companies benefit from tremendous subsidies and protection in the form of modern highways, air traffic control, landing rights, and overall public attention, Washington has largely thrown in the towel when it comes to protecting American shipping. That American-flagged merchant ships survive at all is due to three factors, first among them the evisceration of maritime unions, such as the SIU, which represents *El Faro*'s crew, and the American Maritime Officers union, representing licensed personnel, to the point where they largely exist and negotiate at the sufferance of the shipowners; their ability to leverage higher wages suffers as a result. "Ass-kissers" is how one ex-sailor succinctly describes his union's officials. It's no coincidence that there has not been a strike by American deep-sea mariners in half a century.

The second reason for the merchant marine's survival is the American war machine, which through its federal Maritime Administration (known as MARAD) and subsidized maritime academies* seeks to keep a bare minimum of US-run ships and crews available for the country's next overseas adventure. The third reason is the Merchant Marine Act of 1920, aka the Jones Act, a bill passed just after World War I by congressmen who, rendered nervous by the demonstrated ability of German U-boats to sink ships and strangle commerce, felt laws were needed to ensure the United States maintained a sufficient supply of American merchant ships for future wars. To that end the act reserved intra-American shipping, which is to say commerce from US port to US port, exclusively for vessels built, owned, and operated by Americans.

Tote's ships are all Jones Act ships, and there's a causal relationship here with *El Faro*'s age. Like her sister ship *El Yunque*, she is forty years old when the usual life span of a merchant ship is twenty years or less, and the average age of merchant ships worldwide is eleven years. But it

---

* As well as the federal academy at Kings Point, New York, there are six state maritime academies (Massachusetts, Maine, State University of New York, Great Lakes, Texas A&M, and California), all of which enjoy federal funding through the US Maritime Administration. According to MARAD, "The education of merchant marine officers is an essential Maritime Administration responsibility to meet national security needs and to maintain ... defense readiness. The maritime academies meet that need by educating young men and women for service in the American merchant marine, in the US Armed Forces, and in the Nation's inter-modal transportation system. The Maritime Administration also provides training vessels to all six state maritime academies for use in at-sea training and as shore-side laboratories." (These training vessels are full-size cargo ships that carry cadets for extended tours, often abroad, at least once a year.)

costs three times more to build new hulls in the few US shipyards left, as opposed to building them in China or Korea, so Jones Act owners keep their vessels going as long as possible to avoid the expense of replacement. In 2015, one-third of the remaining US-flag merchant ships are over twenty years old. And since American mariners earn much more than foreign mariners hired on the free market—an American AB earns around $50,000 annually, as opposed to the $18,000 his Filipino equivalent makes—seamen's unions don't complain too much. The Jones Act has hardened institutional arteries on both the owners' and mariners' side, and the frail health of ships such as *El Faro* is the result.

All this is background: stuff known, digested, and assumed by the crew, barely thought about consciously on another day at sea, as the unlicensed mariners coming off the four-to-eight watch, AB Frank Hamm and oiler Shawn Thomas, enter the mess with stomachs growling for breakfast; as Hamm, a large man with an appetite to match, over eggs or waffles probably resumes chatting up his shipmates to buy the rap, house, and rhythm 'n' blues CDs he mixes himself at home, cracking jokes all the while. Hamm is one of the ship's funny guys, usually he shoots off pleasantries about sports that only the initiates fully get but nobody can mistake his laugh, his good nature, his love of dance steps, or his generosity—nobody can think of a bad thing to say about him, and in this closed seagoing environment where petty resentments fester easily, that is praise indeed.

Hamm is a serious churchgoer, like many of *El Faro*'s black contingent; he attends prayer meetings every Sunday he's at home and never fails to give money to the same homeless guy who sets up near his church in North Jacksonville. Though his eyesight is far from perfect and he chronically wears glasses, Hamm was the one who, while standing watch with the chief mate as the ship came into San Juan, spotted a fishing boat in trouble miles distant from the *Faro* and calmly helped direct the rescue. The fishermen waved for assistance; the ship slowed and stopped; and the fishermen climbed up a Jacob's ladder set by Jackie Jones on the ship's lee side, as if they were pilots.

The eight-to-twelve watch, consisting of Jack Jackson and oiler German Solar-Cortes, finish their plates and head for bridge and engine room, respectively. The Polish steelworkers, at their own table, swallow coffee dregs and walk to the outside deck on the aft part of the mess level for a prework cigarette. The day crew—Mariette Wright, Jackie Jones, James Porter, and Carey Hatch—probably pour one last java before reporting to the bosun's store on the port side of Main Deck for the daily muster and assignment of jobs.

But the chronic, low-level tension must have an effect somewhere, even though these men, this woman, are all pros, all proud of their skills and the work they do—this lathe curl of injustice, this thin-sliced tinge of disrespect coming from their officers, their company, their country, can result in a daydream of darker, cooler shades that affects the work environment; that results perhaps in a little less attention paid, a double check to see if a hatch or gate is securely shut waived or dismissed with a shrug; and this can happen even in the shadow of awareness that a storm is out there, because after all, a storm is always out there, somewhere, at sea.

8

Joaquin would be bad enough as forecasters think it is, with winds rising from forty-five to sixty-odd knots (but no higher, or so it's believed), circling obsessively around and around a thousand square miles of ocean, riling up the water into hungry ten-foot combers of somber blue, spitting foam across the jaws of dark between; a big ship could take that in stride, though a small sailing vessel might well find herself in trouble, hove to and trying to ride the waves with a handkerchief of sail bent, her crew tethered by lifelines to avoid being dragged overboard when a wave washes the deck.

But Joaquin, as usual, is not what everybody thinks. Three hundred and eighty miles to the southeast of *El Faro*'s position, the storm has shape-shifted into an early version of the assassin it's destined to become. The shape-shifting, a sixty-hour process, started early the previous morning, on September 29, when much of *El Faro*'s crew was asleep, when the ship herself was moored in still water at her berth on Blount Island.

No one was around to see, no one had dropped data-gathering instruments close enough, the NOAA weather buoys were elsewhere, no experts fully understood what was happening, and what was happening was this: If warm water is what injects strength into an incipient hurricane, Joaquin was spiking into epic overdose. The surface temperature of the waters Joaquin now entered stood at 31.1°C, or 88°F, the warmest ever measured in that area and 1.1 degrees over the previous record; a function, meteorologists agreed later, of overall climate change, the gradual warming of Earth's atmosphere that not only deepens the El Niño effect, which allowed Joaquin to be born in the first place, but contributes to warmer seas overall.

Global warming, aka the "greenhouse" process, is driven by the same physics of heat transfer and changing chemical states that in another form turn *El Faro*'s propeller. The sun blasts "visible" shortwave radiation through the accumulated carbon dioxide in the planet's atmosphere to heat the planet's surface—which bounces much of it back, at cooler temperatures, in longer-wavelength radiation (for wavelengths lengthen with lower temperatures, and Earth is cooler than the sun). Then it becomes a matter of music, almost, of both sympathetic and off-key tuning: longer wavelengths of light make carbon dioxide molecules vibrate in a way the shorter wavelengths do not, and that vibration bounces light rays off-center, deflecting them from their passage back into space; the radiation thus retained mostly stays in the planet's atmosphere, heating it up, cycling it back down to warm the seas beneath.

And so, Joaquin explodes. Its heat pump speeds up, the pressure in its hollow core dropping, sucking in more wind from the surrounding atmosphere and even more heat from the sea, which causes the wet hot air inside its core to rise more quickly in turn, spiraling out the top faster than inrushing winds below can compensate for—although they try, since nature, as everyone knows, abhors a vacuum. All this increases wind speed further still, while the system releases yet more energy, more lightning, thunder, and overarching rain clouds, at the top. At this point the hurricane is an engine that accelerates its fuel pump faster than it runs itself and must speed up to compensate, which only makes the fuel flow faster. At 2:00 a.m. on the thirtieth, while Randolph and Davis are on watch, unbeknownst to them or to anyone else, Joaquin's winds top the 64 knot, 73 mph, mark that officially defines a hurricane. And still Joaquin is not finished, it is right in the thick of this lovely superheated stretch of ocean, and expecting such a storm to slow or stop now is like assuming a thirsty drunk will turn his back on an open bar, an indulgent bartender.

Here lies one reason almost no one saw Joaquin coming, a source for one of the most grievous mistakes in meteorological forecasting of the last decade. While no hard-and-fast rules exist to predict where a system as hugely complicated as a hurricane will go next, one reliable guideline ties the strength of wind shear to the altitude of guiding winds, the airflow that blows it in a given direction. Wind shear saps a storm's strength, or "intensity." If wind shear is low, and the storm thus relatively strong and its massive thunderheads riding high, the hurricane will tend to follow high-altitude winds; conversely, if shear is high and the system weak, it will be pushed around by winds at lower altitudes.

No one, however, knows the specifics of the waters in which Joaquin now thrives, no one realizes how hot they are, and few imagine the storm will develop the intensity it is acquiring. Shear conditions are detected in its vicinity on September 28 and 29 and many forecasts deduce from this that the storm will weaken and drift with the lower airflow, which is driven by a trough over the eastern United States, to the west and north. But a ridge of high pressure over the Atlantic is blocking part of the jet stream and diverting higher-altitude winds toward the south. In retrospect it seems likely that the unexpected bolus of warm-water energy has made Joaquin more resistant to wind shear and therefore more intense—and thus more inclined to follow the higher winds trending south and west.

The lack of understanding is not for want of effort. The National Hurricane Center runs its millions of bits of storm info through a forecasting program powered by two Cray XC40 supercomputers: twin rows of linked, metal-sheathed mainframes, each forty feet long, located in Reston, Virginia, and Orlando, Florida. As of tomorrow—October 1, 2015—the two Crays are due to be goosed to a maximum capability of 2.5 petaflops apiece, one petaflop being equal to one thousand million million floating-point operations a second. A floating point is the smallest unit of coding, equivalent to a single synaptic connection, the simplest form of neural "idea" in the computer's brain, and it all adds up to a total that is mind-boggling: five thousand million million digital ideas, or minicalculations, processed every second.

But the SISO rule of computing applies here, too: Shit In, Shit Out. While the data NHC is gathering are far from "shit," neither are they, in hindsight, complete enough; they do not take into account the über-warmed patch of water, they don't predict the right intensity, and as a result they do not get the trackline right. The SAT-C and TAFB forecasts the hurricane forecast center is generating are therefore far more inaccurate than usual.

NHC experts are not fools; they are dedicated and savvy scientists who are well aware that any model has flaws. Therefore they make sure to incorporate in their final forecast package not only their own model but a spectrum of models run by other forecasting centers, of which the United Kingdom Meteorological Office and the European Centre for Medium-Range Weather Forecasts (known as Euro) models are two of the more influential. The resultant "spaghetti" forecast displays tracks of a hurricane, as predicted by a half dozen different organizations, winding in and out of each other like strands of linguine forked dripping from the bowl, and teasing out more and more as the time frame lengthens and uncertainty factors grow.

Most of the predicted tracks up to September 30 are in line with the NHC's: the storm will skim but not reach hurricane strength; it will continue mostly westward and then veer north as it's steered by winds coming off the inland trough.

There is one exception. The Euro model through September 30 does not see Joaquin turning northward or remaining weak; its track bears southwest instead and is close to the direction that Joaquin, relentlessly strengthening and coasting along with higher-altitude winds, is actually following now, on a collision course with *El Faro*.*

---

* One reason the Euro model proves more accurate for Joaquin, and why it was also more accurate for "superstorm" Sandy in 2012, might be that the ECMWF has increased its program's "resolution," in effect tripling the number of collection points for meteorological data to a level far surpassing that of other models. Another reason might have to do with NHC's brief and the marketing ethic underlying it. Hurricane Center experts are trained to think of their forecasts as "products" they must furnish to "clients," and the overwhelming preponderance of clients are land-based, people living in coastal regions of states most likely to be affected by a tropical cyclone. NHC's focus and therefore its watches and warnings are tailored to specific terrestrial regions such as North Carolina, as opposed to areas of ocean. Moreover, because the principal result forecasters wish to achieve is timely preparation on the part of civilians on terra firma, who have no concept of a storm's complexities, NHC bends over backward to avoid what they call the "windshield-wiper effect": what happens when one shifts forecasts quickly to reflect the newest data. This built-in conservatism means that outlier forecasts, such as the Euro model's in the case of Joaquin, are given less weight day to day than experts examining the data might otherwise assign to them.

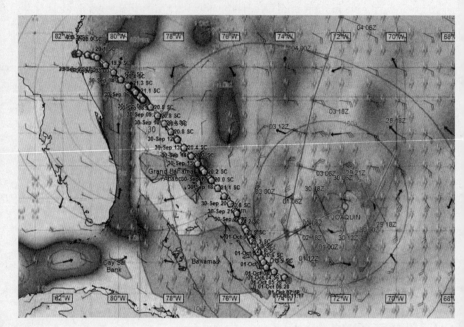

Collision course: Initial forecasts showed Joaquin weakening and moving west, then north, but the storm's actual track shows a steady progression south and west, as if it were deliberately aiming to meet the *El Faro*.

PART IV

IN HARM'S WAY

And once the storm is over, you won't remember how you made it through. . . . You won't be the same person who walked in. That's what this storm is all about.

—Haruki Murakami

1

The day's work begins for the watch standers as they go to their respective posts in the engine-room control station and the bridge for the morning's eight-to-twelve shift. This September 30 the "day" deckhands—Hatch, Porter, Wright, and Jones—also start at 8:00 a.m., but will work right through a normal daytime routine, like their counterparts on any land-based crew, like the Polish riding gang, since much of the work they do is on deck and often requires sunlight; they will knock off in the evening. Sometimes off-duty watch standers, such as Frank Hamm on the four-to-eight, will join the day crew to work an extra four hours of overtime, if Shultz has okayed it.

The day gang shapes up by the bosun's store, coffee breath strong, hair maybe still wet from the shower and drying in warm, oil-and-paint-perfumed wind. The store consists of the outermost port container in a row of three permanent and dedicated freight containers lined up fore and aft on Main Deck's breezeway, one on the port side and two starboard, under the sheltering house. (The other containers hold safety gear such as CO_2 foam and other firefighting equipment.) Deck work is organized by Chief Mate Shultz, and he is there to assign overtime, if any, and generally oversee the shape-up, distributing scratch-pad notes as he organizes the crew. The work itself is run by the bosun, Roan Lightfoot; he holds the same rank and authority as a chief petty officer in the Navy, a master sergeant in the Army, the highest unlicensed position aboard.

Lightfoot is fifty-four years old. One of the crew has described him as an "aging surfer" type—stubble-cut blond hair losing the battle with male-pattern baldness, shortish and muscled and squat—a guy who like some others in the crew likes hanging at Angel's Bar in San Juan, where the beer is cool and the Friday-night strippers are, sort of, hot.

Lightfoot is another who jokes around a lot, but not enough to fool anybody: like many bosuns this guy's a hard-ass and it's his way or the highway, and he doesn't care much if the crew likes him or not, and some of them do not. Still, he knows his job and people respect that, just as some deckies don't speak too fondly of Shultz either, but they're aware he knows his stuff. The shape-up, often enough, is a binary theater of surface "yessir" and subsurface "fuck you," but orders are orders and even grumbling the crew will do what they are told.

Day work on any large steel ship, and especially one as old as *El Faro*, consists of a lot of grunt maintenance, such as chipping off rust with a clatter-banging hydraulic needlegun in areas with the worst corrosion, ear protection mandatory. No shortage of rust around—the twenty-two big vent openings on 2nd Deck, though always left open to draw fumes from automobiles on the decks below, are supposed to close, but they've been corroded so thoroughly some of the baffles that shut them off won't budge. If in some places the metal has wasted away to paper-thin or nothing, the engineers might be called in to patch and weld.

"They were bandaging that ship with steel all the time," Chris Cash, a former crewman, says of *El Faro* later. "They didn't want to put money into the ship, [they would] patch up instead of fix." One of the Polish gang tells his wife there is "rust everywhere, I have never worked on such a hulk."

If the work is done properly, the metal should be ground down, washed with fresh water before welding, protected with primer and heavy-duty oil paint afterward. Today, with swells growing from aft and port, and the occasional crest of a higher wave slurping through the big openings on 2nd Deck, any maintenance on that deck will probably have to be done on bulkheads or elevated areas to starboard, away from the spray; or else on Main Deck or the house or the enclosed lower levels below 2nd Deck.

Shultz will certainly check with Jeff Mathias, who's organizing the Polish riding gang's work, to ensure the two gangs don't get in each other's way. Then as a matter of routine he'll make another round of the cargo, running into Louis Champa as the electrician starts his thrice-daily monitoring of the cooling systems on the refrigerated cargo—and these, too, might echo in a mate's subconscious with how hurricanes work, for like cyclones the reefer units depend on a binary system of heat transfer, through evaporation on one side, condensation on the other. Shultz's conscious thoughts, though, must be focused on much more obvious mechanisms. His job here is to double-check lashings on every trailer, each container, a task that calls for experience and muscle memory because there is no mechanical gauge to test tension on the lashings. He is well aware how many of them are tied off-button. Some of the D rings, too, were rusted to the deck, but loosened with a sledgehammer to accept a hook and chain to tie down cargo. The mate knows that the percentage of trailers and containers secured off-button and even to relatively distant D rings conforms to the limit prescribed in Tote's minimalist cargo manual and should be fine for normal sailing and okay even for rough weather.

A hurricane is not "rough weather."

The men don their hard hats, pick up needleguns, hoses, paint, brushes, tarps, sledges, whatever the job requires, and set off down the deck, walking with the practiced saltwater-cowpoke gait that fits their movements to the ship's, which with the wind rising slowly but steadily off the port quarter and swells moving with it includes a fair amount of pitch, of bow-stern action. James Porter, quiet and focused on his job; Jackie Jones, Porter's cousin, an excerpt from the Bible he reads every morning quite possibly still looping in his head; Mariette Wright; Carey Hatch. Those working on lower levels will take the house stairs to 2nd Deck and there, if they've been assigned a job in the forward holds—1, 2, and 2A—they'll thread their way through the massed shadows, the ranked trailers, the humming reefers, the snaking electric cables, the stink of oil and gas, to one of the scuttles, the tight hatchways leading to a ladder that runs to the next deck down.

If Frank Hamm is working overtime today, this will not be his favorite route. These scuttles are scattered, two to each hold,* in alternating pattern on the very outer edge of 2nd Deck. Their coamings, the raised steel lips that prevent water from flowing to the next level down if, as often happens, 2nd Deck gets wet during passage, are just wide enough for the average man's shoulders, but Hamm is not an average man, he is broad in all dimensions, and getting through requires a certain amount

---

* Except for 1-hold, the cargo space farthest forward, which is smaller and requires only a single scuttle.

of twisting, of shipboard yoga. The scuttle's cover opens and closes on a single hinge in the coaming; the silicon or synthetic-rubber gasket underneath seals the circle when it is shut. The cover's considerable weight is augmented by its locking gears and dogs.

These 2nd Deck scuttle hatches are built of heavy-gauge steel in case rough weather should drive seas deep among the hatchways. Unlike the watertight doors such as those between the different holds, or between 3-hold and the engine room, they are not routinely listed in any checklists as open or shut, since they will be in fairly constant use throughout the voyage. Also, because the rules requiring it apply only to ships built after 1992, they are not fitted with electronic sensors that would indicate, on a panel on the bridge or engine-room consoles, whether they have been dogged.

The gaskets in particular are not inspected. They are made of either heavy silicon, a polymer that is normally resistant to salt, ultraviolet rays, and rushing water; or EPDM (for "ethylene propylene diene monomer"), a hard synthetic rubber. But neither substance is eternal, and both have been known to fail. When serially washed in water that contains chemicals, the component molecules of silicon, aligned in a polymer chain, can be cut, in a process known as chain scission, by the corrosive molecules of solvents and hydrocarbon compounds. And EPDM is highly vulnerable to erosion by gasoline and motor oil. Seawater sprayed or slopped onto 2nd Deck, with the fuel and oil drips of yard pigs, of old automobiles (around half of the cars shipped to Puerto Rico are used), of exhaust residue, of cleaning fluids used to wash the deck, quickly becomes a light cocktail of such chemicals. Presumably, over a long time, the cocktail saps a gasket's integrity, its insulating qualities. And a "long time" is what *El Faro*'s all about.

"Set," too, will reduce the seal's effectiveness. Set is the effect of strong compression, in this case the repeated dogging down of heavy steel hatch on hard steel lip with the gasket buffering the two, not to mention the sailor's habit of letting the hatch slam on its bed. All this will tend to change the gasket's shape, the way a pillow crease leaves its line on a sleeper's cheek, and such change also lessens the sealant qualities of polymers. But why should anyone pay attention to something that routinely works well*—why, with everything you have to do, and maybe some constant irritation at the mate or bosun to bug you, or perhaps a shoreside issue elbowing in on your concentration, look twice at the scuttle hatches as they are opened, banged shut, opened again; reliable, sturdy, ignored?

"Ignored" is not a term that can be applied to the lifeboats, which theoretically are the principal means of escape off the ship. Lifeboats have ranked high on the list of international inspection rules since the loss of the RMS *Titanic* in 1912. *El Faro*'s are two nearly identical boats, twenty-three feet long, made of heavy, cored fiberglass, and suspended from twin sets of cranes, called davits, one on each side of the engineers' level of the house. The boats are open, meaning they afford no shelter from the elements. The starboard boat is capable of holding forty-three people, the other forty-eight. They are painted white outside, orange inside, with benches, or "thwarts," arranged across the boat's width. The portside boat is powered by a diesel engine, the starboard by a construct of gears and push bars, called a Fleming system, moved back and forth by crew seated on the thwarts the way slaves pushed and pulled at oars in Roman galleys. The Fleming gear, like the diesel, turns a shaft and propeller at the stern. Except for the propulsion, however, and the davits' electric motors, *El Faro*'s lifeboats are little different in design or in their launching systems from the lifeboats of the *Titanic*, and they suffer from the same drawbacks, in particular the near impossibility of launching an upslope boat, or loading on the downslope, if the ship is leaning heavily to one side.

Modern cargo ships don't use these antiquated boats. Today's American ships are legally mandated to be equipped with totally enclosed, engine-powered boats, often launched like a torpedo down a chute off the ship's stern. In this system, when abandoning ship, crew members climb through a hatch into the boat, lock the hatch, strap themselves in, start the engine; then the boat's coxswain hits a switch that triggers the unlocking device. The lifeboat, acting more like a rocket at this stage, plunges into

---

* One ex–*El Faro* deckhand has stated at least one of the scuttles doesn't close all the way, but this is not corroborated by other mariners. One ex-bosun claims the scuttle on the fo'c'sle—the top, raised part of the bow—which leads down to storage areas and a locker where anchor chain is held, is damaged and would easily be popped open by waves breaking aboard.

the sea, its tapered bow allowing the craft to dive briefly, damping the shock. When the lifeboat bobs back to the surface, the crew member in charge revs the engine and speeds his boat away from the distressed ship.

El Faro, however, is grandfathered. Because of her age, her owners are not legally obliged to replace these old boats with the modern, chute-launched version. This grandfathered status, and the lack of obligation to modernize, must be key to Tote's bottom line; when the vessel was converted from pure roll on, roll off to Ro-Ro/container in 2006, the Coast Guard initially flagged the work as a "major conversion," which could have required, among other safety-equipment changes, a lifeboat upgrade. State-of-the-art lifeboats cost upward of half a million dollars each. But Tote fought that designation, lodging a protest that resulted in a turnaround by the Coast Guard Marine Inspection Office, which eventually ruled that the work had been, technically, a "minor" conversion and thus did not mandate safety upgrades. And so the antiquated lifeboats remained. So did all other safety features that conformed to the 1975-era "International Safety of Life at Sea," or SOLAS, regulations, even if they did not meet modern standards.*

Third Mate Riehm, inspecting the boats, must clamber inside to check the stores: filtered water, rations, first-aid kit, emergency flares, fuel for the diesel. He makes sure the electric winches that lower the boats are working properly and carefully inspects the davits themselves, including the padeyes, half circles of steel, welded to the deck, that anchor some of the cables. A short time ago the old padeyes, rusted out, were replaced. *El Faro*'s sister ship *El Yunque* had to obtain temporary permission to sail from classification-society inspectors because her davits were corroded. But *El Faro*'s davits have been inspected recently, new clutches and brake pads were installed on the electric winches just before sailing and the system seems to be in good shape.

Riehm, with his usual diligence, would also check out the life rafts, of which there are five, all of the sturdy, tent-covered variety, orange-

---

* Tote's argument was that other ships had undergone similar conversions, and these were not described as "major." The Coast Guard will later criticize its own flip-flop because while the precedent cited in Tote's argument did exist, inspectors nonetheless were obligated to treat each conversion on a case-by-case basis, according to which *El Faro*'s conversion should have been deemed "major."

colored and self-inflating:* two, capable of holding twenty-five people apiece, are strapped inside protective fiberglass shells to cradles just behind the lifeboats, one on each side of the house. Two more twenty-five-man rafts are lashed to railings or brackets near the boat deck, and a six-person raft added as a precaution when *El Yunque*'s lifeboat system was found to be deficient is stowed up forward. The third mate, like every other mariner aboard, is aware of the lifeboats' shortcomings and knows the rafts offer his best chance of survival if things really go south.

2

For a stateroom captain, or at least what Tote considers to be a stateroom captain, Davidson is pretty active on deck today as *El Faro* steams farther to the south and east, skirting the Bahamas chain. Early this morning he went four levels down from the bridge to the galley and spoke to Lashawn Rivera and the stewards about securing their china, sauces, and cooking equipment for rough seas ahead; he is conscious of the mess that happens when a violent roll sends jars of mayonnaise and catsup flying to the deck.

Then Davidson took the stairs another four levels deeper to the engine room to carry the same message to the engineers. The mates worry about the Polish riding crew. "They leave pipes lying around," one of them remarks, and someone will mention this to Jeff Mathias, the chief engineer in charge of the conversion work the Poles are doing, though it's almost certain that Mathias, with his experience and sea savvy ("A born sailor," Hearn says of him later), is already conscious of what's going on and will be taking safety measures accordingly; making sure any equipment not currently being used among the welding cables and bottles of oxyacetylene, the spools of wire, the hulking new winches and heater, are securely tied down and out of the way.

---

* The rafts, which are inspected annually, carry water and food, lights, and baffles underneath that, once the raft is inflated and launched, are supposed to fill with water to prevent the rafts' being blown over. Manufactured by Denmark's Viking Group, each weighs over three hundred pounds and requires at least two strong people to throw over the side. The manufacturer's instruction video shows the rafts being launched and inflated in a perfectly calm, flat sea. Launching methods under stormy conditions are not addressed in the video.

The winches and heater in particular would need to be lashed down hard because they are heavy. The heater is a big steel furnace called a Butterworth, used to make steam for deicing the regular ramps as well as the five extra ramps that will be added to *El Faro* for use in Alaska; the vessel is due to go to shipyard shortly for a final overhaul before traveling to Alaska the following month. The eighteen winches, with electric motors that will raise and lower those ramps or cinch the ship in tight against ice-encrusted docks, all add up to several tons in weight, and it's not clear, then or later, if their combined weight and location have been added to the CargoMax stability algorithm.

The presence of five Polish men adds an extra zest of the surreal to *El Faro*'s human soup. Because of the language barrier, communication is rare or nonexistent between the riding gang and the ship's regular crew. Some bridge watch keepers refer to them as Team Poland and make jokes, not unkindly, about their tastes and proclivities. Describing Team Poland at mealtimes, an AB says, "The cook or the steward comes out and goes, 'Do you want meat or fish?' . . . And they all go 'Fish! Fish! Fish!'" And when later the likelihood of their coming close to a hurricane is explained to them, one of the mates says the foreigners seem excited, smiling, not concerned, even eager to undergo the experience, crying, "Hurricane! Yes!" . . . "Ah, if they only knew," the mate adds wryly.

Generally, the Poles are looked on by the rest of the crew with the sort of bemused tolerance that characterizes Americans forced to deal with non–English speakers, people who don't understand what quarterbacks do. The general impression of the riding crew is that, though foreign, they're good-natured, assiduous, too. Piotr Krause, the twenty-seven-year-old pipefitter, seems particularly easy to get along with; he loves cars and history programs and is liked for his sense of humor, though his recent jokes might conceal an underlying tension. Krause and his wife, Anna, are devoted to each other and to their one-year-old son, Viktor; he took the job on *El Faro* because his family needed the money and the pay was good compared to similar work in Poland, but the long months he spends working on another continent have been hard on all of them. Krause longs to leave the ship and find work in Europe; he is thinking of looking in Norway, where he could make good money and live with his family as well. Krause is happiest working with his hands, fixing stuff. He spends a lot of time with Jeff Mathias, the conversion supervisor. Mathias has no problem working with Team Poland, but Mathias tends to get along fine with most people and especially people who care about machinery as much as he does.

Mathias grew up in Kingston, one of the more rural areas of south-eastern Massachusetts, not far from where the Pilgrims got off the *Mayflower* mumbling prayers of thanks for their salvation from the sea. His family owns cranberry bogs and, as with most farming, the care and maintenance of working acreage requires a lot of machinery: excavators and front-end loaders to overhaul the bogs, pumps to flood the plants over winter, rolling pickers, mechanized conveyor belts to load the harvested berries, trucks to carry them, tractors to drag the machinery from bog to bog. Cape Cod Bay isn't far from Kingston and Mathias did his share of sailing small boats, but what fascinated him was engines. He grew adept at running bog machinery, fixing it when it broke, scouting around for replacement parts; little pleases him more than scoring what he calls a "smokin' deal" on a used fuel injector or water pump, unless it be creating hayrides and other kid-oriented events the Mathias farm puts on around Halloween. When he applied to "Mass. Maritime," only twenty miles south of his home, on Buzzards Bay, the engineering department was what interested him. And there, like Rich Pusatere, he came under the spell of steam engines, to the point where he chose the Tote assignment deliberately so that he could work on a steam plant—although he, like others on *El Faro*, has no illusions about the ship's condition and talks of it openly with fellow engineers. He once asked rhetorically, "How long will Tote keep spending money to keep this ship running?"

Today, despite the freshening wind and the subtly increasing freshness of the ship's motion, he supervises the Poles as they configure overhead cable conduits and new steam lines for the ramps; tells his crew also to weld on a new railing below the bridge, for which the paint and underlying steel must be ground down to bond clean metal to clean metal. Most of this should be dockside or shipyard work but Tote, having recently sent *El Morro*, one of its three ships in the "Ponce" class, which includes *El Faro*, to the scrapyard, is scrambling to get *El Faro* to Tacoma for the Alaska run by December 8·. This is so that one of their Alaska ships, in turn, can be sent to Singapore for conversion to LNG-powered diesel. Dry-docking for *El Faro* is scheduled for early November, the time slot already reserved at the Bahamas shipyard where she is to be worked on. The Coast Guard and Tote's client regulatory body, the American Bureau of Shipping, have been notified so inspectors can be on-site to sign off on repairs. That inspection is scheduled for November 6 to 19. According to Mathias, the decision to scrap one of *El Faro*'s sister ships, *Great Land*, was made too quickly, without any plan to cannibalize the decommissioned ship for spares, which means a lot of unnecessary hours must be spent finding used parts elsewhere or jury-rigging others to refit the *Faro*. This is work in which Mathias, the widget wonk, finds pleasure, but still . . . Because of the extra duties, Mathias recently chose not to stay shoreside, but to ride with the ship to make sure the conversion is pushed through on time. "How do I know what needs to be done if the ship's only in port for one day?" he explained to his wife.

Doubtless Mathias also keeps some portion of his mind on projects Rich Pusatere has going on below. As a licensed chief engineer, as a lover of machinery, Mathias thinks about the whole plant, the entire mechanical enchilada, whether it's his direct responsibility or not, and *El Faro*'s forty-year-old machinery provides plenty of mysteries to worry at. Mathias is known, one could almost say famous, for being single-minded about his job. He was engineer on a ship running to Hawaii when his wife, Jenn, was pregnant with their first child; when news came through the ship's email that Jenn had given birth, the captain called him up to the bridge; but Mathias, once assured that mother and child were well, replied that he would first finish the job he was engaged in, then come topside to celebrate.

His focus on work notwithstanding, like most mariners Mathias holds consciousness of his family ever present in the background, as if they were a favorite show playing on TV in the next room; all the more so because he's scheduled to leave the ship after this trip, to help set up a maze/slide structure he designed for "Pumpkin Patch Weekend," the series of autumn activities due to take place over Columbus Day on his family's cranberry farm.

3

The swells build further, still out of the north. The troughs between get deeper, and the indigo and jade colors inside them darken. As the day progresses, the long northern waves take on even more of an easterly component. People often see their world in terms of overlapping stories, all marked and girdered by the convenient theories of sequence and causality, one event being triggered by a previous event and causing, in turn, a third, with all the time and miles of road between forgotten in the telling; and so they tend to miss the slow, often uneven progression of things, the budding of a flower, the turn toward evening, the rise or fall of tide, the building up of seas. From high up, through the windows of *El Faro*'s bridge, the waves look the same from minute to minute, even over the course of an hour. What sticks out, what makes the navigators notice, will be signals they are trained to observe, such as a greater number of whitecaps, the symptoms of wind speed as defined by the Beaufort scale: "Force 5, wind 17 to 21 knots, fresh breeze, moderate waves taking a more pronounced long form; many white foam crests; there may be some spray."

They will notice, too, the unusual—when a tarpaulin is ripped off by wind from the bridge wing, or when the ship lurches unexpectedly.

Davidson is back on the bridge at midmorning. "Ship's solid . . . ," he tells Riehm. ". . . Just gotta keep the speed up so we can get goin' down. And who knows, maybe this low will just stall—stall a little bit . . . just enough for us to duck underneath."

It's a scenario of wishful thinking in the skipper's mind, uncomplicated by new facts; a scenario strong and plausible enough that it extrapolates trouble to a later time, when Joaquin has stalled and hung around, once *El Faro* is safely past and in Puerto Rico and her officers are prepping the trip back.

At 10:22 a.m. Davidson sends an email, transmitted by satellite via the Inmarsat device, from his office computer to Tote's safety manager, John Lawrence. The email, noting that Joaquin is "erratic and unpredictable," says Davidson expects to be safely on the storm's back side by morning. It then asks for authorization, if Joaquin is still hanging around causing trouble in the area after *El Faro* loads in San Juan, to return to Jacksonville via the Old Bahama Channel route.

Lawrence doesn't see the email immediately; he is busy attending the National Safety Congress convention in Atlanta, the biggest such event of the year for safety officers. At the convention—perhaps ironically, given the tension existing between crew and officers on *El Faro*—he may well have listened to one of the keynote speakers, a former US Navy commander named Michael Abrashoff, detailing the increase in safety that results at sea when a captain takes the time to interact meaningfully with his crew.

In Lawrence's absence the email is fielded by another Tote officer, Jim Fisker-Andersen, who replies, "Understood and authorized." But Fisker-Andersen does not send this for several hours, and in the interval Davidson will for some reason fret as nervously as a teenager waiting for a girl to accept his invitation to the prom.

"I have to wait for confirmation from the office, but I put it out there," the captain says later. And later still: "That's why, you know, I just said, 'Hey, you know—I would like to take this [Old Bahama Channel] going northbound. I'll wait for your reply.' I don't think they'll say no. I gave them a good reason why, because if you should follow this down, then look what it does on the third [October]—fourth and fifth. And it's right where we're going. . . . So I just put it out there."

On three additional occasions, in the interval between sending the message and receiving the go-ahead, Davidson repeats these or similar statements, and all of them sound as if they're coming from someone desperate for approval; all indicate a substantive worry on his part, that Tote might refuse. What is also clearly implied in how he frames the issue on the bridge is this: Davidson believes that if Tote disputes his request, he might feel pressured to take a route back that is close to a storm that could put his ship in danger.

Why Michael Davidson is so nervous about Tote's approval of his change of course is relevant to what will happen later, but the tension audible in his worry is not new. Shipowners make their money by delivering freight safely and on time at the lowest feasible cost, and the consequent need to stick to schedule is thus a normal part of shipping. If a ship is delayed—if her captain, for whatever reason, takes a detour—the companies whose freight she hauls will receive, and deliver, their goods later, which in turn might cause them to lose money.* Sometimes, as in the case of Walmart, a client can penalize the transportation outfit for the delay, especially if spoilage (as in rotted foodstuffs) results. In all cases the possibility exists that recurrent delays will cause the freight owners to switch to a different, more punctual shipping company.

The result of all these factors is pressure: direct pressure, in the form of a shipowner's schedules and the expectation, spoken or implied, that they be met; indirect, in the form of awareness on a captain's part that if he is consistently late—if, for example, he acquires a reputation for excessive timidity in the face of weather that results in chronic tardiness and higher associated expense—he will find himself eventually without a job and blacklisted throughout the industry to boot.

Against these pressures has always stood the tradition of the all-powerful captain, of his, or her, status as ultimate authority on board ship; as the saying goes in the French merchant marine, "Sole master aboard after God." The reason for this unitary authority is simple. It's the same as for any other group of people, such as army commandos or astronauts, seeking to fulfill a specific mission in a risky, potentially lethal environment. For a patrol behind enemy lines, for a ship beset by storm, the ability to make swift and firm decisions in the face of fast-changing threats is paramount, because nearly any action ordered quickly and firmly is better than hesitation, and in such a situation it makes sense to delegate authority to a single experienced and decisive commander with the expectation that she or he will get the group out of trouble as swiftly as possible.

Two hundred, even seventy-five, years ago, while the commercial pressures on a captain always existed, their potency was far less because of the practical impossibility of second-guessing a captain's decisions, or of changing them if one did. Before wireless radio became common on merchant ships after World War I, a seagoing ship had no contact with shore and the shipowner no possibility of knowing what obstacles—such as adverse winds, pirates, or storms—might affect a captain's route. Even

* The insurers' cooperative known as Lloyd's of London was created in the seventeenth century to alleviate the risks associated with the delay or loss of seagoing freight.

through the 1980s, when satellite navigation and weather observation were starting to come online, a ship's master had to make decisions in good part based on personal observation and experience without real-time reference to land; it was up to him to weigh an eventual reckoning with the ship's owner against his immediate duty to keep vessel, crew, and cargo safe.

It was this balancing act that Joseph Conrad, himself a former ship's master, described in his novella *Typhoon*, in which Captain MacWhirr weighs whether to flee a hurricane, expressing his thoughts to the first mate much as Davidson does to Shultz:

> "If the weather delays me—very well. There's your logbook to talk straight about the weather. But suppose I went swinging off my course and came in two days late, and they asked me, 'Where have you been all that time, Captain?' What could I say to that? 'It must have been dam' bad,' they would say. 'Don't know,' I would have to say; 'I've dodged clear of it.' See that, Jukes? I have been thinking it out all afternoon."*

Over the last twenty years, MacWhirr's dilemma has become somewhat anachronistic. To take an extreme example, it is now possible for a shipowner to operate, navigate, and command a fully automated ship, without captain or crew aboard, almost anywhere in the world, using real-time links to satellite images, weather forecasts, CCTV, radar, GPS, and engine and steering controls. Fully automated vessels, though prototypes already exist, have not been authorized to travel internationally, but the same technology allows company officers to hire routing services that will plot the most efficient route possible given weather, sea state, and other factors for an individual ship, and to ensure that the vessel's systems capture that information. Having done so, the company will expect the master to go along with what the service recommends, and if the master does not, the shipowner will know and can demand explanations immediately, by radio, emails, and satellite telephone calls.

Since Tote does not subscribe to the BVS routing service, the company's officials have no easy way to track *El Faro*'s route in relation to the

---

* MacWhirr's eventual decision was to avoid risking the owners' displeasure: to stick to his planned course, and run the storm.

elements. And those corporate officers in closest touch with the ship, probably dulled by the routine, back-and-forth tag team *El Faro* and *El Yunque* run on this short and mostly trouble-free route, are not in the habit of keeping close track by any other means of either ships or weather. Certainly they are not keeping track of either *El Faro* or Joaquin on this trip. Yet it seems clear that *El Faro*, her crew, and especially her master fall victim here to a peculiar dead spot in the evolution of ship management: before the advent of fully automated ships, but long after the era of fully independent captaincy.

This limbo is reflected in the well-demonstrated belief on the part of Michael Davidson that he must clear major detours—such as taking the Old Bahama Channel, a route that were he to follow it on the run south, as will be clearly suggested by his subordinates, would take *El Faro* out of Joaquin's grasp—with the company beforehand. Tote's officers later will vehemently challenge that assessment and state that they would never interfere with a captain's judgment on safety issues; in the words of safety manager John Lawrence, "We don't tell masters what to do." Tote's operations manual notes a captain must check any route change or delay with management, but does not state he must obtain permission for the change.

In later hearings, one captain will testify that his DPA, or "designated person ashore" at Tote, told him that if he did not reveal his route plans, the DPA would relieve him of command within two hours. But other captains who work for Tote will affirm that the practice of notifying the company of a route change does not mean they have to obtain company approval.* And a company executive claims in testimony that Tote always implements a "safety first" policy for its ships and crews.

Still, Tote's officers will never be able to explain away Davidson's obsession with getting the company's okay for his northbound detour, as demonstrated in the de facto request for permission Davidson makes at 10:22 a.m. on September 30 as *El Faro* heads south; and in repeated, informal statements by Davidson to the effect that he must await approval from Tote to plan the longer route.

---

* For example, Jack Hearn, *El Faro*'s former captain, says the master is supposed to consult with the company on route changes, but doesn't need permission to make them.

Davidson has his own reasons for being particularly sensitive to the opinions of his employer. He told his wife he was forced to resign from his previous job with Crowley Maritime when the ship he was commanding developed steering trouble in the Chesapeake and, on his own initiative, he hired tugboats to escort the vessel out of the bay in case her steering failed. Davidson believed that this decision, which on the face of it was justified on safety grounds, cost Crowley money and Davidson his job.

Davidson's sensitivity to safety decisions that might irritate Corporate was probably exacerbated recently when Davidson was passed over for a master's position aboard one of the two new "Marlin" class ships, the LNG/diesel-powered *Isla Bella* and *Perla del Caribe*, that Tote has ordered built in San Diego for the Puerto Rico run. (Company officials initially recommended him for promotion, then changed their collective mind, and while they have not formally notified him as yet, Davidson seems to have got wind of the verdict before leaving on this voyage.) Though Davidson apparently was not given an explanation, the previous censure of his crew handling, and his reputedly hands-off command style, were cited internally in Tote's decision to reject his application. Melissa Clark, the human resources officer, reported "dwindling confidence" in his leadership as one reason she and another manager counseled against posting him to a new ship. The ship-management director, Jim Fisker-Andersen, paid Davidson a left-handed compliment: while he was the "least engaged" of all four captains on the Puerto Rico run, Davidson was great at "sucking up" to office staff.

Other *El Faro* officers, particularly on the engine side—Pusatere, Griffin, Kuflik—have been tapped to serve on the Marlin ships, so it's no surprise Davidson feels that he is not appreciated in this company. In an earlier email to his wife he writes of Tote, "I feel taken advantage of . . . but they pay real good." Later today he will talk bleakly to Chief Mate Shultz about being "on [Tote's] chopping block," a sentiment Shultz shares regarding the mate's own prospects at Tote. In such circumstances it makes sense to assume that Davidson's state of mind when reaching decisions that affect *El Faro*'s safety will be influenced by what he apparently believes will be the punishment, even dismissal, he might expect if the company disagrees with those decisions. The captain's two daughters are of college age—though both will go to

Southern Maine University, a relatively inexpensive state school—and the watch keepers he has talked to say he's concerned with the bills he must pay, and the need to hang on to a good job. He is fifty-three years old, competing now against younger officers, men more familiar with the automation technology that will eventually replace them all. He is truly, in the words of his fellow captain, Earl Loftfield, someone who's "not going in the direction Tote is going in."

4

If a ship is a complex world that in its detail and isolation starts to feel like a distinct form of life to her crew and passengers, a large corporation—if usually less attractive and unitary and certainly less seaworthy in aspect—can be at least as complicated and full of quirks as an aging freighter.

Enough has been written about bureaucratic pathologies to suggest that, just as a ship sometimes seems to adopt a distinct personality, a corporation too acquires idiosyncrasies and characteristics that build, memo by memo, email by email, conference call by conference call, rumor by rumor, a collective personality of sorts; and that personality ultimately affects the people within.

The transcript of the bridge recording makes clear that Tote, in its various guises concerning the Puerto Rico trade, worries the hell out of Davidson and Shultz. Davidson at least seems to take it for granted that he needs some sort of permission for a major course change, even if such a change is warranted by safety concerns; and even Randolph, who is very far from a complainer, while talking on the bridge to Larry Davis about an engineer who worked long unpaid hours in a shipyard, slags the company's indifference toward employees. "Tote has its favorites," the wife of another *El Faro* officer said recently; those not favored, in her view, could expect punishment in the form of piecework, arbitrarily assigned.

Former crew, including Jack Hearn, one of *El Faro*'s captains, as well as AB Bruer and oiler Hearman, have mentioned Tote's slowness in addressing safety-related issues brought to the company's attention by mariners. Hearn, in public testimony, has drawn a causal link between his demands to report safety concerns on Tote ships to the Coast Guard, and his eventual firing on supposedly unrelated grounds. But all these judgments, while relevant, are based on symptoms. To find out the core reasons for Tote's behavior one must scalpel deep into the tendon and bone of company personality, history, and ownership.

The company that would become known, on the waterfront anyway, as Tote was born in 1983 in Chester, Pennsylvania—a city with a long shipbuilding tradition—in the shipyard that built *El Faro* and her four Ponce-class sister ships. Sun Shipbuilding, also known as Sunships, went into the freighter-owning business, in partnership with individual investors, under the name Totem Ocean Trailer Express, running first a single freighter, the *Great Land*—Sunships hull number 673—and then in 1977 adding *Westward Venture* to the fleet. Totem, or TOTE—essentially a Jones Act outfit precisely engineered to shuttle cargo between Washington State and Alaska—was soon bought out by a consortium of eight individual partners, mostly men from Sun's senior management. Their number included the director; a couple of lawyers, Michael Garvey and Stanley Barer; and another Sun exec, a World War II vet named Leonard Shapiro. TOTE Resources, as the new company was called, soon changed its name to Saltchuk Resources, borrowing the word for "salt water" from a trading jargon spoken by the Chinook tribe of the Pacific Northwest.

Saltchuk expanded steadily, focusing on niche markets similar to its original Alaska route, buying up Foss Maritime, one of the oldest Pacific Northwest tug companies, as well as Interocean, a ship-management corporation. Another Ponce ship, the *Puerto Rico* (Sun hull number 670), was renamed *Northern Lights*, lengthened by 90.9 feet in a Mobile, Alabama, yard, and assigned to Tote's Alaskan freight run in 1993. In 1998 Saltchuk bought the Sea Barge towing operation, which transported freight between Puerto Rico and Florida, and renamed it Sea Star Lines.

Still Saltchuk expanded, snapping up air cargo, trucking, fuel, and port-logistics firms—companies such as North Star petroleum, Northern Aviation Services, Aloha Air Cargo. In 2006 *Northern Lights* was converted to a Ro-Ro/Con ship—a "minor" conversion, as the company's lawyers contended—renamed *El Faro*, and transferred to Sea Star's Puerto Rico route.

Saltchuk's original owners, the Sun Shipbuilding crew, were eventually bought out by the lawyer Mike Garvey, who became majority stockholder in '93. His son-in-law, another attorney, named Mark Tabbutt, became president of Saltchuk Resources in '99. Garvey transferred ownership to his three daughters, Nicole, Michelle, and Denise (Mark's wife), in 2009, making Saltchuk one of the largest private companies in the United States to be owned solely by women.

In 2010 a ship managed by a Saltchuk subsidiary delivered aid to Haiti following the devastating earthquake of that year and remained in Port-au-Prince over two months, providing the only large-scale unloading facility for relief efforts in that harbor.

Judging by their surface record, Saltchuk and its subsidiaries seem a well-run, dynamic outfit focusing on precisely defined markets liable to produce steady if undramatic returns. In 2015 Saltchuk was Washington State's largest private company, with over $2 billion in assets, $3 billion in revenues, and almost eight thousand employees; in that year Saltchuk companies gave away $2.5 million in donations to various communities. In 2014 Saltchuk Resources was awarded the title of "world's most ethical corporation" by the Ethisphere Institute of Scottsdale, Arizona.

If one looks closer, though, cracks start to fan out across Saltchuk's shiny facade.

For one thing, the Ethisphere Institute is a for-profit, Arizona-based corporation that takes money from a limited stable of corporations who pay to join, then nominate themselves for 144 "world's most ethical company" titles. Ethisphere's due diligence, according to the *Los Angeles Times* and slate.com, is token at best.

Another crack in Tote/Saltchuk's benevolent front concerns the record of Foss Maritime, a Saltchuk subsidiary that will be sued in 2017 by a West Coast longshoremen's union for retaliatory layoffs during a longstanding dispute over overtime and work-shift limits. The International Longshore and Warehouse Union also accused Foss-chartered tugs of breaking picket lines during a 2013 Columbia River strike; an unsurprising action for a corporation, perhaps, except that Mike Garvey's father was a committed union man, a stevedore who was part of a dockworkers' gang that threw scabs off ships during strikes in California ports.

Tote has also engaged in illegal price-fixing activities on the Puerto Rico run *El Faro* works. In 2002—this according to federal criminal charges against Sea Star and Tote Services—following the bankruptcy of Navieras de Puerto Rico, a major rival on that run, Saltchuk cofounder Shapiro told Sea Star Lines president Frank Peake and pricing director Peter Baci that the Tote subsidiary, Sea Star, which had lost $20 million the year before, must start turning a profit. Later that year, in the Park Hotel in Charlotte, North Carolina, Peake and Baci met executives from the two other major Florida–Puerto Rico shipping companies, Crowley Maritime and Horizon Lines. At that meeting the three companies secretly agreed to fix, for the Puerto Rico trade, uniformly higher prices that would guarantee fat returns. The scheme worked, and next year Sea Star posted a profit; the arrangement continued until 2008, when the colluding companies were sued by some of their major clients, including Walmart, Walgreens, Kraft, and Kellogg's. Baci and Peake were sentenced to four and five years in jail, respectively: harsh punishment that a federal prosecutor said "Reflects the serious harm these conspirators inflicted on American consumers, both in the continental United States and in Puerto Rico." The Saltchuk cofounder Shapiro was accused by Baci of ordering the price-fixing strategy, but never charged.

Peake and Baci, of course, are no longer employed by Tote companies. Tote, Inc.'s director since 2010 has been Anthony Chiarello. Its general counsel and chief ethics officer is a lawyer named Michael B. Holt. Both executives came to Tote from the giant Japanese shipping conglomerate NYK; they worked for the company's US arm headquartered in Secaucus, New Jersey. Coincidentally, NYK was prosecuted for price-fixing in the port of Baltimore between 1997 and 2012, a period during which, at varying times, Chiarello and Holt both worked for NYK. A plea bargain that forced NYK to pay $59.4 million to victims of its restraint of trade was agreed upon with federal prosecutors in March 2015.

Chiarello was deputy administrator for the Port of Baltimore until the early nineties, long before NYK allegedly got involved in price-fixing activities there.

Under Holt's stewardship as top ethical counsel for NYK's US group, the company was selected as one of the "world's most ethical" companies in '08, '09, '10, and '11 by an Arizona business-ethics consultancy called Ethisphere.

That Saltchuk also seeks to improve its regulatory environment by contributing to, on average, a third of the election war chests of US House and Senate subcommittee members charged with overseeing the merchant marine would of course be routine for a big corporation and accepted as perfectly ethical by current business standards.*

Despite the record of Peake and Baci, Saltchuk and its Tote subsidiaries do not normally appear to behave in a manner that can be construed as illegal or even unethical by current business standards. But it's also fair to say that the record suggests a pressure both standard and significant exerted by Saltchuk on subsidiary companies to maximize profits irrespective of labor sensitivities or, at times, the sensibilities of its employees; and such pressure might well have resulted in behavior that generates risk for those employees.

At Tote, the evidence for a link between pressure to maximize profits—which for any company must include cost cutting—and the experience of *El Faro*'s people becomes, at least circumstantially, important. Jack Hearn, in later testimony, will say he noticed a change in office support when he joined the Puerto Rico run in 2012. Cuts in staff numbers tend to be one of the first tools a company uses to reduce costs, and inadequate staffing was cited by Tote's HR officer, Melissa Clark, and also by Jack Hearn as causing glitches in ship/office relations. "I felt at the time I could have used additional staff," Clark will comment in testimony. An audit cited a company reorganization in 2012, under Chiarello's supervision, as being at least partially to blame for delayed maintenance and poor ship/office communications; a foreman of longshoremen working on Tote vessels in Tacoma around that time says he noticed a definite change in style, from a fairly low-key, paternalistic company that didn't mind putting money into equipment, to an outfit with a more hard-edged and stingy management persona.

---

* The subcommittees are the House Coast Guard and Maritime Transport Subcommittee, and the Senate Subcommittee on Surface Transportation and Merchant Marine Infrastructure, Safety, & Security. Saltchuk also, quite logically, funds a good percentage of Alaskan, Floridian, and Washington State politicians, whether or not they belong to committees immediately relevant to their maritime activities.

In 2013, a reorganization at Tote Services Inc., *El Faro*'s operator of record, resulted in its marine-operations team being reduced, from a team including ship's officers tasked with offering real-time advice on offshore operations and weather, to one officer, a person holding no merchant marine license and with little direct experience of seafaring. The company's president also refused to hire a safety coordinator, whose job apparently would have included tracking ships, although the job was listed in the organizational chart and at least one candidate was interviewed before the hire was prohibited. Later hearings will determine that the safety department overall consists of only two persons, one of them Lawrence, charged with overseeing the safety of twenty-five ships worldwide; 85 percent of their workload, according to evidence presented at the hearings, is devoted to the LNG fleet.

El Faro's port engineer, Neeson, will testify at the same hearings that he is always working the equivalent of two and a half to three jobs at once. His workload must certainly have been increased last month by Tote's decision to get rid of the "port mate" who helped out with loading. A former chief engineer on *El Faro* will state at the hearings that whereas, before the company's reorganization, he could count on support from multiple Tote officers in Jacksonville, afterward he could turn to only one: the port engineer. This kind of reorganization could certainly have had an impact on safety and overall maintenance, at sea and in port. It is important to reemphasize as well that pressure to keep to schedule and reduce operating costs, coupled with a human resources culture that fosters insecurity among some officers, might lead employees to cut corners in an effort to satisfy company expectations.

Tote, of course, will deny any negligence, let alone malfeasance, in what is to happen to *El Faro* during hearings on the loss. Tote will refuse to comment on any matters pertaining to *El Faro* in the writing of this book. Multiple lawsuits brought by families of *El Faro*'s crew will be settled out of court. Tote will prove to be fairly humane in its response to individual families and will help pay for memorials to its crew members. And looking at the issue through accountants' eyes for a moment, one must admit that no company—especially in a niche market in which the bills for replacing equipment are high—can stay 100 percent safety conscious or maintenance obsessed. Nor can such a company afford to be 100 percent profit-oriented at the expense of safety and maintenance; that is, if it wishes its operations to run smoothly.

Every corporation builds an operational rheostat on which it seeks a right setting between the two poles of employee safety and profit. It seems very possible if not likely that Tote, used to the tranquil Puerto Rico run, and encouraged by a more bottom-line-oriented regime at Saltchuk, allowed its setting to creep too far to the profit side, and this resulted in a slacking of effort devoted to safety concerns. An important example of this might be the failure to keep close track of ships and weather, of *El Faro* in relation to Joaquin; relying instead and solely on the noon report, the time-honored practice of having the captain notify the head office of position and status daily at midday.

As Michael Garvey will say in an interview after the price-fixing incident, most business sins are sins of omission rather than commission. Tote's line managers, some of whom were mariners themselves, are certainly far from indifferent to *El Faro*'s fate. Many of them, it appears, will be personally devastated by what happens to her crew. But overall the evidence seems to point to Tote's responsibility for a number of sins of omission: "a colossal failure of management" is how Tom Roth-Roffy, the leading National Transportation Safety Board official investigating *El Faro*'s disappearance, will express it during hearings;* and this will have a measurable part to play in the fate of one of Tote's ships over the next twenty-one hours.

It is ironic that the ship in question should have been one of the original Sun fleet present at the conception of Tote and Saltchuk—come back, an unshriven ghost, to haunt the company's offices in Jacksonville, Princeton, and Seattle, for years to come.

5

The first SAT-C forecast to predict Joaquin's elevation to hurricane status comes chittering out of the Inmarsat console on the bridge at 10:57

---

* Roth-Roffy, shortly after making this statement, which by some standards implies prejudging of fault in the investigation, will quit the investigating panel, and the NTSB, for a job at SUNY Maritime.

a.m. and is torn off the printer at 11:00. It shows the storm, which (it is also predicted) will generate winds of seventy knots, is going to move to the southwest, heading 230 degrees; ambling along, still slowly, at five knots. This prediction will turn out to be off by sixty-two miles and thirty knots. It heralds a Category 1, blowing between 64 and 82 knots (74 to 95 mph),* the least strong of hurricane ratings. Yet the forecast for the first time gives some definition to the beast Joaquin is at heart, some clue to what it is becoming.

On the bridge Jeremie Riehm and the captain confer. A few min-utes earlier, before the SAT-C came in, Riehm talked about being on a "collision course" with the storm, and Davidson tweaked his "nice little diversion" a handful of degrees farther west, pressing the change into the ship's GPS and putting the ship on a course of 138 degrees. He and Riehm think the ship won't experience winds stronger than forty-five knots when they brush by the circling tumult of the storm. When he looks at the newest forecast, though, Davidson compares it to the Bon Voyage prediction he has already scanned, and curiously, he repeats the same line he used before, almost as if it were a prayer: "Yeah, I think we're gonna—we're gonna duck underneath it."

Davidson puts a lot of faith in BVS and the clarity and resolution of its forecast package, and so does at least one other officer: Shultz at 3:33 p.m. today will say to his opposite number on a radio call to *El Faro*'s sister ship, "We're really lovin' that BVS program now." The red zone of highest winds at the center of a cyclone, the orange/yellow of lesser turbulence around, the easy greens and blues of relative calm; the black projected track of a storm, sharply defined on a chart; these seem to offer solid, concrete choices, as opposed to the small gray print and implied uncertainties of the longer meteorological analyses offered in text. Against these bright, colorful pictures one can plot a ship's evasive tactics as clearly and simply as in a video game.

One thing Davidson cannot know, however, and nor can anyone else, is that the BVS track he is relying on is misleading, and not only

---

* Category 1 on the so-called Saffir-Simpson scale packs winds of 64 to 82 knots (74–95 mph); 2 is 83–95 knots, or 96–110 mph; 3 (qualified as a "major" hurricane from this point on), 96–112 knots (111–129 mph); 4 blows 113–136 knots (130–156 mph); 5, 137 knots or 157 mph, and higher.

because of the underlying inaccuracy of the National Weather Service forecast. A glitch in Advanced Weather Technologies' mainframe computer in Sunnyvale, California, has resulted in an uneven refresh of the BVS forecast package. The text portion has been changed to reflect the newest NWS/NHC data, but the track portion of the graphics has not been reworked. It is the old track, and this means that if you tot up the time that NWS takes to convert raw data into a forecast (three hours), plus the time BVS needs to create their package (six hours), plus the wait period before the next transmission cycle, the trackline Davidson and his officers are looking at through most of the morning of September 30 represents *yesterday*'s predictions for Joaquin, well before it became a hurricane. Graphically speaking, the forecast is twenty-one hours old.

This is not a terrible delay for the clients NWS most cares about, who are wondering whether to put their bikes in the garage or nail plywood over the picture window, but it's a matter of life and death for mariners depending on BVS to show them the likely path of a cyclone.

If we imagine Michael Davidson on the bridge or in his office, focusing on the clearest and most visually effective representation of Joaquin—a BVS track that shows the storm, a circle of bruised scarlet, separated by a collar of lighter and cooler colors from *El Faro*'s projected course, and visually just far enough away to allow the ship to "duck" beneath, through winds and seas that will resemble, as Davidson likes to repeat, the usual day's work in Alaskan waters—it is not entirely surprising that he doesn't stop to reassess his thinking and opts instead to keep the ship on course.

It seems clear from the VDR recording that *El Faro*'s officers in general are not aware of the lag between data and prediction inherent in either forecast; or if they are, they do not pay sufficient attention to the extra uncertainty such a lag must entail.

6

Danielle Randolph is up and running well before the change of watch at noon, in part because that's the etiquette for relieving the previous watch; in part, very likely, because the second mate's brief, as well as navigation and keeping the bridge in order, is to back up the chief mate on cargo work, so she would walk the narrow canyons on Main Deck between the stacked containers, their crossed breastwork of chains and rods; thin rectangular views of sea, clouds, a flat horizon slowly moving up and down against the ship's roll, and a stubborn spangle of bright sun glimpsed between the forty-foot-high steel walls; random spray of thrown spume, warm but still refreshing, when she moves between the outboard railing and the outermost boxes; and there, a heart-salving sensory overload of wind and the crash-wash-crash of wake.

Then, down the companionway to the decks below, opening a scuttle to clamber down the ladders, past 2nd Deck to 3rd Deck, where she might run across Champa and one of the goodies doing another ritual check of the refrigerated trailers; down yet another level to the Tank Top, where the only company among a crowd of parked, silent cars might be an engineer checking on the complex of pipes and pump valves that is the core of the ship's firefighting system, ranked against the bulkhead starboard-aft. Sensory overload of a different kind happens inside these cargo spaces at sea, everything half-dark yet alive with the ship's motion, the vast, echoing, exhaust-blackened garages inside *El Faro*'s hull, most of the holds over a hundred feet long and ninety wide, sectioned off by the gates, and through those gates you walk into the next vast space, hold after hold, each an abode of steel girders and close-packed trailers and great black shadows fighting the occasional blare of neon light; smell of oil and gas from the cars, pervasive roar of reefers all around, creaking springs as the trailers rock, the distant, regular boom of waves on the thick metal that keeps the sea out. Throwing your weight on the levers that dog the watertight doors inside the gates, you make your way from the forward areas, 1-hold back to 2-hold and 2-A (a "plug" hold, the section added in 1993), to the ass end of 3-hold, making sure you close and dog every door behind you; then through the watertight door kept open for ventilation to the engine room on 3rd Deck, or back up to 2nd Deck to another hatch, and a final check of 5-hold aft.

Then, most likely, a quick lunch in the officers' mess. Afterward, Randolph and Larry Davis make their way to the bridge, where Riehm and Jackson have been looking over the forecast—"Got it forecasted all the way up to one hundred and twenty [knots]," Riehm says, and Jackson responds, "Holy shit," but that's a forecast for October 3, and the men agree they'll be in "safe harbor" before that: ". . . We'll probably see forty-five [knots]," Riehm says. While Davis and Jackson complain about the union meeting that woke them up this morning—"If I were you, I'd come out with a hammer and just whack! Whack! Get the fuck outta here!" Jackson advises—Riehm shows Randolph the GPS waypoints for the tweaked course Shultz and Davidson planned earlier. The new course is "one three eight," Jackson tells Davis. "One three eight," Riehm repeats, and "One-three-eight," Randolph confirms; and wishes Riehm and Jackson good day.

Once Riehm has left the bridge, though, Randolph seems to fall prey to doubt about the new course. Maybe because she is less focused on the BVS graphics and can pay more attention to the raw NWS text data on the SAT-C, she is starting to doubt her captain's reasons for not taking more drastic action to evade Joaquin. She acts it out, in a way, for Davis's benefit, pretending to be Davidson: "'It's nothing and it's nothing!'" and "'Uh, I'm going up here fucking way off course.' Of course it's nothing—then why the hell are we goin' on a different track line? I think he's just tryin' to play it down because he shouldn't have come this way . . . saving face."

"We're getting sea swells now," Davis says, referring to the deeper period waves that might be expected from the hurricane.

"Well, Larry," Randolph says, presumably showing him a chart or forecast track line, "we are here and the storm is here. . . . We're entering it."

At noon a bell sounds, on the bridge and throughout the ship. It's the test signal for the general alarm, a ringing that sounds throughout *El Faro*, which at any other time would signal to everyone that the ship is in peril. At this time also, Davidson, from a computer terminal in his office, sends Tote an email via Inmarsat. This is the routine noon report, a standard form including average speed (19.8 knots), amount of fuel consumed (580 barrels), distance remaining to San Juan (828 miles), as well as various engine temperatures and pressures. In the "notes" section of the report, he adds one terse line: "Precautions observed regarding Hurricane Joaquin."

Clouds scud before the sun, the ship seems to rock 'n' roll from dark to bright sea. Jeff Mathias shows up on the bridge, looking for an update on the storm or maybe just Randolph's famously excellent coffee. The two are friends and do favors for each other. Randolph once went on a shopping raid into San Juan to buy presents for Mathias's kids when he was too busy to get off the ship. "Is it gourmet?" he asks now, referring to the java, and Randolph assures him, "It's freshly ground. . . . We do not joke up here when it comes to coffee."

"I guess not," Mathias agrees.

As they sip their brew Randolph shows the engineer where Joaquin is in relation to the ship, offering him "the pretty colors," presumably on the BVS map. If it is the BVS, though, she is not as confident of its accuracy as her superiors, or maybe she's more aware of the overall lack of comfort in being at close quarters with something so big, the way someone might feel about edging around a bad-tempered gorilla, though the gorilla is just beyond arm's reach.

"Okay," Mathias agrees finally.

"We're not going far off course."

"Well, hey, this is a fine cup of coffee, so thank you." As Mathias is leaving, Davis advises him to pack up his metal pipes and conduits, and the engineer replies, "Absolutely. Acetylene bottles secured . . . pipes are all lashed down."

"Lash down your workers?" Randolph asks.

"They're all excited."

"I don't think they realize what they're getting into," Davis comments, and, disgustingly, mimes someone being sick on the deck.

7

Down in the hissing, rumbling, wheezing, chugging chiaroscuro of the engine room, though this is its own closed world and you have no visual of the weather or sea state unless you leave it, the ship's livelier motion is noticeable; you have to compensate a bit more for the deck shifting beneath your feet, rocking fore and aft mostly but lately with a bit more sideways to it; the motion has more of an effect here, lacking a horizon to keep track of what's up and down, the vestibular system in your inner ear has to work harder. Sometimes it helps to hold the handrail set at waist level on the control panel, not to save you from falling, the motion is not yet so violent, but to hold steady, give the semicircular canals a break while you check gauges in sequence or jot down settings.

All of this is normal; to the engine-room crew, motion sensed and seen, the shifting dark areas and glaring lights, the gleam of those lights on sleek, oiled machinery casings, warm breeze from fans and vents, the smell of grease, steam, and hot metal wafted on that breeze are all objective correlatives of home—the rocking is as comforting in its way as the rocking of a porch swing. Here amid the regular thrumming sounds of *El Faro*'s engine room it seems everything is in its place, all of these sense impressions evidence that the engineers' world is working, doing what it's supposed to do, turning and pressurizing, spinning and squirting, roaring and driving the ship through whatever the sea might lob at them now.

Captain Mike came down earlier, in the second watch, to warn of heavy weather, and everything loose that can be stowed or tied down is secured, so that even in the context of the upcoming storm everything is right with this world, top to bottom—top being the uppermost level of the engine room, just a platform and steel stairs, but the flat includes a space with a good selection of gym equipment, Exercycles, weights, StairMasters; though the third engineers are not on watch between four and eight, you might well find Mitch Kuflik here, working out. Maybe because he's six foot four and there's more of him to feel confined and bogged down by shipboard claustrophobia, he likes to stretch his muscles and spends more time exercising here than most; just as, having recently moved with his fiancée to Brooklyn, he spends a lot of his spare time out of the city, hiking in the summer, skiing in winter. He proposed to Brittany on Sugarloaf Mountain in Maine, prepared the whole thing with an engineer's attention to detail, delegating friends to shepherd her to the mountain's very top just before sunset so he could pop the question with half of New England shining in blue-tinged snow and golden light beneath them. It wasn't his fault he couldn't foresee everything, couldn't know beforehand that Brittany, a ski novice, though more than willing to learn a sport her future husband loved, by the time late afternoon rolled around would have hit the wall of chill and muscle cramp and would flatly refuse to ride back up to the mountaintop. Eventually, worn down by the weird insistence of Mitch's buddies, she consented to do one more run on the bunny slope, and Mitch ended up proposing to her on the kiddie lift while his chums, chortling, snapped pictures of them from the next chair.

Next level down, to the control bank between the mass of boilers and sloped housing of the reduction gear. The second engineer, Howard Schoenly, earlier was busy blowing tubes, channeling steam at high pressure back into the boilers to knock accumulated soot, the carbon detritus of burning, off the pipes through which water circulates. Diverting steam in this way reduces the amount driving the turbine and therefore brings down rpms, something the bridge noticed and took in stride, though speed is a big part of the captain's safety equation, the ability to zip quickly around Joaquin implied—but blowing soot is necessary to avoid the fire-side clogging up, which eventually would slow the system down anyway.

At this hour Schoenly is probably busy on the engine room's lower level, cleaning out the strainers on the fuel-transfer pump. *El Faro*, per company policy, did not fill her fuel tanks to the brim; she took on eighty-five hundred barrels of RMK 500, a viscous golden liquid, known as bunker oil, somewhere between regular diesel fuel and home heating oil, from a barge at Blount Island; enough for the Puerto Rico round-trip plus a 50 percent safety margin. Most of that is stored in four tanks, two on each side in the lowest part of the ship, below the Tank Top Deck; it is then transferred to a service tank as needed. The company mandates the partial fill-up, some say to preserve its ability to top up the tanks at lower cost if bunker prices drop, although to anyone with awareness of seagoing stability, the idea of half-full tanks is bothersome because of "free surface motion." In a full (or "pressed-up") tank the liquid, whatever it is, stays put because it has nowhere to move. In a half-full tank, if the ship tilts to one side, the liquid follows gravity and sloshes to the downhill side of the tank, adding weight to that side and causing the vessel to list farther in an exponential, self-sustaining chain reaction that can have serious consequences for a ship already in trouble. It is not clear however, now or later, whether free-surface motion in the fuel tanks is an active factor in what is going to happen, now only fourteen hours in the future.

The burn-off of several thousand barrels of fuel also affects stability, decreasing weight low in the hull and raising the center of gravity so that the ship's average GM margin, when arriving at destination, typically decreases to .25, still safely above the minimum. One ex-captain believes this change also is noticeable on the bridge, the ship becoming more tender as her roll period, the time she takes to tilt from side to side, increases from roughly ten seconds to twelve or fifteen.

The strainers Schoenly is working on are part of the pump that moves fuel from storage to service tank, from which it is squirted into the boilers. They screen out impurities to prevent clogging in the burners; the burners atomize the fuel that, once lit, heats the steam that keeps the turbine spinning. It's therefore important to clean the strainers daily, even more vital to do so if heavy weather is anticipated, since a lot of rolling and pitching will stir up accumulated rust and other sediments in the main fuel tanks, which will clog the strainers' pores. There are two strainers, one of large mesh set at the suction end of the pump, where the raw fuel comes in; the other, of finer mesh, screens the discharge end, whence the fuel goes straight to the burners. Each strainer has two baskets, one in use and one off-line: turning a handle between them diverts flow to the second filter, which allows removal of the first for cleaning. The engineer then cleans the used filter and replaces it in the unused basket, ready for the next switch tomorrow, or sooner if the pressure differential between suction and discharge ends of the pump starts to climb, indicating blockage.

And Schoenly can do this in his sleep, having been a second engineer for so long. Like Jackson in his able-seaman's post, Schoenly has reached the level of responsibility he's content with and has no desire to become chief or even first engineer and no fondness for the paperwork those posts entail. He is a large man with a big salt-and-pepper mustache, a fondness for beer, and, ironically perhaps, a near-total lack of filters when it comes to saying what he thinks. One engineer he has worked with says that if you ever want to vent, but don't know how to do it diplomatically, tell Howard; he will do it for you, in the *whaddya* accent and high volume of his native New York but usually in such a manner, laced with insults that are not really offensive—"Ya snapperheads," he calls the deck officers—that no one gets truly pissed off. The targets of his harmless abuse just shake their heads and mutter, "That's Howard," although they'll have heard the message, too.

The second engineer has his own spectrum of duties, most having to do with the boilers: fuel and strainers are part of that, as is checking the "water side" of the system, the vacuum feed pumps on the lower, port-side level that supply water to the boilers, the condensers that capture and cool the steam. He might have Griffin, the first engineer, working with him or elsewhere in the engine room, since engineers often stand normal watch at the controls then add on two hours for maintenance duties. Schoenly's regular assistant on the four-to-eight watch is Shawn Thomas, a hardworking oiler, or engine-room hand, a man who's as quiet as Howard sometimes is loud and knows the routine as well as Schoenly. The routine on this ancient ship is a bit more heavy-duty than it would be on a modern vessel; it's like crossing the street with your grandmother as opposed to a buddy you're going to play squash with, you know you have to take more care, look out for the old lady, be a bit more attentive to avoid granny breaking her hip—shun a malfunction that might shut down propulsion.

As regards the boilers, two hoary Babcock & Wilcox D-type super-sized kettles, the granny analogy is no exaggeration. They are original, like the rest of the main propulsion plant, thus forty years old. They were checked at the end of July by an inspector from Walashek Industrial & Marine, an engineering firm that specializes in seagoing boilers, and reinspected earlier this month. During that process the portside boiler was cooled down over a day and a half so that engineers could crawl inside and directly examine the pipes and burners. The starboard was not inspected that way, but the chief assumes it's in the same shape, since it suffered from even worse problems on a previous inspection.

Those problems do not prevent the boilers from working at their present capacity, generating steam at a pressure of 850 to 900 pounds per square inch, a somewhat lower level than their original rating of over 1,070 but adequate for pushing the turbines. Deterioration of the boilers, as of granny's innards, is a foreseeable consequence of age: the "throats" of the burners, where fuel is sprayed into the heating chamber, are worn, and the tubes that hold the water as it's heated to steam are bending outward because the wall of insulating bricks lining that chamber is also starting to bow outward. Although a September survey cited concerns about oil buildup on all three burners because of cracks in the metal, nobody seems to think the problem is grave enough to stop the ship from sailing. The company has deferred repair till *El Faro* goes to shipyard for her refit in November, before she goes to Alaska. The Walashek inspector has advised that the repair be seen to as soon as possible—"not prudent to leave" is how he puts it—but it's also true that he has pressed no panic buttons, does not foresee an immediate danger to the ship, and his report was sent to no one excepting his supervisors at Walashek and Tote.

8

Through early afternoon the wind does not stop freshening. The barometer drops, which is hardly a surprise to anyone, given that a cyclonic system revolves around a node of deeply low atmospheric pressure, and the first effects tend to spread far from the actual storm. Davidson comes back to the bridge.

"Weather pattern . . . is crazy erratic," he comments.

"It's a good thing I'm the swell whisperer," Randolph quips. ". . . I can feel it." She taps a rhythm with her fingers. "Like, this way." Tap, tap, tap. Then she asks if their sister ship *El Yunque* took the Old Bahama Channel on her opposite trip, northbound, and Davidson says, "She did not," and explains: by speeding up (which is possible in part because, Puerto Rico's resources being what they are, the ships on the northbound route carry less cargo and so can move faster) they have stayed ahead of the storm—and yet they encountered gusts gauged at one hundred knots on their anemometer. Because *El Yunque* was driving at twenty-plus knots into the wind, this meant the wind was blowing at less than eighty knots, but it was still hurricane force.

Randolph points at the anemometer dial. "That's not been workin' accurately so it's not—" Now she points at Larry Davis. "We'll just stick

Larry out there; we'll do the Larry gauge." Still looking at Davis: "If you get blown off the bridge, we'll be, like, 'Aah, it was about a hundred, ninety.'"

"We're gonna be far enough south," Davidson says confidently, "not gonna hit the damn thing. Watch . . . these ships can take it."

The waves galloping around are increasingly crowned with white, they tumble into troughs already laced with the torn shrouds of previously broken combers. The wind has picked up further. The VHF, always tuned to 16, the marine call-up and emergency channel, crackles as a Coast Guard aircraft, invisible above the hurrying clouds, sends out the latest brief for mariners: a warning for the central Bahamas, including San Salvador Island. A warning, though it is exactly that, announcing merely the possibility of a hurricane's reaching a given area, is a step up from "watch" status.*

Davidson, speculating now, says that when they get closer to the storm, they might have to alter course to steer into the waves. "I'll be up all night for the most part," he promises. ". . . We may just steer one twenty-five [roughly southeast, riding with the wind and waves as they would be when the hurricane was past]. Or we may just steer one thirty . . . get us through the storm. Weather ride."

"Might as well be comfortable," Randolph agrees.

Chief Mate Shultz and AB Frank Hamm relieve Randolph and Davis just before 1600 hours, 4:00 p.m. *El Yunque* is over the horizon, steaming on the opposite track; Shultz knows when she left San Juan and can figure out when *El Yunque* will be within range of VHF radio, which, as a line-of-sight transmission system, has a maximum range limited by antenna altitude and Earth's curve, in this case roughly thirty or forty miles, more if the corresponding ships bear their antennas high. He calls the other ship, therefore, on Channel 16. On the *Yunque*, thirty miles to the east, the chief mate, Ray Stith, immediately answers, and they switch to the channel used for normal traffic.

After a few minutes of chitchat, of ribbing about mislaid supplies and

---

* Five ships respond to the aircraft's call with requests for further info on the hurricane. *El Faro* is not one of them.

broken lightbulbs, Shultz says, "Ya know we're watching the weather, uh, you guys are all in the clear, right?"

"Yes," *El Yunque*'s mate replies, "don't worry, we sped up just ahead . . . of the storm."

"And that's why," Shultz says, "we're not side by side here, 'cause we're tryin' to give it an extra thirty to fifty miles from the predicted center as we, uh, scoot around here."

"The captain," Stith comments a little later, referring to *El Yunque*'s master, "says you're going the wrong way."

"No, you know, we're really loving that BVS program now."

"Okay," *El Yunque*'s mate says, and adds, with irony perhaps intended, "bon voyage."

Shultz, having repeated Davidson's term for the hurricane evasion plan, goes back to the BVS, gauging the ship's distance from the cyclone as the storm, proceeding southwestward and spinning counterclockwise, conceptually at least skirts the left-hand facet of *El Faro*'s track, sideswiping the ship with the outer skein of winds rocketing off its own left hand and then lower-left arc, on *El Faro*'s backside.

No one mentions it at the time, perhaps because this seems self-evident to any navigating officer, but the strategy of staying on the left-hand side of a typical cyclone's course in the northern hemisphere makes sense for three reasons: first (and for this it's helpful to visualize the circle of a storm spinning counterclockwise, with directional indications all taken from the storm's point of view), because winds on the right-hand curve of an advancing cyclone will tend to scoop a ship toward the hurricane's center; second, because winds in the right-hand quadrant, blowing roughly in the direction of its advance, will be stronger by the speed of the hurricane's motion; third, because hurricanes approaching the North American continent typically veer rightward, to the north, at or shortly after this stage of their development, and thus away from a ship on its left-hand side.

Dead reckoning now puts *El Faro* off Elbow Cay, the southeastern corner of Abaco Island in the central Bahamas. A big stone lighthouse is built on the cay, easy for radar to spot, and it shows on the ship's long-range screen, twenty-five miles to the right, or starboard, and a little behind the ship.

Davidson returns to the bridge. "That's a pretty healthy swell building there, Chief Mate," he says.

"Not totally unexpected," Shultz replies. "It's on the port quarter [the back, left side of the ship]."

"As expected. I like the period of the swell, too. Ride nicer. We are really comfortable actually."

The "comfortable" nature of a ride is not just a matter of physical ease for the crew. Rough rides mean, almost inevitably, some cargo damage.

Both men now look at the charts and forecasts for the return trip, which the captain says, if Joaquin does what's predicted, will mean a miserable ride northbound ("Watch this thing morph like on the third, fourth, and fifth. It then explo-o-o-des," he says a little later). And once more he reiterates the pitch he made to the company for going north up the Old Bahama Channel route he decided *against* for this run south: "What I'd like to do is get away from all this. Let this do what it does. [He's talking about the return trip, up the Old Bahama Channel.] . . . I would expect anyone in the office would say, 'Absolutely, you're the only one, you're the one here.' Yeah, but you know I'm extending them a professional courtesy," he continues, "and saying, 'Hey man—you know—these are some of my thoughts and you got any objection to that?'"

"So what did you say?" Able Seaman Hamm breaks in shortly afterward. "There could be a chance we'll turn around?"

"Oh, no, no, no. We're not gonna turn around," Davidson replies firmly.

Around 4:21 p.m. the captain leaves. Presumably he consults his emails and finds Fisker-Andersen's reply, for he comes back a few minutes later, announcing to Shultz, "We can go Old Bahamas Channel comin' home." They remind each other to tell Randolph when she comes back from supper, presumably so she can get charts ready, and then Davidson, clearly relieved, exclaims, "Old Bahamas—northbound!" and Hamm joins in happily, "Woo-ooh!"

The second mate, coming back to relieve Shultz and Davidson so they can eat dinner, sorts through the paper charts that the ship will use to go through the Old Bahama Channel. And then the 5:00 p.m. SAT-C forecast chatters in. Randolph examines it intently. "Looks like the hurricane is right over our track here. Our old trackline . . . so, two in the morning . . . it should be right here." She starts chuckling. "Looks like this storm's coming right for us. Aah, you gotta be kidding me."

Her chuckles swell to outright laughter, and this might be a measure of real worry on Randolph's part. Her roommate at Maine Maritime, Claire Lewis, now captain of a seagoing tug with Crowley Maritime in Alaska, says later, "[Danielle] used her sense of humor as a way to deal with situations she either didn't like or was uncomfortable with. I clearly remember her stressing about a paper due in one of our classes . . . and how she wasn't going to get it done on time. Instead of freaking out about it, she instead was laughing. Laughing and joking about how, if she botched this paper, it would be the first step on her road to ruin."

"Max winds eighty-five—gusts to one hundred and five knots," Randolph reads now.

"We're gonna get our ass ripped," says Larry Davis, who has just come up to the bridge to relieve Hamm.

"We are gonna go right through the fuckin' eye."

"Kiss those containers good-bye."

"Gonna get to sleep fast tonight," Randolph adds, "'cause I think you and I are gonna be the lucky ones—we're gonna get the brunt of the storm during our normal . . . watch hours."

Later, when the regular watch standers return to the bridge, Randolph and Davis head for their cabins. Able Seaman Frank Hamm is still nervous. "Doesn't look pretty," he tells Shultz. They both are looking at the SAT-C forecast, each adjusting his glasses to read. Davidson is currently in his office, looking for the BVS package, which comes in as a Microsoft Outlook attachment to an email sent via Inmarsat to the office computer; if it's visible on the bridge, that's because the captain forwarded it there. This is one of the little quirks of *El Faro*'s system, not very important in itself, but even the small delay it causes might affect decisions under the pressure of time, on the bridge in later hours. And it prevents mates from reading BVS forecasts if the skipper neglects to send them. "That don't look too good right there," Hamm continues. "That red . . . I don't like that."

Hamm mentions the CDs, of R&B and house music, that he mixes and sells to crew members; he doesn't want his stock-in-trade flying around in rough weather.

Shultz points to his coffee mug. "See, this here is my favorite coffee cup. It's goin' in the sock drawer. I'm not gonna let it sit out on my deck." As if it were the same topic, which it is in a sense, Shultz adds, "I've seen water chest deep on Second Deck . . . it's no joke." Clearly the image of water flooding 2nd Deck triggers another image in the mate's mind, of what might happen if seawater found access from 2nd Deck, the lowest semi-open deck in the hull, to the supposedly watertight areas below. "Yeah, when I said you know those scuttles need to be dogged—not just flipped down—they need to be spun and sealed."

Hamm has a similar nightmare running. "I mean—I've been on ships . . . ya get your sea legs—and we was like, 'Whoa, whoa,' you know what I'm sayin'? And it's cra-a-azy, spray came all the way like basically over the top . . . of the trailers like this, like when waves and spray just come back.

"I ain't never seen—these containers with chains—dropping, destroyed," he continues. "Know what I'm sayin'? Just, I ain't never been in nothin' like that before. Knock on wood, I won't be part of nothin' like that."

Then Davidson's back on the bridge. Shultz looks at him and clears his throat, probably wondering, because of how firm the captain's been about not giving too much ground to Joaquin, if he should bring up the idea of diverting farther. Finally he does.

"Umm, would . . . would you consider goin' the other side of San Salvador?"

But if Shultz is worried about the captain's reaction to such relative prudence, Davidson surprises him: "Yeah, I thought about that."

The two men move to the chartroom, to a big desk on which the paper chart of the Central Bahamas is laid out; a function, perhaps, of *El Faro*'s lack of an operational electronic-chart display,* but also because a paper chart, typically three and a half feet wide by three deep, affords a physically more generous view of the waters they travel in; given their need to take in the big picture, it makes sense. The captain and mate discuss the details of leaving *El Faro*'s current track, which skirts the Bahamas chain to the northeast and doesn't break through, in order

---

* Generally speaking, US ships over sixteen hundred gross tons are required to carry paper charts as backup to their ECDIS systems.

to cut inside: dip behind the island of San Salvador, through a channel between San Salvador and Rum Cay, and then out to open ocean again.

They work out the changes the detour would entail, where the ship will alter course to steer her half circle around the island, dodging behind land in one of the few places there's enough deep water to do so.

"That's what I was aiming for," Shultz says, "lots and lots of deep water." And later: "We'll stay well clear of that shallow spot."

The dodge is a step in the right direction given that *El Faro* should be in position to veer southwest behind the island, taking advantage of its protection, at the very time they are due to be close to Joaquin's projected track. It's not a big detour, just a tactical dogleg that soon brings them back to their previous track line and will add less than twenty miles to their overall route: a quick duck in, duck out. But if the storm stays far enough northeast it will give the ship a crucial respite from the roundhouse swings of the hurricane's wind and waves.

Even so, the mate urges Davidson to prolong the detour by a few miles around the next island to the southeast, a glorified sandbar named Samana Cay. "If you agree—well—we'll stay south of this island as well before we come back out . . . in this area here."

"I don't think we'll need to," Davidson says.

Possibly emboldened by Davidson's ready agreement to the San Salvador detour, Shultz proposes extending it through a channel that would take *El Faro* even farther south, from the San Salvador channel to another skirting Crooked and Acklins Islands, and onward through what's known as Crooked Island Passage, which finally rejoins the lower portion of the Old Bahama Channel off the eastern end of Cuba. Then they could continue eastward to Puerto Rico.

"No," Davidson replies curtly.

The two men plug course changes and waypoints into the ship's GPS, and in the midst of navigating, perhaps because Davidson finally got his reply from Fisker-Andersen, their dialogue veers to head office and scheduling, and from there to the opinion both believe their corporate superiors at Tote have of them.

"When they lay this up [in shipyard], they're not gonna take us back," Shultz says.

"No, I know."

". . . I hear what you're sayin', Captain. I'm in line for the chopping block."

"Yeah, same here."

"I'm waitin' to get screwed," Shultz says, and "Same here," Davidson says again.

One can imagine the two men staring forward out the bridge windows as they talk, looking into what they see as overcast, even storm-bound career paths; observing the sea, always, for they are mariners. Even with the bridge's air-conditioning the air is dense with humidity the hurricane is pushing ahead of itself, vapor drags at the men's clothes and weighs down their lungs a bit. It is almost 7:00 p.m., and the sun setting behind and to the right of *El Faro* stabs blades of light, sharp and sparkling as a killer's knife, between the thick ribs of clouds, bloodying the sky above, the dance of whitecaps below.

9

Back in the engine room, Schoenly and Thomas are on watch this evening, their rounds not limited to the second engineer's sphere; they cover the system entire. The gauges at the control station show the different working pressures of water and steam, tracking the change of state as water turns to vapor to superheated steam, then cools back to water again. The gauges show the various temperatures of fuel and lube oil, pumps and bearings; the wellness of the electrical circuit, the rpm of gears and shaft. Glass bull's-eyes through which the golden fuel, the darker lubricating oil, can be observed show no evidence of movement, which paradoxically means the oil, the heavy fuel, are in fact flowing well, without visible interruption or air bubbles. Everything is okay, no one has to call the bridge to report problems, as the chief would certainly do if necessary; personal issues, such as not getting along too well with Davidson, are irrelevant to a guy who does things as conscientiously and by the book as Pusatere does.

Schoenly might not be interested in the bureaucracy of higher rank, but that doesn't mean he's uninterested in his duties as second engineer, his experience having given him the sense of balance all good engineers must have, of how any one component of the plant depends on the rest, of how malfunction in one part can weaken or bring another down. Therefore he more than likely pays particular attention to the reduction gear, which has been vibrating more than usual of late. He looks closely, as well, at the gauges monitoring lube-oil flow in three areas: the main turbine's forward "journal" bearing (a circle of ball bearings surrounding a shaft), which is running six degrees hotter than normal; the strut bearings in the propeller-shaft tube; and the sump under the reduction gears. Much as a doctor sends patients' blood and urine samples to Quest, samples of lube oil from different parts of the machinery are sent at regular intervals to a shoreside laboratory for testing. The strut bearing is a stout steel appendage under the ship's stern through which the propeller shaft runs, spinning on those oiled bearings, and the results for that area came back with an "alert" score for high levels of tin, indicating the metal there was breaking down. All of these items have been scheduled for inspection at the Bahamas shipyard.

The oil lubricating the turbines themselves, as dripped down and collected in the engine's lowest sump, deep aft under the reduction gear, tested fine; and the electrically powered oil pumps, two DeLaval-Imo screw-type machines each big as a full-grown man, whine smoothly, powerfully moving the pure, viscous fluid through a spiderweb of yellow-colored pipes. The pumps' operating principle, supposedly invented by Archimedes in the third century BCE, is as reliable as it is ancient, one or more screws (or helices) driven by a shaft that scoops up, at one end, liquid that is carried along on a screw's continually winding thread to the other end. In these machines the oil is sucked into a pipe that hangs ten inches over, and twenty-two inches to starboard of, the sump's base in the lowest part of the gear housing. The oil is then "screwed" upward, splurting over the pump's innards as well as up and over the turbines. Like the turbines and boilers these pumps are part of the original plant; but with few moving parts, and all of them self-lubricating, they usually cause no trouble. The seal on the forward pump is due for replacement, and this is standard maintenance. The aft pump is running 3 psi lower than normal, which calls for a complete rebuild. But even if trouble were to occur in one pump, setting off multiple alarms at the control console, the second would kick in and take over; and if for some reason both pumps went off-line at the same time, the backup, gravity-fed tank would dump its load of oil into the turbine, giving engineers between two and ten minutes to shut down the turbine before it seized up.*

Still, an unexplained leak occurred in one of the pumps several months ago, with a significant quantity of oil lost, lowering the level of oil in the sump to twenty-two inches. The incident, according to a Tote manager, was probably due to malfunction of a seal or gasket. Reporting it to the Coast Guard would not have been required. But history such as this causes an engineer to gaze carefully and long at the machinery responsible, feeling under it for leakage, resting his hand almost sensually on the casing to check for arrhythmia. Like any engineer he thinks his way inside the pump, imagining its guts, from the suction pipe that dips into the sump, siphoning oil, to the whirling helix that drags the thick fluid to spray over the hot spinning machines. As he works he might well discuss what he's doing with Mitch Kuflik, come down from the gym a little early for his eight-to-twelve watch to see how everything's going and lend a hand if needed. Kuflik's sense of involvement, of responsibility, is strong; like Davidson, Kuflik's normal schedule should have taken him off *El Faro* this trip, but he opted to stay on because Dylan Meklin was joining the ship. Training a green-horn third takes a lot of time, and Kuflik didn't want to saddle Mitch Holland, the other third engineer, with extra work.

Mathias, too, has a strong sense of responsibility and doesn't mind extra work. Anyway, it could be that the headaches of maintaining an old plant, like keeping used farm machinery running, give him pleasure; at any rate he rarely complains about them. The oilers are sometimes less reticent. Eddie Pittman, a former oiler on *El Faro*, said of the ship's engine room, "The question was not what wasn't working, the question was what *was* working." He describes part of his job as standing at the console to keep an eye on the gauges, then making rounds to see what

---

* The ten tons of extra oil in the reserve tank behind the turbines are also available, in theory at least, in case of lubrication problems, but the supply line from that tank is only one inch in diameter. According to Chief Engineer Brad Lima, of Massachusetts Maritime Academy, even a one-and-a-half-inch pipe would restrict flow to 10 percent of what would be required to significantly increase oil levels in a sump the size of *El Faro*'s. A one-inch pipe would allow less than that, making it useless in an emergency: for example, if it suddenly became necessary to increase the volume of oil in the system overall.

problems are surfacing up close and personal. "Anomalies all the time; if the vacuum pump's gauge goes down, if a feed pump leaks, you go to see what's happening." But the complaints rarely go beyond the griping stage. "You don't want to be, 'Why'm I doing this?' If it's working, I'm not going to be a nuisance about it, anyway I didn't feel it was that much of a danger. . . . It's a steam culture, everyone knows what to do."

Below the pumps and the deck plates under the engine room's nether level is the dark underworld into which oiler Shawn Thomas sometimes peers to check for telltale leaks from engine systems or from the hull itself. Some oilers do not much trust the hull. They have found water in the bilges, over and above what one might expect from condensation or wash-down pumps or from spray that somehow made its way through the vent openings on 2nd Deck all the way down to the Tank Top. *El Faro* is strongly built compared to some modern ships, but even in deepest steel her age shows: last January, a classification society inspection revealed holed and wasted steel in a transverse bulkhead in the forepeak. And a 2015 hull survey found that fillet welds—joins burned into the trough between two angled slabs of steel—had fractured over a length of several feet in a portside ballast tank, causing the tank to crack away from two supporting frames. These flaws are due to be repaired in shipyard.

Also, *El Faro* was lengthened. That extra section of hull, 90.9 feet in length and 92 feet wide, was constructed in 1993 at the Bender Yard, in Mobile, Alabama. *El Faro* (or *Northern Lights*, as she was called at the time) was then dry-docked next door and sliced clean in two at the forward bulkhead of 3-hold, between frames 134 and 135. The two halves were dragged apart and the new section rolled into place and welded, front and back, to the corresponding sections of the ship.

There was nothing out of the ordinary about this procedure; it is done all the time. The molecular bond between new steel plates and old can be fine, though it depends on thorough and expert welding to achieve the required strength. Frames and stringers reinforcing the hull must also be welded together perfectly for them to resist the bending, flexing, and torquing forces to which the lengthened ship will be subjected by the sea.

Given both the high quality of Coast Guard inspections and the general indifference of the American public to maritime matters, what happens if welds and the overall hull structure of a lengthened ship fail is rarely spoken of in the United States. But catastrophic hull failure is a real danger that might, for example, have contributed to the celebrated loss of the American ore carrier *Edmund Fitzgerald* in 1975, the year of *El Faro*'s birth;* a tragedy burned into America's consciousness thanks to a hit single by Canadian folksinger Gordon Lightfoot. Catastrophic hull failure is an affliction that has particularly beset large, foreign-registered bulk-cargo carriers, such as the UK-flagged MV *Derbyshire*, which disappeared in a typhoon in 1980. At one point in the eighties and nineties, bulk carriers were sinking from hull failure at an average rate of one a month. Other types of ships have suffered as well. In 1997 the hull of the *MSC Carla*, a Panamanian-flagged container ship, split in two in heavy weather at the spot where the ship had been lengthened. The *Marine Electric* also had been lengthened, like the *Carla*, like *El Faro*, and while rotten hatch covers were found to be primarily responsible for her loss, a subsequent report indicated failure of the hull plates might also have been a cause.

Two sister ships of *El Faro*'s have suffered serious hull failure. The *Great Land* was forced to return to Tacoma, Washington, after her main deck and supporting hull structure developed cracks in rough Alaskan seas in February 1998. The *Lurline* suffered a "class one" structural failure of hull plates and frames in 2008. The *Westward Venture* once suffered flooding in the bilges of 3-hold. It took over eight hours to evacuate the seawater through rust-clogged pump inlets, or "rose boxes." One officer says the flooding was never fully explained.

With these old ships it's a virtual certainty, especially in areas where complex welding is required, that metal fatigue will occur; in fact, the question is not whether fatigue occurs but whether it happens to an extent that will be problematic. Fatigue happens in two ways: by repeated stress, as when a hull is subjected to uneven cargo loads or to bending in heavy seas; and by "working." In the first case, the molecular

---

* The twenty-nine-thousand-ton ore carrier sank in a severe storm on eastern Lake Superior on November 10, 1975, at the same time as *El Faro* was being built; her loss exhibited several characteristics similar to what is going on with *El Faro*. The Coast Guard determined the *Fitzgerald* probably sank because she started taking in water through deficient or unsecured hatches, then capsized; other experts raised the possibility that hull failure might have contributed to the disaster. The *Fitzgerald*, too, sent no Mayday signal.

structure of the steel, which in its pristine state is regular and crystalline, after being subjected to the ten thousandth or one hundred thousandth stress event, starts to twist and knot up, opening microscopic pockets in, say, a weld—pockets that will in time widen into a crack. The crack will then lengthen in a typical branching pattern, caused by resistance from a "moraine" made of molecules piled up ahead of the lengthening, which forces the metal to split off in a different direction.

"Working," the second form of metal fatigue, describes the tendency of repeatedly stressed steel undergoing similar molecular changes to stiffen instead of flex—anyone who has ever broken a paperclip by bending it back and forth is familiar with such stiffening, which increases until suddenly the metal snaps. This snapping is a quantum event in that the number and state of molecules are not directly measurable. The time and place at which a tipping point occurs and a weld or steel plate actually breaks is dependent (as chaos theory would have it) on the process's "exponential sensitivity to initial conditions"—initial conditions being the near-infinite number of variables such as metal composition, types of stress, length of exposure, and so on that determine when a break will occur.

Not everyone places much importance on the presence of water in the bilge. One former chief claims it's a result of inefficient draining and filling of the tanks of fructose, which after discharge in Puerto Rico are destined to boost the commonwealth's already astronomical obesity levels via the Coca-Cola bottling plant in Bayamón. Some stevedores, he says, are sloppy when hooking up and disconnecting the hoses, and gallons of the sticky syrup drain into the bilges. The bilges therefore require washing down, and not all of the wash-down water is removed by the pumps, but instead accumulates where an oiler might come across it, under the Tank Top and lower-engine-room deck plates.

10

The seas Joaquin churns up at its center, according to the latest forecast received, must by now be well over fifteen feet in height, driven by winds of seventy knots. As night falls *El Faro* is navigating an ocean environment far less dramatic, but the wind is still increasing in strength.

swells from the northeast have not stopped building, they are approaching ten feet and the ship, which thanks to her sea-kindly lines still rides easily, is nonetheless feeling the storm's deeper motion the way a person on a king-size mattress will jiggle when her partner, though on the bed's other side, rolls or shifts.

In the galley, Lashawn, Quammie, and Jordan have prepared and served a supper menu featuring jerk chicken, rice and peas, a dish popular with the unlicensed crew, though less so with some of the mates—"It's just food," one of them comments dismissively. After the meal is officially over at seven thirty, they load the dishwashers and once again secure for weather, stowing anything loose or breakable in lockers or refrigerators.

Captain Davidson is still on the bridge when the watch changes at 8:00 p.m., and he oversees the transition from Chief Mate Shultz and four-to-eight deckhand Frank Hamm to Third Mate Riehm and AB Jackson. Davidson briefs the incoming mate on the San Salvador detour: "Before it got dark we altered course, picked a new route to get farther from the hurricane," he explains.

The new course is 150 degrees. Their present speed is nineteen knots, which, as the captain remarks, is a good clip, though the ship is capable of more. The diversion should keep them well away, or forty miles in any case, from the storm's center. "San Salvador is gonna afford a lot of lee. . . . We'll just bust on to get down. . . . We'll be passing clear on the backside of it. Just keep steaming, our speed is tremendous right now. The faster we're goin' the better," the captain insists. "This will put wind on the stern a little more, it's gonna give us a push." Even tomorrow morning Davidson will repeat, almost as if he's trying to convince himself, his ship "will be on the upside"; the storm will have raged on past.

In most disasters there exists a moment in the timeline, of which observers say later, "Here is where such and such a factor might have halted the chain reaction of accident." And it's tempting now to refer back to the broken anemometer, because if Davidson had benefited from a constant, accurate read of wind direction, coupled with data from the (working) barometer, he soon would have realized that a consistent northeast wind and falling atmospheric pressure meant that the ship could not be "clear on the backside" of a tropical cyclone. But the anemometer is broken, and the idea of coming safety remains intact, for the captain at least: and surely the image in everyone's mind as they hear the captain talk must be of clearing skies, a horizon-wide brilliance of sun striking sparks of warmth and colors of jade and lapis from the softening seas, a welcome injection of ease after a dark night fighting clear. Yet despite or because of what sounds almost like a pep talk, the captain warns his third mate, "The safety of the ship comes first." He also advises, "Keep one foot on the deck," a mariner's way of advising caution.

And then at 7:57 p.m., 19:57 in ship's time, Davidson descends the single set of companionway stairs to his stateroom. He will not come out until over eight hours later—4:19 the following morning—when the ship is fully engaged with the lethal weather system he believed they would avoid.

Riehm has listened respectfully to the ship's master, only once re-marking that the Weather Underground website has predicted the storm's winds will blow harder than forecast. "They're saying it's more like eighty-five . . . ," he said. Once Davidson has left, Riehm checks the forecast against the chart. At 2:00 a.m., he calculates, the ship will be seventy miles from Joaquin. Referring to the Weather Underground prediction, still marking positions on the chart, he says to Jackson, "If [the forecast] is off by forty knots, then—sixty, here. . . . It's just, I don't like being so close to something here."

Checking the chart would put Riehm in the classic navigator's stance, bending over the big chart table at the bridge's aft end, perhaps walking the dividers: a brass instrument, like a compass used to trace circles in geometry, with which to measure distances. Though the chart table faces forward, he would draw the curtain behind him, once the AB has returned to lookout position, to keep the chart light from opening Jackson's pupils and harming his night vision. The rasp of rings on metal rod as the curtain is opened and shut is a chronically recurring sound in the voyage-data recording. . . . The meat and potatoes of watch keeping in the twenty-first century is electronic, with electronic chart display and GPS, along with autopilot, steering the ship, and radar furnishing distance off and relative bearing of obstacles and traffic; yet tradition and practical experience require keeping physical lookout as well. The GPS, usually reliable, can nonetheless go off-line, and radars can miss a target, especially in rough seas.

The traditional language a mariner is trained to obey, like the tradition of a captain's absolute authority, is unchanged from the days of sailing ships. Rule 5 of the International Regulations for Preventing Collisions at Sea, aka COLREGs, the corpus of basic traffic and navigation rules that ships' officers must obey at sea, states "Every vessel shall at all times maintain a proper lookout by sight and hearing as well as by all available means appropriate . . . so as to make a full appraisal of the situation and the risk of collision." COLREGs concludes, "Nothing in these Rules shall exonerate any vessel, or the owner, master or crew thereof, from the consequences of any neglect to comply with these Rules or of the neglect of any precaution which may be required by the ordinary practice of seamen, or by the special circumstances of the case." The "ordinary practice of seamen" is usually interpreted to mean physical lookout and other traditional methods of keeping watch and tracking position and weather.

Riehm keeps up his commentary to Jackson. Perhaps by talking out his thoughts he can clarify his doubts to himself and strengthen his resolve, should it come to that, to question his captain.

"It's more powerful than we thought. It's supposed to . . . stop . . . getting any closer, it's gonna turn toward the north. What if it doesn't? What if we get close—we get jammed in those islands there and it starts comin' at us? . . . Maybe I'm just being Chicken Little here," he adds gloomily, "I don't know."

Riehm's commentary has vector, and following the direction of his spoken thoughts, he starts to imagine an alternative course.

"There's a gap in the chart," he adds, apparently referring to the passage Shultz spoke of, south of San Salvador, that leads southwest past Crooked Island and eventually to a continuation of the Old Bahama Channel. He starts to plug waypoints for the new course into the GPS, ready for use should the need arise.

"Some captains," Riehm remarks, "would have taken one look at that and said, 'We're gonna go the Old Bahamas Channel—we're not takin' any chances here.'"

"That's what I thought we—we were gonna do," Jackson says.

"'And we'll go well south of it,'" Riehm continues, still quoting a hypothetical captain, "'and we'll be gettin' in a little bit late. We'll be off schedule . . . but we'll catch up.'" A few minutes later though, as if to reacknowledge his captain's authority, he vows, "I'm not gonna second-guess somebody."

"Well, I'll never have faith in the fuckers like I used to though," Jackson remarks, chuckling. "The captain of [name redacted]* sailed us right through one." He describes Hurricane Hugo and the ship's path through it in 1989. "I got thrown to the deck—I could hear the captain screamin', 'Yaaaah!'" Jackson laughs as he mimics the terrified skipper. "We were goin' over though, this big wave. . . . It came in and slammed us. . . . I mean, we came to this shuddering stop. I mean, I was sure we were goin' over—positive. . . . It's like death was actually—I mean, it *was*—we were fated to die. . . . No one hardly spoke for like about two, two to three days, before people even started talkin'.

"I mean," Jackson continues more somberly, "everyone felt death was like right on us, man. It was like this presence, you know?"

Jackson, it seems, cannot let go of this memory. "Oh, man, that thing—first it started you know—pitchin' and rollin', and then it got worse, it started, like some kind of wild animal, just tryin' to break out of its—like a fuckin' bull in a stall, you know. . . . Then all the cargo broke loose and, aaah my God.

"Speaking of cargo lashings," Jackson adds, "I found two little [twist] screws stripped . . ." The two men talk of there not being sufficient spares to replace broken twist screws on the container lashings, and how they don't complain at safety meetings for fear of being labeled "that troublemaker." Riehm is still focused on the storm.

"I was just walkin' up Second Deck this afternoon," he says a little later, "and just goin', 'Oh, man.' Guess I'm just turnin' into a Chicken Little, but—I have this feeling like something bad is gonna happen."

At 10:53 p.m. the latest SAT-C forecast comes in over the printer. This forecast is far more accurate than the ones preceding, placing the storm only twenty-five miles too far northwest, a mere five knots too low in intensity. Ten minutes later Riehm gets on the phone to the stateroom where Davidson is sleeping.

"Hey, Captain—sorry to wake ya. . . . The latest weather just came

---

* NTSB investigators deleted multiple names and chunks of dialogue that they judged irretrievable or irrelevant while editing the VDR transcript. In all, the NTSB excised over half of the twenty-six hours of recording.

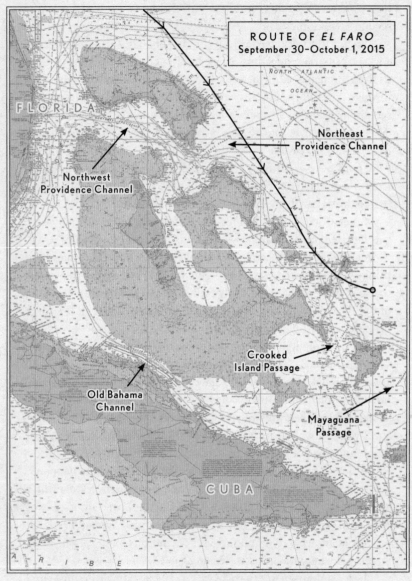

ROUTE OF *EL FARO*
September 30–October 1, 2015

NORTH ATLANTIC
OCEAN

FLORIDA

Northeast
Providence Channel

Northwest
Providence Channel

Crooked
Island Passage

Old Bahama
Channel

Mayaguana
Passage

CUBA

Escape routes: *El Faro* could have taken the Northwest and Northeast
Providence Channels, and finally Crooked Island Passage, to escape Joaquin's
clutches; she did not have time to make the Mayaguana Passage. Shaded areas
mark both solid land and shallows *El Faro* could not navigate.

in, and, umm, I thought you might wanna take a look at it." He listens to Davidson's response, then continues, "Just lookin' at the forecast and lookin' at our track line, which way it's goin', and, uh—thought you might wanna take a look at it. . . . The current forecast," he goes on, "has it . . . maximum winds, umm, one hundred miles an hour at the center, and if I'm lookin' at this right, umm, it's moving at—at two thirty [degrees] at five knots. So I assume it stays on that same—moves that same direction for say the next five hours and . . . so it's advancing on our trackline and puts us real close to it. I could be more specific—"

Davidson tells Riehm to plot out the new forecast against the ship's planned track and to call him back. Riehm plots the bearings, commenting to the AB, "Well, he seems to think that we'll be south of it by then—so the winds won't be an issue."

A half dozen minutes later the third mate rings Davidson again.

"So at oh four hundred we'll be twenty-two miles from the center with, uh, maximum hundred with gusts to one twenty and strengthening so—the option that we do have . . . is at oh two hundred we could head south. And that would open it up some—so I mean of course I'd want you to verify what I'm seeing. I do understand you expect us not to get into the quadrant dead ahead and expose us. Just so you know that—that's how close we'll be."

A pause in Riehm's run-on as Davidson replies.

"You're welcome," Riehm says at length, and puts the phone down. The two men are silent for several minutes. Eventually Riehm speaks up.

"We'll be as close as we're gonna get," he tells Jackson, "according to the forecast—four, four thirty."

"And the wind speed now?"

"One hundred max—gusts to one ten."

"Shit," Jackson says. "Shit."

". . . What he's saying is, 'Well, we'll be in the southwest quadrant, wind will be coming from the north.'"

"Nantucket sleigh ride," Jackson comments, referring to the headlong trip endured by an old-fashioned whaleboat roped to a harpooned, wildly fleeing whale.

"I trust what he's saying," Riehm says. "It's just being twenty miles away from hundred-knot winds—this doesn't even sound right."

"No matter which way it's hittin' ya—still hundred-knot winds. I got a feelin', gonna get my poopy suit* and my life jacket—laid out. . . . It's good to know," Jackson continues, laughing, "that Lonnie and Lashawn will get the EPIRBS, man."

EPIRBs are emergency position-indicating radio beacons, self-contained transmitters usually stowed on an open deck, that broadcast automatic distress signals when activated manually or after immersion in salt water. *El Faro* has one; it's unclear whether anyone else aboard owns a personal beacon.

A little later, watching the radar, spotting a band of rain that might be one of the first signs of the actual hurricane, Riehm says, "We don't have any options here. We got nowhere to go."

"Jesus, man," Jackson replies, "don't tell me any more. I don't even wanna hear it," and the third mate laughs. Jackson continues, "Th-th-th-th-th-these are ba-ba-ba-ba-ba-ba-big waaaves." He's imitating Elmer Fudd: "Jesus, it's a *hurricane!*"

11

Investigators will later determine that the gut feelings of Riehm and Jackson are far from misguided. Most prudent mariners would agree with Riehm and aver Davidson is making a mistake. With just one glance at the chart, even the flawed weather charts *El Faro* has been receiving, a cautious skipper would react instinctively to that angry red swirl apparently coming after him and decide not to try outguessing the storm, just get the hell out of the way and never mind the bureaucratic consequences.

Earlier Riehm talked about Davidson's experience as captain, and even now he seems to have faith in his skipper's overall judgment; he certainly does not put up a fight when Davidson dismisses his suggestion

---

* Survival or immersion suit; the nickname comes from the obvious fact that a survivor might be stuck in the suit for hours with no way to relieve himself outside it. The totally enclosing garment, of thick orange neoprene, with hood and face flap to protect the head, will in theory keep the occupant warm and floating for hours if not days. The suit is also called a Gumby suit, from the rubbery cartoon character it resembles.

to escape the storm by steaming southwest through Crooked Island Passage. Taking that channel, or else turning tail and fleeing at full speed back to Jacksonville, are probably the only two paths to survival left open to *El Faro* at this point.

And yet Davidson not only rejects Riehm's idea, he seems to do so summarily. He doesn't bother climbing one flight up to his bridge to eyeball directly what the situation might be, given the new forecast. (SAT-C data don't transmit directly to his office computer, though the terminal receives the BVS version; that he asks the mate to do the tracking suggests Davidson doesn't get out of his bunk to check BVS either.) Nor does Davidson immediately download the BVS forecast that came in at 11:00 p.m. Of course, as an experienced mariner, even one who's okay with relying on GPS to thread tricky passages in bad weather, he can visualize twenty-two miles, or a hurricane's swirl, in his mind's eye and sense on some level the fanged gauntlet of reefs and islands *El Faro* would have to run to flee south.

But the human imagination is heavily visual, and eyeballing spatial relationships on screen or paper is important to our understanding of them. With the grace of hindsight, we can imagine that coming up to the bridge and visually measuring the tracks of ship and storm might have allowed Davidson to accord a bit more weight to Riehm's advice.

Instead, Captain Mike apparently settles down in his bunk and closes his eyes again.

We will never know for certain why. We can never be sure why, as Davidson considered his options when safely moored in Jacksonville, he seemed so convinced that taking the inside route through Old Bahama Channel, traveling at the greatest distance possible from Joaquin, was an option not even worth considering, except for the return trip. He had done it once before, in August, when Tropical Storm Erika threatened, although in that case he probably felt encouraged to take the longer route south because of emails from Tote that strongly counseled safety precautions. Faulty forecasts, unrefreshed BVS track lines, and the momentum of habit certainly played their part in his thinking for this trip. So, perhaps, did overconfidence in navigational options: the tendency, as Delgado says, to forgo the ordinary, cautious practice of seamen and "tickle the dragon's tail." Davidson also seems excessively

confident of *El Faro*'s overall strength in stormy seas, due perhaps to
the relative unfamiliarity of a hands-off skipper with the salt-and-steel
vulnerabilities of his ship. He may not realize that the Ponce-class ships
he knew in Alaska handled better because they didn't carry a tall deck
cargo of containers.

Michael Davidson's insecurity about his job at Tote clearly played
a major role in his initial decision. He knew from his experience at
Crowley Maritime, and possibly from scuttlebutt surrounding Hearn's
dismissal from Tote, how professionally risky it could be to make decisions based solely on safety concerns that would cost a shipowner money;
his near-obsessive reiteration of how he asked Tote for permission to
take the safe route back seems evidence enough of that. All these factors
combined would provide strong psychological pressure for Davidson
to focus hard on his ongoing "shoot under" strategy, to the detriment
of other options and of *El Faro*'s eventual safety.

Deeper yet, among the complexities of the captain's mind; lower than
those synaptic annexes of fear and confidence, lies a subtler and possibly
just as fateful psychological quirk. For Michael Davidson, according
to several crew members with whom he discussed the subject, was a
"doomsday prepper," one of that subgroup, more common in America
than anywhere else, that expects the end of civilization to occur quite
soon, and possibly tomorrow, from any number of causes: nuclear war,
economic, social, and political breakdown, global pandemic, widespread
terrorism, peak oil, rising sea levels, earthquake, meteor strike—even,
on the fringes of the group, alien invasion and zombie apocalypse.

Preppers believe also, and this is just as important as the fear component, that the end is survivable as long as one gets ready for it. To that
end they dig blastproof bunkers, buy canned foods and water filters,
stock up on guns and ammo. More productively perhaps, they learn
how to grow vegetables, set up solar panels, and generally live off-grid.

It's not clear how far down the prepper road Davidson has traveled,
but he has talked about building bunkers before. And he listens to the
podcasts of Alex Jones—the same Alex Jones who, when he is not de-
riding the murders of Sandy Hook's children as a government hoax, is
selling prepper products online: packs of iodine tablets for use in case
of nuclear fallout ($19.95 a twenty-pack), tactical body armor ($1,400-

plus per vest), bottles of "male vitality" ($59.95 apiece) for guys who can't really get it up for The End.*

At first glance, preppers such as Davidson would strike one as being more, rather than less, aware of coming disaster; more apt to take measures to neutralize the effects of a coming holocaust. "Holocaust" in the original Greek means the burning of everything, and if one substitutes water and wind for fire, and drowning for cremation, then Joaquin, even if not worldwide in scope, possesses all relevant attributes in as much terrifying volume as one might ever wish for or fear.

But psychologists who have examined the issue have found that, curiously, many preppers are committed optimists. "When an unpredictable or painful experience . . . is predictable, we relax. The anxiety caused by uncertainty is gone," a *Scientific American* article opines.† If one thinks about it for more than five seconds, the idea that a nuclear holocaust, for example, could be survivable thanks to thyroid tablets and a bunker dug in New England clay truly represents an act of optimism, not to mention naive, even illogical, faith. And with such faith comes a curious peace, even complacency, because one has prepared—as if preparation in and of itself has satisfied some moral code only the community of preppers can appreciate; as if the quantum sum of tiny factors that contribute to taking further action, or not, has just shifted by one psychological unit to the "chill out" side.

Safe in that knowledge, peaceful in his complacency, the prepper can pull up the covers, close his eyes, and finally sleep.

---

* 2017 prices.

† Authored by Daisy Yuhas. "There may also be comfort in being able to attribute doom to some larger cosmic order . . . such as an ancient Mayan prophecy. This kind of mythology removes any sense of individual responsibility," Shmuel Lissek, a professor at University of Minnesota, writes in the same article.

Old-style lifeboat: *El Faro*'s lifeboats, of the same basic design as the *Titanic*'s, could not be launched in a hurricane. (The boat pictured here, nearly identical to *El Faro*'s, was carried by her sister ship, *El Yunque*.)

PART V

THE QUANTUM OF SHIPWRECK

The sea—this must be confessed—has no generosity. No display of manly qualities—courage, hardihood, endurance, faithfulness—has ever been known to touch its irresponsible consciousness of power.

—Joseph Conrad

The ocean is so vast, deep, and complex—so infinitely varied in the way its black canyons and pulsing life, its currents and dolphins, rages and calms, moon and weather, all interplay—that no mariner can afford to go to sea while thinking about or trying to fathom such scale and infinite roil. It's just too big. He or she deals with the unknown inherent in the marine environment by focusing on what can be measured and understood, weighed and manipulated. She or he cuts down the infinity of sea to a smaller, digital view, of ship and crew, task and routine, coffee, food, and cabin; confident in the great likelihood that discipline, tradition, and the sheer scale and strength of a ship such as this will see her safely to harbor.

The wind, though still northerly, has yet more east to it now; blowing probably twenty-five or thirty, gusting to forty. The swells, northerly earlier, are also starting to swing east a bit but *El Faro*, on her new course of 150 degrees, a little east of south for the channel behind San Salvador, still drives mostly perpendicular to the long ranks of dark rising water. The waves are more than ten feet high, long ridges increasingly driven by the southwest spin of Joaquin approximately 120 miles to the northeast; they are barely visible in the night except for where a porthole's glint touches froth whipped up by wind or wake or the smash of a wave collapsing, but the wind is starting to draw out the crests into streaks of foam that run like thin groping claws down the combers' flanks. Ten- to fifteen-foot waves are nothing to a ship this size—as Davidson says, she used to plow through twenty-footers on a routine journey between Tacoma and Anchorage—but waves are not reducible to their official height. They are not, in fact, waves in the sense we imagine them, as serried crests marching like soldiers from horizon to horizon, but rather a heaving of the sea itself, rubbed harshly by wind into humps that rise in a roll of trillions of individual molecules of water, salt, weed, plankton, and amino acids that shift on the vertical, describing a circle that brings them back to the same place, but which shoves at the next stretch of water so that the action itself, the humping up of water, continues in a forward surge of un-furling liquid, a tumbling rhythm of great might—a single storm wave, by some calculations, carries 1.7 megawatts of potential power in its every square meter.*

The varying rhythms of waves, tuned by the strength, direction, and duration of wind, not to mention the area and topography of the ocean they inhabit, can interfere with each other, causing rips and cross seas. Or they can join forces as two oscillations of water, period shrinking to nothing and amplitude rising commensurately, almost double in height to create a rogue wave. The general rule is that one in a hundred waves will be a third higher than the average of higher waves, and one in a thousand will be double the size; thus even now, if the waves average thirteen feet, *El Faro* will occasionally be riding nineteen-footers, and twenty-six-footers more rarely.

The waves' rhythm can determine how a vessel will move as it navi-gates a rough ocean. For container ships, with their relatively high center of gravity—and specifically, container ships heading perpendicularly into or away from the watery ridges—the interval between waves can matter a lot.

A ship moves in six different ways: pitch, as bow and stern alternately lift; the sideways roll; "yaw," as her direction changes port to starboard and back. "Surge" is a longitudinal movement of the entire vessel; "heave" is the vertical equivalent, and "sway" is a bodily movement sideways. For a ship heading perpendicularly into or away from a wave field the most important motion would probably be pitch, but if the waves' period, the space between them, is equal to the ship's length, and if the ship is traveling at more or less the same speed as the waves' motion, and if the waves are big enough, she can start to roll with great violence. That's

---

* One megawatt of electricity would power between four hundred and nine hundred American homes for one year. Even a smallish storm wave covers a thousand meters in area and could, if its power were harnessed, illuminate Washington, DC, for a year.

because the waves curling from aft give her stern a shove at the same time as her bow plunges into the next crest forward (or vice versa); the ship's two extremities being shaped very differently, they react differently to the two humps of water, and that difference twists the hull and causes it to roll hard to one side. Such movement, unless heading and/or speed are changed, can become self-sustaining and self-aggravating to the point of peril. This is known as a synchronous roll.

The ship's motion can also be affected by parametric roll; basically, a bad tuning between the vessel's roll period (the time she takes to roll to one side and back) and the rate of encounter with swells; if the period of encounter corresponds exactly to the vessel's roll period, and she's traveling at the same speed, the roll can also deepen.

El Faro, right now, moves easily enough. Despite his earlier concern Frank Hamm has cut down worry to the scale of his CDs and likely stashes them carefully in a drawer, or in a box he stows in his closet or under the bunk.

In the galley Lashawn Rivera, Ted Quammie, and assistant steward Lonnie Jordan have put the last of dinner's dishes in the industrial washer. To prepare for heavy weather—they have been warned several times now, by Davidson, by the mates—they must already have triple-checked that everything loose, including the sauces Davidson particularly worries about, has been stowed; that the lockers holding china and pans are closed and latched tight. They have prepared the usual "night lunch"—sandwich rolls, cheese, roast beef, sliced turkey, mayo, lettuce, tomatoes, and the like—for the crew on watch, maybe less copious than usual so the chow won't overflow serving trays if the ship rolls hard. The night crew can take more food if they need it from a fridge in the mess. The coffee urn is strapped down. The stewards can't be sure what the weather will be like tomorrow, but they know the crew will want breakfast, and the galley staff will have pancake batter and scrambled-egg mix ready to go, covered and sealed in the galley fridge.

Back in his cabin Rivera makes sure to put extra towels under a deckhead that always leaks when it rains. As a native Floridian he knows full well that hurricanes, even if they don't hit you directly, will bring rain, crazy amounts of it. As most mariners do, he has pictures of his family, his girlfriend and son and two daughters. Maybe he gives them a longer look than usual, utters another silent prayer for his people and himself as he makes sure nothing important lies within range of the leak, and that the breakable items in his cabin are as well secured as those in his galley.

Jackie Jones, as a day man, is quite possibly still up; in the crew's mess maybe, playing dominoes with Carey Hatch or shooting the shit with his cousin James Porter; most likely of all, with this crew of family men all doing their own thing, he's in his cabin, tending a Crock-Pot of beans and rice, playing video-football games, or watching DVDs of classic Super Bowls, and videos of his sons throwing passes.

Assuming Larry Davis took Randolph's advice, he is fast asleep, storing up energy for the midnight-to-four watch. Davis is a veteran, not just of the merchant marine but of commercial fishing boats as well, and knowing what rough water is like he will have taken out the bulky orange life jackets stored in his closet with his Gumby suit and wedged them against the bulkhead on one side of his mattress. By narrowing the bunk's width to that of his own body he ensures that he won't roll around as the ship moves. If she rolls too hard your body will rattle like popcorn in a hot pan, and you won't sleep, and sleep is precious at sea. Right now the motion isn't so bad and anyway, to a sailor, the rock and pitch of a moving ship, like servosystems' noise to an astronaut, can feel comforting, reassuring. With the rattle and creak of joinery and machines, it says the ship's world is doing what it's supposed to do, moving fast and consistently in the direction of shelter.

At the heart of *El Faro*'s world, however, some of the quantum details that must stay in order, lined up within the spectrum and parameters of safety to work right, instead are starting to skew—to pass from the known quadrant of tolerance, the okay strains and foot-pounds, to the unfathomed, the quantum possibilities of breakdown.

Here's one example: the gasket between lid and lip in one of the scuttles on 2nd Deck, those hatchways leading from the cargo sections on 2nd to the watertight holds below. It could be that the serial wash of hydrocarbons onto the scuttle, and the ongoing scission or wastage that derives from it, has cut one chain of silicon molecules too many or eroded a wider patch of synthetic rubber on this particular gasket, which has created a tiny void in the seal. Hardly a big problem, or not at first. Except that this deck, though covered, is open to the elements through those fifteen wide ports on each side of the ship, several as big as a car or pickup truck. As soon as the waves reach a certain height they wash through the ports across the decks; and because of the dearth of bulkheads on this deck, they have more room to run. The trailers slow them down inboard, but the scuttles are all set at the deck's outer edge, an area that, except for the occasional vent housing protruding from the side shell, is as open as it gets in a cargo hold. In heavy weather big waves will find the scuttle, smash against the coaming, build up against a nearby vent housing, and submerge the hatch; they will blast into any void or pocket in the gasket and exert strong pressure there, widening the pocket. In a big enough void this pressure can grow fierce and repetitive enough to shift the dogging mechanism, especially if that mechanism has not been fully engaged—it can even move the bolts themselves, if they're already worn, just enough so that they barely touch the coaming lip. When that happens, a strong wave jetting against the damaged hatch is enough to flip it open.

And maybe, much deeper in the ship's structure, beside one of the longitudinal stringers that reinforce the section between ribs 134 and 135—the spot where a section of hull (subsequently named 2A-hold) was inserted between 2- and 3-holds when *El Faro* was lengthened in 1993—in one of the plates of the hull at that point, here, too, a void has formed. Molecules of steel, their crystalline structure perhaps uneven to begin with because of a faulty weld, have been subjected to repeated and uneven stress. Possibly a crack has branched outward from that void. The crack is tiny, undetectable; it's not even big enough—assuming it's within, or affects, a hull join—to allow water through. But it weakens the metal and in an environment of increasing stress, weakness must feed on weakness. This is a classic example of chaos theory, a branch of complexity studies that seeks to understand situations in which a near-infinite, and infinitely complicated, number of elements and physical relationships too small to see or analyze—elements that normally work together within a certain framework and rhythm—start to collapse under stress, one grain of dysfunction weakening the structure and pulse of the next, making it easier for the grain neighboring it in time and space to break or malfunction in turn. When and how the exponentially growing cascade of breakdowns reaches a tipping point at which the whole structure fails, given the endless number of variables, is impossible to determine except in calculations of probability.

But however the math of chaos works, breakdown has started. The waves and wind are building relentlessly, water spraying then sloshing then cascading onto 2nd Deck as the ship pitches and rolls, harder and harder. And deep down the hull moves; a hull is a living thing, it flexes and twists, which is right and desirable as long as the welds are healthy. But if there is a flaw, the hull's torque in heavy weather weakens it further.

2

It should not happen this way.

Because of the Jones Act, which has had a whipsaw effect on American maritime transportation by protecting the coastal US market for American shipowners while also forcing them to build their vessels in expensive stateside yards, *El Faro* is one of many older ships in service between American ports. Yet she was also well built in that Pennsylvania shipyard—more steel, her crewmen tell each other, heavier steel even than in her sister ship, the *El Morro*.

US construction and maintenance regulations are among the toughest in the world, another reason *El Faro* should not suffer the harm she courts; except that she, and other ships of her class, have slipped through loopholes in the laws. The difficulty and cost of maintaining ships beyond their shelf life, or so owners affirm, demands relief in the form of less stringent regulations, and in 1995 they lobbied for and won an exemption in the rules for older ships. It's called the Alternate Compliance Program, or ACP, and under this regime older vessels are not required to update some of their safety features to current standards. Another loophole superannuated vessels can take advantage of, separately from the ACP, lies in the Coast Guard's authority to exempt such ships from safety upgrades unless they undergo a "major conversion." The exact definition of this term became very relevant in 2006, when *El Faro* was converted from a pure roll-on, roll-off freighter to a Ro-Con, a mixed-container and Ro-Ro ship. The conversion included structural changes to Main Deck and effectively lowered the vessel's freeboard—the vertical footage between waterline and top watertight deck—by two feet.

The changes were not insignificant. A high load of containers is apt to make a ship—even if she stays within the stability requirements set by regulatory authorities—more top-heavy than a roll-on, roll-off configuration that keeps her cargo below decks. This was the chief factor cited by Jack Hearn, who commanded *El Faro* when she was a pure Ro-Ro in Alaskan waters, to explain why the vessel became more list-prone after her conversion. Lowering the freeboard also means more water will come aboard in rough seas. But the Coast Guard, on appeal by Tote, went back on its decision and ruled the 2006 changes "minor." This was the about-face that allowed Tote to keep running *El Faro* with antiquated lifeboats.

The ACP loophole has further consequences. Thanks to this program, much of the inspection of lifeboats and other features of the ship is now carried out by an independent "classification society" instead of by the Coast Guard. These societies are nonprofit organizations that collect fees for carrying out inspections. This builds a conflict of interest into its operation, since the inspection outfit will have an institutional prejudice against being too hard on a given fleet, so as not to annoy a shipowner to the point where he will switch to another society, thus depriving the first of fees. The classification society can examine ships by the standard of an "equivalent level of safety" to government rules, a benchmark that has left room for interpretation.

The classification society Tote hires is one of the biggest, the American Bureau of Shipping. It also turns out that ABS has been seriously remiss in inspecting *El Faro* and her sister ships. For example, the society did not advise pressure-testing *El Faro*'s boiler tubes while the ship was operating, despite their obvious and ongoing problems. And when *El Yunque* was examined by Coast Guard inspectors following *El Faro*'s accident, her twenty-two watertight fire dampers and vents were found in many cases to be rusted through or seized up or missing gaskets, and inoperable. The Coast Guard concluded *El Faro* suffered from the same deficiencies on her last voyage, an assumption clearly corroborated by one AB's comment on the voyage data recorder: "Vent's rusted fucking solid, man!"

One reason for the vents' poor condition is that they have been left permanently open because closing them has never been necessary in the kind of placid weather *El Faro* usually experiences on the Puerto Rico run. Why they were left open to begin with is due to a regulatory inconsistency: the ship's "certificate of inspection" allowing her to sail requires that the vents be kept open to disperse gasoline vapors from the cars below deck. Yet the same rules allow *El Faro* to be loaded deeper on the assumption that closed vents will prevent flooding of the hull in a storm.

After *El Faro*'s accident ABS will recommend repairs to *El Yunque*, which will supposedly be carried out before the ship is reassigned to the Alaska route, but a diligent Coast Guard inspector examining the ship in Puget Sound will find that her vents still exhibit "longstanding uncorrected wastage"; Tote will promptly send *El Yunque* to the junkyard. After *El Faro*'s last voyage, other ships sailing under the ACP will be inspected; three will be found in such poor condition that they have to be scrapped, two others will be banned from sailing without repairs, and several others exhibit "significant deficiencies," according to the Coast Guard. One maritime expert, Captain William Doherty of Nexus Consulting Group, says of the ACP, "What they have done over the past twenty years is lower the bar. Their definition of seaworthy gets lower and lower because the ships are getting older and older."

In 2016, 10 percent of ACP ships were prohibited from sailing by the feds. And all this happened under rules set up after the *Marine Electric* disaster, which were supposed to make it impossible for vessels with rusted-out working parts to venture seaward at all.

Following what will happen to *El Faro*, the ACP program as a whole will be judged "not effective" by the NTSB.

3

Shortly before midnight on September 30, Randolph and Davis appear on the bridge to relieve Riehm and Jackson. Riehm shows Randolph a new band of rain and clouds on the radar, then leads her to the back section of the bridge, to the chart table, closing the curtain behind them. Together they look at the ship's current track, course, and projected stroll around San Salvador Island in relation to the latest forecast, which shows Joaquin bearing down in roughly the direction of that island, though still with that twenty-five-mile error allowing a thin belief they could squeak past. And Randolph starts laughing uncontrollably.

"We would have been better off staying on our old track line," she says.

"It's gonna be a party in a few hours," Jackson tells Davis.

"I know," Davis agrees. "I just seen a little TV." (*El Faro* is at the outer limits of TV broadcast range from South Florida stations; reception will shortly fail.)

The two mates are still leaning over the chart, probably touching the paper as they point out different positions, a finger on Joaquin's predicted track, another on the ship's course. "Here you are at zero-four-hundred [October 1]," Riehm says. "All right, so this is twenty-five miles."

"So you think that's gonna happen at two?" Randolph asks.

"That's what I just said."

"About two hours."

"Gettin' my flashlight—life saver—my Gumby suit out," Jackson tells Davis.

Davis worries about his TV set. "It ain't tied down or nothin'—but I gotta feelin' it's gonna bite the dust."

"At oh two hundred," Riehm suggests, "you could head south."

"This is the second time we've changed our route," Randolph comments, referring to their dip around San Salvador, "and it [just] keeps comin' for us."

"Well, anyway," Jackson says, heading for the stairs, "we're the only idiots out here." And like any competent seaman handing off the watch, he repeats the course to his replacement: "One fifty."

Riehm and Randolph earlier talked about the third mate's idea, that apparently he will not let go of despite Davidson's stubborn adherence to plan, to escape down the route behind San Salvador, running a southward gauntlet between the shallows near Crooked and Acklins Islands on one side, Rum Cay and Long Island on the other, to finally rejoin the Old Bahama Channel off Cuba.

Now Randolph fixates on this idea as well. "I was looking at the chart," she explains to the AB at twenty minutes to one, "we can try to connect with the Old Bahamas Channel if we, I don't know . . . go due south. . . . We wouldn't have to worry about it until two o'clock. Our tentative position—our dead reckoning for zero-two-hundred gets us in a good angle, in a good spot that we can alter course south to one eight six, and that course line . . . keeps us five miles away from any kind of shallow area, which is . . . not a lot of wiggle room, but right now where we're going, we don't have much wriggle room right now. We got land . . . coming up on either side of us."

The ship, following the course Davidson and Shultz set out earlier, is now running into the narrow slot of deep water between San Salvador Island, Cat Island, and Rum Cay.

Randolph must take a breath after that long and, so it feels, passionate explanation; yet Joaquin and its perceived obsession with pursuing *El Faro* has prompted doubts again. "Unless . . . this damn storm goes further south. Can't win. Every time we come further south the storm keeps trying to follow us."

"It ain't gonna do nothin' but sit down here, growin' up. Keeps getting stronger and stronger," Davis agrees.

"Now we're gonna hit it at four o'clock in the morning."

"What's he thinking?" Davis asks rhetorically, about Michael Davidson. "Jack said he had his survival suit ready to go," he adds, and Randolph chuckles.

One reflex Randolph has in order to deal with tough situations is to laugh. The other is to make coffee, and she does so now. The sound of a coffee grinder takes over the bridge.

"I don't know if he can sleep, knowing all this," Randolph says later of the captain. She yawns, adding, "I slept pretty good last night until nine o'clock. I guess that's when my ZzzQuil wears out. It's just like,

Bing! I'm awake." She chuckles, and adds, "They were doin' that work";
she's referring to the riding gang. "Bangin' around."

"Yeah."

"So I put in my earplugs," Randolph continues ". . . tossed and turned
for a little bit, and fell back to sleep. . . . Earplugs—ZzzQuil. That ZzzQuil
knocks me out. I love it."

Later, Coast Guard investigators will focus on fatigue as a factor in
what happens to *El Faro*. The frenetic pace of loading, in particular
for the third mate who has to be on his feet all day in Jacksonville and
then take the first navigating watch till midnight, has to be exhausting. Randolph's usual watch-standing routine is four hours on, eight
off, but at sea she is expected to put in an extra couple of hours doing
inspection and maintenance chores after her midnight-to-four shift.
This works out to six hours on and six off.

International regulations specify a minimum period of rest, for
mariners as for air crews, but the inspectors will find serial flouting
of these rules on Tote's Puerto Rico run, as well as deficient keeping
of records intended to document and enforce rest periods.* That being said, what constitutes sufficient rest for watch-standing officers
at sea—when even a four-hour-on, eight-off routine, not counting
time needed for eating or personal chores during break, plays hell
with normal biorhythms—is a tricky question. Were consistent and
sufficient rest periods enforced consistently, it would still be hard to
find an officer to swear he has never stood watch when sleepy or exhausted. That a former chief mate on *El Faro* was discovered at least
thrice to be sleeping on watch and was not reported by the captain
possibly speaks to two issues: first, Davidson's lenient treatment of
rule-breaking crew; and second, an empathy, however misplaced, for
the stress and fatigue involved in watch-keeping routines, especially for
navigating officers. The chief mate, for example, works at least twelve
hours unloading and loading cargo; the third works a twelve-hour
cargo shift, followed by his four-hour bridge watch; and Randolph

* Three specific rest violations by Tote ships will be cited. Serious collisions in 2017 (with
multiple fatalities) involving the US Navy ships *Fitzgerald* and *McCain*, in which both fatigue
and inexperience were listed as contributing factors, have increased regulatory concern about
fatigue issues among watch-standing officers on American ships.

has confessed to a Maine Maritime friend that, working under Davidson, she is forced to put in twelve-hour shifts on a regular basis. "She couldn't stand it," her roommate testified. ". . . She was always exhausted and tired."[*]

One should also bear in mind that, while Davidson is the single officer who appears to get sufficient snooze-time during El Faro's final voyage, judging by the VDR record he's also the only navigating officer impervious to the clear peril the ship invites by running so close to a major storm. Meanwhile his mates, Riehm and Randolph, neither of whom benefits from the long stretches of rest Davidson enjoys, display "situational awareness": they are alert, cautious, and clued in to what's going on.

This brings up another issue: Why do Riehm and Randolph not challenge Davidson on a question that objectively threatens the safety of every man and woman aboard? Again, the tradition of a captain's inviolable authority is a sound one, especially in emergency situations, its importance attested to by the severity of punishments reserved for those who infringe it. To defy an order from your superior at sea defines you as a mutineer who, in time of war, would be shot; in the merchant marine you probably won't get shot, but your career will end.

Yet a precedent exists for opposing a captain's decision that is considered clearly wrongheaded or dangerous by his junior officers. Merchant marine academies, with their federal funding and strong Navy connection, drill uniformed cadets on the parade ground, encourage enlistment in the naval reserves, and pound into students' heads the duty to unquestioningly obey orders from a superior.[†] It

---

[*] The author, while standing watch six hours on, six off, as mate on British tramp coasters, made a practice of drinking strong tea and nibbling on cola nuts to stay awake—then, off watch, downing a shot of whiskey to help him fall asleep (alcohol was not taboo on those ships, in those days). He never fell asleep on watch, but the specter of doing so, and the underlying fatigue, never left him either.

[†] They have also set up classes in "bridge resource management," a team-oriented approach to handling risky maneuvers at sea that emphasizes concepts such as a "shared mental model" that will encourage consultation and cooperation between officers when danger threatens. And yet, as recent collisions involving Navy vessels have shown, cooperative captaincy can be self-defeating in tight situations, and the tradition of a captain's absolute authority remains very much alive in both the US Navy and merchant marine academies. Tote's lack of interest in BRM will be cited by the NTSB (but not by the Coast Guard) as a factor in El Faro's fate.

seems likely that for Randolph at least—less so for Riehm, who did not attend an academy—the habit of obedience slammed into her by military-service parents as well as by Maine Maritime prevents the second mate from kicking up the kind of fuss that would at least get Davidson out of bed to deal with her. While the US Navy Code does not condone disobedience on grounds that an action ordered by an officer is perceived as dangerous, it is generally accepted that on commercial ships a mate has the right, not to mutiny, but to disagree with a superior's order and officially note his or her objection in the ship's log—before obeying the order anyway.* Such behavior, of course, would have knock-on effects in terms of corporate evaluation, promotion, and overall reputation, and maybe this is where the fatigue factor truly comes into play, because it takes not only great self-confidence but a boatload of energy to butt heads with your commanding officer—especially one who is in bed, rested, and apparently quite convinced of the rightness of his actions.

El Faro's motion quieted down to some extent as she approached the channel between Rum Cay and San Salvador. Now she starts to roll and pitch harder. Randolph and Davis sip coffee, watching the radar screens as ghost shadows of land slide by on either side, keeping a close eye on the next waypoint that will swing them around the western arc of San Salvador and back into the Atlantic. One of them turns on the Sirius XM satellite radio. The brash banter of an advertisement fills the bridge, followed by a news bulletin. She, or he, turns up the volume. The announcer speaks of Joaquin. " . . . Category Three storm . . . expected to pass near the Bahamas before heading toward the East Coast of the US."

"Oh my God," Randolph says, ". . . now it's a Category Three."

"A hundred and thirty-five miles an hour?" Davis says of the wind speed.

"I have it to a hundred and twenty."

---

* A mate also has the right to change course while on watch if the master is not present, but practically speaking a major course change would require his approval.

"Biggest one since I've been up here."

"We're right between the islands—so-o-o. Wonder why we're rolling?" Randolph laughs.

"This is fixin' to get interesting."

"Mista-a-ake," Randolph drawls, "yes." Then, a few minutes later: "I'm gonna give the captain a call and see if he wants to come up and look at it." She rings Davidson. And waits, phone pressed to her ear. And waits. Finally, Davidson answers.

"We'll be meeting the storm," she tells the captain. ". . . It's up to Category Three." She then suggests the Crooked Island escape route. "Alter course straight south and then we'll go through all these shallow areas . . . umm . . . and the next course change gonna be through the Bahamas and then just gonna turn."

A short pause as the captain replies.

"Okay, thank you," Randolph says finally, and hangs up the receiver. She turns toward Davis.

"He said to run it. Hold on to your ass, Larry."

And Randolph laughs.

"So we're gonna stay on this course?" Davis asks.

"Yeah. The one you see programmed on the radar."

El Faro is now at the waypoint, after passing San Salvador, at which she is supposed to turn toward the ocean again. Together Randolph and Davis go through the routine of course change, a swerve eastward from 150 to 116 degrees. It's what professional mariners do, take care of ship's business no matter what their thoughts or opinions, fears or doubts.

But these few minutes—as Davis turns the wheel leftward, to port, steering *El Faro* onto her next programmed course and then setting the autopilot for that heading; as Randolph watches the radar picture change, San Salvador the pivot point of the ship's swerve to east-southeast—mark a passing of the last chance *El Faro* and her crew have to escape the increasingly powerful, grasping talons of the hurricane advancing on them from the northeast. With the San Salvador feint over, and the one feasible escape route, to the south, finally nixed by Captain Davidson, ship and crew are returning to the track line that brings them back into the domain of storm. Into a trap—of space, for *El Faro* is reducing, instead of increasing, the distance between her and the storm; of time also, for starting now the effects of the hurricane will only grow until, quite soon, wind and waves will be so powerful that the ship will have no option but to confront them as best she can, in whichever direction causes least harm, because any other direction could sink her. And then the ship will no longer be running the storm, she will have been taken into the hurricane. Escape will no longer be an option, and her only chance for survival will be to ride it out and hope to come out the other end alive.

"Things are fixin' to change here," Davis comments as the ship turns onto her new course. "Here we go . . . a little rougher."

"One-one-six," Randolph reminds him.

"Wind heel," Davis announces, shifting his weight as *El Faro*, coming out of the shelter of San Salvador, shoved by the wind now blowing against her port side, her high wall of containers, leans to starboard. "Yea-a-ah."

"You can hear it," Randolph says, looking at the radar screen. "Rain squall comin' up."

At 1:33 a.m. the engine rpm dial shows a drop in speed. The ship meets a big wave, staggers. A loud clunk sounds on the bridge wing. "Not too bad," Randolph jokes. "I can stand up straight."

Flashes of light briefly light up the clouds dead ahead of the ship. Joaquin's collection of secondary storms, their lightning and thunder, vortices and rain, is within sight. Randolph asks Davis if he wants more coffee. The ship seems to stumble again.

"Whoa, that was a good one," Randolph says. "Definitely lost some speed."

"Damn sure don't wanna lose the plant."

"Nah," Randolph agrees.

"Do a lot of things," Davis adds, "but you don't wanna do that."

More clunks. Some damage is starting to happen. The waves are suddenly a lot bigger; in the light of the forward range light they can see a swell crash over the ship's Main Deck, water "breaking green" in a muscle of dark motion topped by froths of foam over the railings. The ship's speed falls again, to sixteen knots. The wind, still mostly from the north, is picking up significantly, Randolph remarks. At 2:47 a.m. she adds, "We're pretty much committed now."

"Figured the captain would be up here," Davis says.

"I thought so, too. I'm surprised."

"He'll play hero tomorrow."

Randolph laughs, then something else breaks.

"Oh!" Davis exclaims.

"Shit, oh, shit," Randolph groans.

"That was a big wave."

"She won't be able to take more of those."

The waves—no surprise here—keep building; they're probably approaching fifteen feet much of the time, coming at the ship's left rear, her port quarter. *El Faro* may be starting some parametric or synchronous rolling, the period of waves front and back accentuating her rolls port and starboard, but if so she breaks out of it serially and never gets into the self-fueling, lethally increasing cycle of bad rolls characterizing that condition.

In any case the ship reacts gamely, pitching and rolling yet moving steadily forward. "I had to sit down for that one," Randolph comments, laughing; then the helm alarm goes off. The ringing signals a wave has knocked this 790-foot ship more than three degrees off a course the autopilot is trying to hold. There's another sound, of something coming loose outside the bridge, and inside, an ashtray, a water bottle, go flying.

Randolph mimics the voice of Scooby-Doo, the dog who is first in his team of ghost-busting cartoon detectives to spot trouble and get the hell out:

"Rhut-row," the second mate says.

"Yeah, it's startin' good," Davis agrees.

And Randolph greets the hurricane: "Hello, Joaquin!" she says.

4

Thus in the early hours of October 1 the navigating officers of *El Faro* are split, mostly between their own doubts as to the wisdom of playing footsy with a hurricane, and the stubborn confidence displayed by their captain that this storm will stick to its predicted track—will hew to timetable as well and by dawn have spun off north and west of *El Faro*'s track, allowing her to be flicked out of Joaquin's swirl of winds in the southwest quadrant like a kid slung by centrifugal force off the edge of a merry-go-round.

But Joaquin seems to have no such doubts. Later evaluation of the hurricane's track shows it continues to resist wind shear and is therefore steadily following the upper-level flow of Atlantic air currents from the northeast, trundling southwest in the direction of the lower Bahamas so single-mindedly as to appear to be driven by its own internal scheme.

The storm has been moving in one direction long enough now that forecasters (other than the European, who were onto it from the start) are starting to catch on. The NWS predictions thirty-six hours out were wrong by a wide margin: this was the early forecast on the twenty-ninth that was 180 miles too far north and sixty knots too low. By the night of September 30 the error had shrunk to twenty-five miles, with wind speed five knots too low. But the predicted *direction*, twelve and even eighteen hours before, turns out to be about right and is reflected in the NWS and BVS packages *El Faro* is receiving. With the 4:00 a.m. watch change on October 1, therefore, her officers and ABs poring over weather charts can visualize the vast, circling, blood-hued wound that is the hurricane staining thousands of square miles of Atlantic only slightly north and east of their intended course; they can eyeball the increasingly turgid bands of rain that mark Joaquin's outskirts, and gauge the narrowing gauntlet between island chain and storm their captain reckons they can safely run.

What they cannot visualize, for none of the people on watch have gone through a full hurricane before, is the raw power of this storm. By now Joaquin, as a Category 3, spins sustained winds of 100 knots, or 115 mph, and gusts far stronger. The huge thirst of this system, the driving force of heat at its core, evaporation at the bottom, condensation on top, the circular plunge of everything the Atlantic—the whole northern hemisphere, it feels like—can gather together into this vast swirling system, this climatic engine gone berserk, continues to intensify: still sucking ever more fuel into itself from beneath by its bulimic consumption of fuel on top, Joaquin's tearing dearth of pressure generates yet more vacuum from the superheated water it rides.

It is worth remembering that the Central American deity Hurakan, who gave his name to this type of weather, used flood and storm to utterly clear the world of human beings.

An average hurricane, through the energy generated by its changes of state, from water through heat to vapor and back again; by the kinetic force of the resulting winds, over the course of its life unleashes power equivalent to that released by ten thousand to five hundred thousand nuclear bombs. Gauged another way, every day it puts out energy equal to over two hundred times the total electrical power the planet can generate in twenty-four hours. But those numbers are impossible to imagine fully, the gap in understanding is like that between the bad shock you'd get from grounding a car battery, versus being fried to overcooked bacon by the world's entire voltage. You're extrapolating Hiroshima from a kitchen fire. "Duck and cover" is a joke, "Kiss your ass good-bye" is all anyone can say trying to imagine such power, shrugging in defeat. The reality is something else—it even *looks* evil from afar, a towering country of wraithlike clouds reaching well in advance of the storm, a superheated humidity that enfolds you like a sweaty sumo wrestler; then a darkness that takes over the world and rain comes down, hiding the monstrous thunderheads now taking over the sky; a few drops, sheets of it, finally a vertical flood. Lightning sears every which way from the tumbling vapor. And the wind starts up, low rush at first, the 1–10 scale of volume ratcheting up to 11, to a keen, a howl, a million screaming ghouls busting through your ears, your skin, into your very nerves; strong enough to make you fly or slice you in half with the junk it blows around.

Joaquin is all of that, and within its eyewall—the vertical circle of clouds surrounding the storm's center—as if dissatisfied with this single engine of impossible power, minihurricanes form. The process here is similar to the collision of Coriolis winds that spin a hurricane at its inception; the difference in speed between winds around the outer and inner cores spins smaller vortices that, in a process akin to the larger storm's, pull warm air upward even faster than through the eye—hot towers they're called, or heat elevators, zooming a thousand floors up the express bank to condensation—and what this looks like to a person in the middle, at sea, is waves higher than houses, and combined waves twice that size, each tall and wide enough to smash and destroy a village; wind that carves off their tops and hurls the water in what feels like white sheets of salty razor a hundred yards long, at speeds that will turn a truck into an airplane.

But no one is near Joaquin's center yet. No one in his or her right mind wants to be anywhere close.

5

Not much communication is happening between engine room and bridge, now or at most other times. It's not clear if some personal tension between captain and chief engineer has a role in this, or if the relative silence is just a function of the usual semi-joking professional rivalry between deck and engine departments. Davidson is not on the bridge when the engine slows at 2:15 a.m. for no discernible reason, but the mate in charge, Randolph, doesn't call down to ask what's up, even though reliable operation of the engine, as she and Davis note, is crucial to the ship's safety in a storm. It can be assumed, and the bridge officers clearly so assume, that the engineer on watch will call the bridge if anything unusual occurs. The senior third engineer, Mike Holland, and the oiler on duty, Joe Hargrove, came on watch at midnight, and one of the first things they'd have done once the changeover was finished, and once they had checked the control console and noted everything in the log, would have been to swap out the fuel strainers again to make sure any sediment stirred up in the tanks by rough waves would not be sucked into the burners. The burner throats are bad enough, they don't need any clogged fuel lines on the fire side to complicate things further. And God knows what plaques of rust or clouds of sediment from bunker barge or pipelines lurk in the various fuel tanks and are being knocked off by the sloshing of fuel; all would clog the engine's arteries absent those strainers. Now with filters swapped the bunker flows golden and sweet through the pumps, past the glass bull's-eye inspection port. The lubricating oil, too, is clean. That system is closed, so there is no need to swap oil filters frequently; the gauges measuring the oil's flow around different parts of the system, inflow and outflow, show no difference in pressure readings that might indicate a problem.

As for the readings in the minds of the third engineer and the oiler, these must be pegged to the "so far, so good" level. The same is likely true of Chief Pusatere, who has certainly been present, making sure everything works right for the coming watch, which is bound to be rough. So most likely has the other licensed chief, Mathias, who, while charged only with oversight of the riding gang and the retrofit of *El Faro* for Alaska, is far too experienced and committed an engineer to not leave his cabin and come below to help when the going gets a little hairy. Hell, most of the engine-room gang has probably been down, possibly because sleep is getting harder and harder to come by, even if wedged into your bunk with life jackets. Mitch Kuflik, the third in charge of showing the ropes to the greenhorn, Meklin, would be on duty by choice; and Meklin no doubt feels some excitement, if not heightened concern, radiating like a mild fever from the older men as they walk up and down and around the deep confines of their workplace, holding on to rails and support stanchions for balance, keeping an eye on the wonky hangers across which some steam pipes run; listening harder through the noise. The quality of noise itself is always a tool for diagnosis, and there's more of it than usual now. Although the engine room is insulated from outside, both by the sound of its own machinery, which takes up auditory wavelengths the storm uses also, as well as by its location, which is largely under the waterline, the ship's more violent movement as she moves into ever-higher waves boosts the overall sound level as stressed joints and pipes increasingly complain and squeak.

The boom of water slamming against the side shell fills holds forward of the engine room, and those sounds echo in the palace of cargo areas and come through the watertight doors between 3-hold and the engine room, which are pegged open, even in rough weather, to keep a draft going, to help cool the machinery spaces. Should Dylan Meklin, for example, peer forward through those doors he would get a loud dose of echo from the bang of waves as well as the creak of trailers and cars rocking on their springs to the pitch. He'll also find it a little spooky—the minimal lighting conjures memories of every clichéd movie murder committed in a half-lit underground parking garage; and the massive, serried ribs and girders of the ship's structure, visible down the narrow corridor between trailers and side shell, twist ever so slightly as *El Faro* rides over a swell, the vertical beams forward all leaning one degree to port in relation to the ones aft, then reversing that movement, as the ship rides the swell; like a snake sliding over a stick, as Conrad once described it.

Of course no one in the engine room can physically see the waves, but because it's night and the air is filled with wind-driven spray, nobody on the bridge can either, except when the ship plows bodily into the side of a wave and black-green ocean bleeds briefly under the port light and raises spume against the containers, or when foam smashes in a million gallons of phosphorescence against the ship's side. The bridge is high, totally enclosed, and fairly quiet despite the wind; the officers' cabins are well insulated, and even if the navigating officers could see, this is no yacht small enough that everything is perceptible to everyone, rhythm of engine, sea state, wave sound, and wind-feel all up close and personal. The bridge staff are attuned to the ship's motion, but lacking visuals they cannot describe the sea to the engineering crew, and no one is correlating the relative size of waves to the shimmy of the ship as she moves.

If they were, they might be wondering why *El Faro* moves as energetically as she does; rolling, as Randolph remarked, even when she is between two islands that should be sheltering her from rougher seas.

6

El Faro now holds close to her course of 116 degrees. She's heading for an ocean waypoint from which she can resume her track to San Juan—except that the swells are suddenly high enough to make steering by autopilot clumsy, and Randolph and Davis have adjusted course somewhat, from 116 to 114 degrees; and, when a particularly large wave bangs in, to 110. As is typical at this stage of and proximity to a hurricane, the wind, still out of the northeast, is starting to whine, mutter, shriek at times on the lower registers of the banshee opera. The ship's movement is suddenly harsher, the twist of her hull tangible to everyone, to the men in the engine room's deepest level; to Lashawn Rivera and Jackie Jones, now wedged into their bunks on the unlicensed-personnel deck, four flights up from Main Deck, three down from the bridge.

If some divine observer, some Poseidon with a nightscope, could see *El Faro* now, he would observe a shape massively long and dark, the edges of which are defined by the ghost-pale crash of waves smashing at her bow and from behind and to the side, faint spray blasting off the rows of containers, the white, green, and red shine of her navigation lights arcing slowly but considerably up and down, left and right; blurred pinpoints of yellow from the lounge windows on mess deck, from a cabin on the deck above where one of the crew lies sleepless; pinkish glow of bridge windows high up; occasional shine of lightning on metal enameled by rain and blasting wind and more spume from the ranks of rearing waves.

Her speed has come down further. From 3:45 a.m. on, this ship that can move at twenty-two knots, that desperately needs power to escape the storm, will never go faster than eleven or twelve. As she moves she wobbles a bit, causing the helm alarm to ring again on the bridge; lifting to one swell, aft first with port side surging higher, starboard thus lower as well, and water washing solid through the starboard side-shell openings on 2nd Deck, bathing the trailers lashed there. The wind blasts from the north and east and, with the ship running a little south of east, heaps more water against her port side. Then the stern dips down and the swell now lifts her bow and she leans to port, but not as much due to the ongoing shove of wind from that direction. Because of the wind, when she rolls back to starboard, she sags perceptibly deeper on that side. At reduced speed she's still slugging it out, gamely crushing into the backs of storm waves, and overall this Poseidon-type, assuming he's a mariner, would not find much amiss, except perhaps her heading: a big ship moving strong, confidently steered into darkness.

But disaster, and we have seen signs of this already, starts as small as it gets, and as *El Faro* edges back into the Atlantic, what starts to kill her most likely begins on 2nd Deck, at those big openings through which the avid ocean slurps. The ports are fifteen-odd feet above the waterline, two feet closer to the sea than they were before the ship's "minor" conversion. The waves still average between ten and fifteen but the foaming commotion they make when hitting the ship drives them higher; those higher than average reach eighteen, even twenty feet, tall enough to reach the ports when the ship is level. When she rolls, bringing ports on the lower side close to the waves, even average swells can smash in bodily, pouring and white-watering on 2nd Deck to a depth of four or five feet.

Given the pressure of the strengthening northeast wind, the roll to starboard must now be consistently deeper, and the slices of solid North Atlantic water wash that much fatter through the starboard ports. Black and monstrous in the sparse neon, glinting evil, the waves crash against the chained trailers, make surf against the steel baffles and half bulkheads built on 2nd Deck to shelter the many vents against seas that normally wash in, then wash out again via the same ports they came in through; the waves don't care, they come back, outflank the bulkheads and throw themselves bodily against more trailers and curl against the scuttles leading down to 3rd Deck; roar hard and strong as if shot through a fire hose, swirl in grins of froth around the lashings, slop into the angle between the hull's starboard side and a vent housing where the scuttle leading to 3-hold is located, deepening and churning there against the scuttle's coaming, deflecting upward: the jetting water will hit any void where rubber rotted, peeling away the rest of the gasket with power strong enough to move a car, which the waves most likely are starting to do as well—and now that gap, that chink between gasket and lip, is wide enough that hundreds of foot-pounds of pressure are pushing through it against the scuttle's lid.

Or it could be that the hatch was not dogged to begin with; given the frenetic rhythm of loading work, and the amount of maintenance the day crew have to do on this old ship, and the fatigue the ABs working overtime experience, who the hell knows for sure if they remembered to dog down that particular scuttle or just assumed they had?

Which wave doesn't matter. Nor does it matter what the original conditions were, which added ounce of pressure was needed to edge the bolt that extra millimeter or jet between lid and gasket lip; what molecule was first or last to break the gasket's synthetic chain. If the hatch was undogged to begin with, it happens more directly. But one last, big comber coming aboard finally does it, *this* one: crashing upward against the hatch cover's edge and popping the cover like a church key prying off the cap of a beer bottle—slamming it up, over, and back.

Now water from each wave coming through the ports pours down the open scuttle into the dark booming cave system of 3rd Deck. Cascades of warm salt water, thick with foam and the occasional sea-nettle jellyfish, gush down every time a wave surges into the deck above; thinning to a stream, spray, or fan of drips as the ship rolls away, till the next wave comes aboard and rushes in turn down the open wound in *El Faro*'s gut.

The water now in 3-hold roils around the trailers there, rocking them hard. Following the basic rules of gravity, it finds the open ramps and companionways from 3-hold to the lowest deck, the Tank Top.

It has no visible effect at first. Seawater sloshes back and forth with the ship's motion on 3rd and Tank Top Decks, a great, broad puddle of ebony liquid, laced with salty drool, reflecting the lights; becoming, as the sea continues surging down scuttle ramps and hatchways, a deepening and sloshy pond. The waves outside grow taller yet, easily fourteen feet high on average now with occasional twenty-footers. The flow becomes more consistent and eventually a near-steady pour of ocean invades the vessel's lowest level. And no one is around to see, watch standers are either high up on the bridge or standing at the engine-room console, while everyone else is sleeping or at least resting in his or her cabin or the lounge.

El Faro is barely wounded. A hatch three feet in diameter, above the waterline, in a ship almost eight hundred feet long and ninety broad, is no big deal in normal circumstances. But the water accumulates steadily at the ship's lowest level, in the depths of 3rd and Tank Top Decks. Now free-surface effect starts to come into play because the liquid, washing in the direction the ship rolls—this was taken into account in calculations for bunker fuel sloshing around the fuel tanks, but not for this—adds weight to the downhill side, making the roll worse by that amount of tonnage. Which is cause enough for concern if the ship is rolling evenly back and forth, but when the ship rolls deeper and more often to one side, then the ship will start to lean more in that direction, and the weight of accumulated water there will make it harder for her to roll back, and water from the next roll will also run to the lower side. On the bridge *El Faro*'s officers are keeping her heading as close to 116 degrees as possible, with the wind well on her port side, so the hull is rolling ever harder, deeper, to starboard.

It's impossible to know for sure if the scuttle's opening will be the chief contributing factor to what is going to happen. The total continuous flow of water through a hatch three feet in diameter is enormous, but there's no way of ascertaining how often or consistently waves cover the hatch, at least at first.* The time is 3:45 a.m., and on the bridge Randolph and Davis are getting ready to switch watches with Shultz and Hamm. The slosh of water in the ship's belly has not affected her movement or balance enough for her crew, whose vestibular systems are fully occupied keeping their bodies upright, to notice; feet splayed on the wheelhouse deck against pitch and roll, hands grasping the engine console's railing, the crew tend to the usual duties of their station.

7

Shultz and Hamm get to the bridge at a quarter to four to relieve Randolph and Davis. The second mate tells Shultz they've adjusted course again to make steering easier through the swells. She cracks a joke about "crawling" to her cabin, and leaves.

The helm alarm rings again, but Davis reassures Shultz, "She'll come back. She did that a couple of times because, uh, she pitched so bad. When you get, uh, the good slams and the good pitches she might lose it a little bit but overall she's been holdin' good, knock on wood."

Shultz stares out the bridge windows at the invisible storm. One

---

* A rough calculation of continuous flow of water through a hatch three feet in diameter, with zero pumping pressure, works out to a total intake of water of 14,100 gallons per minute, or 846,000 gallons per hour, which is equal to 3,638 long tons in weight. No one knows, now or later, how much is actually coming through the scuttle, given the intermittent nature of the flooding on 2nd Deck and the uncertainty as to when it started.

of the windows has a clear-view screen, a rotating disc of glass that keeps rain off by centrifugal force, but it is useless against the night, the volume of water. "It's hard to tell which way the wind's blowin', huh?" he comments. "I assume we're heeling to starboard because the wind must be blowing port to starboard."

Davis wishes his relief "a good one," and disappears down the companionway.

"Don't like this," Shultz says, almost to himself.

"What's the gusts out there?" Hamm asks. "I don't have any idea," Shultz says, "we don't have any instrument that can measure it."

One deck below, sitting at the public computer terminal in the ship's office, Danielle Randolph taps out an email to her mother, Laurie Bobillot: "Not sure if you've been following the weather at all, but there is a hurricane out here and we are heading straight into it. Winds are super bad and seas are not great." Then the normally undemonstrative second mate types the sign-off that will strike panic in her mother's heart: "Love to everyone."

Captain Davidson must be awake in his stateroom, sitting at his own computer; emails from the ship's other workstations collect in a file on that computer and don't get shunted to the Inmarsat satellite transmitter until he clicks on the "send" icon. While they sit in his terminal, the captain could theoretically read or delete crew emails at will, and some family members will later voice suspicion that the captain read and censored messages voicing doubts about his decisions; their relatives or spouses say the crew usually send several a day, but not on this trip. No evidence exists to prove this one way or another. Davidson clicks the send icon now. Still at the workstation he downloads the BVS forecast package that came in at 11:00 p.m. the previous evening. It's an enhancement of the same forecast, on the SAT-C terminal, that Riehm told Davidson about, but given Davidson's reliance on the BVS version it's surprising that he has waited so long to download it.

Then Davidson climbs to the bridge. It is 4:09 a.m.

"There's nothing bad about this ride," he tells Shultz and Hamm cheerfully, and adds that he's been "sleepin' like a baby."

Others aren't sleeping that well, Shultz remarks.

"Well, this is every day in Alaska, this is what it's like . . . a typical winter day in Alaska."

Silence for a while on the bridge. Everyone is leaning, compensating now for the ship's tilt to starboard. The windows are utterly blank with night and rain and spray. The mate states the obvious, which is that the wind's on the port side, and Davidson says, "The only way to do a counter on this heel is to fill the portside ramp tank up. Heel is not so bad." He adds, "Oh, it's howlin' out there," and the chief mate says the wind should come around to hit the starboard side later, which is what the forecast implies could occur once the storm has passed as its lower arc of counterclockwise wind swipes from north and west of *El Faro*. Davidson agrees.

A 4:15 the engine revolutions slow. Davidson calls down to the engine room. Second Engineer Schoenly, who has just come on watch, picks up. "How you guys doin' down there?" Davidson asks, and Schoenly explains that he's doing the usual on his watch, blowing tubes, which accounts for the drop in speed.*

The barometer stands at 970 millibars at 4:24. At Joaquin's center, according to weather reports, the pressure is around 950. "It's gonna go down before it goes up," Shultz says. But Davidson is still convinced they are already on the back side of the storm. "We won't be going through the eye," he comments at one point, and a few minutes later, "From here it's all downhill as far as the low."

Now Davidson says to the mate, "Sounds a lot worse up here than in the cabin," but it sounds more as if he's musing to himself. "Right now we're poundin' a little bit because we're goin' more easterly . . . gotta let her get up to speed, get a little more toward our course . . . need the rpms."

He decides to check on the galley and disappears down the companionway. Two minutes later the bridge telephone rings. Shultz answers.

---

* *El Faro*'s tubes are blown daily, which is standard practice. However, some engineers will wonder why the engineers on *El Faro* do not systematically call the bridge to warn the navigating officer about the associated drop in rpms, which would also be standard procedure. The likely explanation, yet again, has to do with the "milk run" nature of *El Faro*'s route, whereby events such as blowing soot happen at the same time, on the same day, every day, to the point where warnings are no longer called for or expected.

It's one of the engineers, probably Schoenly, with news that a container on 2nd Deck has come loose from its lashings and is leaning over. "I'll pass it on to the captain," the chief mate says, adding that Davidson is in the galley.

Two minutes later the telephone rings again.

"Bridge, Chief Mate."

It's the chief engineer. He wants to talk to the captain.

Shultz listens for a while, then says, "I understand you." He hangs up and calls down to the galley. "Captain—Chief Mate. The chief engineer just called, and they called back again, something about the list and oil levels."

Davidson comes straight up to the bridge, calls the engine room; he listens, then hangs up.

"The chief wants to take the list off," he tells Shultz, "so let's put it in hand steering."

"Mr. Hamm," Shultz says, and maybe he's making a joking alliteration, and maybe he's taking refuge from worry, as is not uncommon, in the formality of address he's been taught in the academy, "go into hand."

And Frank Hamm, whose height is on a par with his girth, flicks the switch that turns off the Iron Mike, hunches over the small metal wheel set low on the forward console of *El Faro*'s bridge, takes a solid grip on the wheel with his large fists—maybe looks automatically at the windows in front of him, the clear-view spinning, wipers swiping uselessly back and forth as the wind drives rain at them in a smush of twisting drafts and vortices and water—and finally looks lower, in front of the wheel, at the glowing compass and gyroscope dials that tell him in which direction to steer.

8

Even if someone was aware of the busted scuttle and looking at it on 2nd Deck, in the swirl and froth of waves coming in, washing out, it would be hard to tell how much is pouring into the lower decks. But it's sure that by now tons of water must have come in, and thanks to free-surface motion, the ensuing list is bad enough that it's having an effect in the engine room.

Conceivably, the scuttle is not the only culprit in the flooding. Trouble continues to occur in the way chain reactions and accidents happen, through a complicated system in which every part, to some extent, is reliant for its efficient functioning on every other, so that one initial fault puts extra strain on the next, which because of the strain fails in turn, starting a chain of breakdowns that exponentially increases in speed and scope—and so it might be that the list itself is the final stressor that causes the crack in hull plates to creep that extra nanometer, that almost infinitely small subunit of analogue change. For a ship is built to ride, on average, on an even keel; if listing to one side, the bow's curve will capture more waves under that side, which will push the front part of the ship sideways, exerting uneven force down the hull's length. This is never a problem when the stress is regularly relieved as a ship rolls the other way. But if she doesn't, and if the waves are big, the strain can damage an already wounded hull. It might be that two corners of plate between 2A- and 3-holds, right at the turn of bilge, the curve where the ship's vertical side meets her horizontal bottom, were incompletely welded in a Mobile, Alabama, shipyard in 1993. Since then fatigue would have weakened them to the extent that they are held together at this point by a scant nanometer of steel. When that nanometer lets go, the plates start to separate, only a millimeter or two at first; but through that void the sea streams in.

Another actor in this theater of dysfunction is the cargo. Already, according to one engineer, who likely saw it happening through a port-hole in his stateroom, a container has busted partly free of its lashings, whether twist-locks or rod-and-chain tie-downs or both.

Some of the trailers on 2nd and 3rd Decks are off-button, and the lashing manual specifies that, if stored off-button, they be secured by six rod-chain lashings to whatever's available; however, the kind of pounding *El Faro* is starting to experience, plus the constant and egregious stress on port lashings as the list to starboard pulls trailers the other way, inevitably loosens the tie-downs. With more play and bigger waves the heavier off-button trailers start to slide. They are brought up short by their lashings, but forty thousand pounds of trailer busting on a chain rated only to twenty-six thousand will create intolerable "shock load," and a link inevitably will snap, and this will increase stress on other chains till the trailer breaks entirely free on one end or both and slams into the trailer it's moored beside, initiating a similar sequence there.

The same is true of the cars, mostly loaded on the Tank Top Deck, many of which are not individually secured but are instead fastened to those long chains running across the ship, port and starboard; in this case there might be more play for cars to work against, especially as the waves reduce the tires' grip on the wet deck. And if a central chain should break, a number of cars would be set free at the same time, skidding around together in a nightmare version of crack the whip.

The density of trailers parked on a fully loaded ship means that they cannot move far individually, cannot pile on weight to one side of the ship the way the free-surface effect works with a liquid. The same is true of cars. Automobiles might have a different effect, however, in the lowest part of the ship, starboard and aft on Tank Top Deck, where the main inlet pipe for the firefighting system rises out of the seabox; the latter being the manifold through which *El Faro* lets in seawater from outside the hull to quench flames or draw ballast. The inlet pipe is partially shielded by a protective bracket made of six-inch-diameter piping, but the possibility exists that a loose car, weighing a ton and a half, will gain enough momentum to break through the protective steel and bust the pipe; and if that happens, pressurized seawater will pour into *El Faro*'s hold at a volume sufficient to explain by itself how the ship takes on so much water so fast.

If this is what happens, the flow rate of seawater from the firefighting pipe will be greater than the bilge pumps' ability to gush it back into the ocean.

9

Schoenly and his oiler, Thomas, have been checking the lubrication system as a matter of routine, and, to begin with, the oil pressures were okay with no loss of lubricant or anything else to report.

Then the alarm sounded at the control console, piercingly loud to catch everyone's attention amid the machinery noise. Most likely it keeps sounding, sporadically, and a light flashes also next to the lubricating-oil-pump pressure gauges. Low-suction pressure on the inlet side, low-discharge pressure at the outlet, trouble by any other name would look and sound this way.

It's not consistent, and for now the interval between the low-pressure events triggering the alarms must be long enough that the primary pump can regain suction and bring the pressure back up quickly, thus avoiding the automatic trip that brings the second pump into operation, let alone more dramatic emergency moves to cope with the problem.

Probably a small crowd is in the engine room by this time. Griffin, the first engineer, told his wife in an earlier email that he would be up all night because of heavy weather. Schoenly and Shawn Thomas are on watch; the chief, Richard Pusatere, is not the sort of officer to let his subordinates take care of problems when they're apt to occur, as in a storm; the same is true of Jeff Mathias, the other licensed chief aboard.

Thomas and Schoenly might be assigned to keep an eye on the rest of the plant, but Pusatere, Mathias, and Griffin will be taking inventory of all the gauges to make sure they've pinned down the problem. The oil-temperature alarms at turbine and bearings have not been set off. One of the officers certainly moves fast to the lower level to look at the screw pump itself, but it, too, appears to be working well, at least when there's enough oil. Nothing sweats from the seal, no discernible leaks plague the system, so the most likely culprit, the engineers agree, is the one they blamed initially: this list to starboard.

That's when Pusatere gets on the phone to the bridge to tell the captain the list is affecting his oil levels.

The pumps have not been opened up in a long time, and even the engineers probably don't know by heart the exact specs of this lubricating system—how the intake, an eight-inch steel pipe with a flared mouth, hangs ten inches above, and twenty-two inches to starboard of, the V-shaped bottom of the reduction-gear sump. They wouldn't know by rote but could look up the amount of lube oil currently in the system: 1,225 gallons, which corresponds to a depth of oil in the sump of 24.6 inches. This theoretically means the pipe's suction end plunges 14.6 inches below the surface of the oil, more than sufficient depth for normal uptake.

But a serious, chronic list will reduce that depth by spreading oil to the port or starboard sides of the sump, shallowing its depth near the center. Possibly, if the list is severe enough, consistent enough, especially when combined with a lot of roll and pitch, the oil level will shallow sufficiently for the pipe no longer to touch the liquid. The pipe's end will pull out of the oil and the pump will suck dry, if only for a while, creating air bubbles that reduce or even gag off the flow of oil to turbine and gears.

A former chief on *El Faro* will testify that he normally keeps the oil level between twenty-nine and thirty-two inches, and higher for rough weather. The sump can hold 2,020 gallons, which works out to a thirty-three-inch level, enough to ensure suction at any conceivable degree of tilt. Because *El Faro* carries only 1,225 gallons this trip, the oil level in the sump lies well below that mark.

Everyone in the engine room knows what actions to take if oil pressure suddenly falls. The flow of oil must be brought back to normal levels, and if not enough oil is in the sump to maintain suction, the sole remedy is to add oil from the gravity-fed storage tank inside the boiler casing at Main Deck level. From that height a head of pressure will drive spare oil directly to the sump. The gravity tank holds sufficient oil to maintain lubrication for those two-to-ten minutes of respite. And likely this is what the engineers do now, bleeding enough extra oil into the system for the pump to suck normally again, sufficient to restore regular flow and quiet the alarms.

These men are used to little crises in the engine room, especially old engine rooms; they happen often enough. They are trained to think in terms of engine systems, all of whose unitary parts depend on smooth functioning of the other parts, and they are aware of what can happen if one part fails. Especially under Pusatere's regime they have gone through numerous drills; they instinctively follow the engineer's rule of rushing to "the last thing you touched, the last alarm you heard" in an emergency; they know in their bones how the chain reaction works,

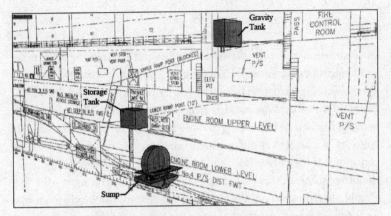

Last-chance lubrication: The topmost, "gravity," tank can cool the engine
for a few minutes at most. The lower, "reserve" (or "storage") tank is useless in an
emergency. Without oil, the engine stops, and the ship lies helpless.

moving at scary speed from a small fail to a minor malfunction to a
malfunction that slows or stops the plant. In this case, if the oil pumps
fail, and they can't fix the problem, they'll have those two to ten minutes
of grace while the gravity-tank oil bathes turbine, gears, and bearings
on its own.* But that oil won't come close to filling up the sump and
when it's gone, as one former chief puts it, "You're shit out of luck."
The throttle, whose valve itself is held open by oil pressure, will close
automatically when the pressure drops. The turbines will slow and stop
to save the spinning blades, the precise gears and shafts, from melting
down. The engine room will grow quiet. The propeller will slow, and
still. And *El Faro*, eventually, will come to a stop as well.

The danger to a ship if the plant fails in a hurricane is something no
one who goes to sea for a living needs to analyze or think much about.
Their job is to keep the plant working, and they will do everything in
their power to achieve that end.

---

* Probably the engineers will also start feeding oil into the sump from the other oil tank, the
ten-ton reserve behind the turbines, although they know that, given the trickle that emanates
from its one-inch feed pipe, it would take hours for this to have any real effect; but they are
trained to take all measures possible.

10

Davidson decides to head the ship into the wind and tells the helmsman to change course accordingly. Looking forward into the blackness, lacking the visual information he needs, a captain tries to get a feel for where the wind and waves are coming from by sensing how the ship moves beneath his feet. If she's rolling and being thrown mostly rightward, the wind and waves are coming mostly from the left and that starboard list continues. If they bring the ship around so the wind now comes from the other side—in this case, from starboard, from the right—the list should switch to the port side, which won't solve the problem either. As far as Davidson knows, the list causing the oil problems is due only to the "sail effect" of wind, which has been screeching from the port side of their regular course, against the hull's side and the containers stacked on Main Deck. If he can get the ship to head straight into the wind, she would only be pitching, bow up, stern down, and vice-versa; the wind would blow from dead ahead, the list should vanish.

"Just the list," he tells the chief mate. "The sumps are actin' up, to be expected." Davidson then directs his attention back to Frank Hamm, at the wheel. Keeping the ship on one heading in heavy seas is tricky enough with visual information or an anemometer to tell you where the weather's coming from; doing so at night entirely by feel requires constant adjustments. "Just steer that heading right there the best you can," he tells Hamm and Shultz. "That'll work for us."

"Okay, steer zero six five," the chief mate says. The wind, as far as they can tell on the bridge, has continued veering easterly and is now coming more or less out of the northeast.

"Zero six five," Hamm repeats—and a few seconds later, as a big wave hits: "Wo-o-o."

"Now swingin' right pretty fast," Shultz says.

Hamm is working hard at the wheel. The position is awkward, he is standing at the bridge console, bending over the wheel while keeping his head lifted to watch the compass or gyroscope. He is probably sweating in the iffy air-conditioning and despite the stream of air coming from the fan.

It might also be that, as the one person on *El Faro* in semidirect contact with the sea's forces, through the wheel's turn, even though mediated by hydraulics to the rudder; by feeling through muscles of arm and shoulder and stomach just how hard it is for her to hold course, how tortured her movements are, Frank Hamm more than anyone aboard right now is conscious of the true might of the waves, the power of this wind the ship is fighting. More than anyone else he may understand in his gut the extent of murder Joaquin holds in its heart, how great is the danger they all face.

The captain does his best to make Hamm's job easier and relieve the helmsman's tension. Though Davidson only occasionally puts his hand to the ship's wheel, he directs Hamm and is thus somewhat conscious of the level of storm and the state of his ship within the storm; and the relationship between the two men will only grow tighter, more intense, as *El Faro* moves deeper into the hurricane's embrace.

"Take your time and relax," Davidson says now, "don't worry about it. Stand up straight and relax." "I'm relaxed, Captain," Hamm replies, which doesn't convince the skipper, who repeats, "Relax—steer the direction we're goin'."

Later the officers will fetch Hamm a chair to ease his back, get him a cup of coffee as he wrestles the wheel.

The barometer is still dropping: it now reads 960 millibars.

Hamm and Davidson adjust the course toward where the wind seems to be coming from now: fifty degrees, almost due northeast.

Someone relays a message: a trailer has busted its lashings and is leaning over on 2nd Deck.

Jeff Mathias shows up on the bridge at 5:10 a.m. "Things are slappin' around," he says, "down on Second Deck."

"There's not much to see," Davidson says. "You know that's our biggest enemy. We have no visibility, ya know. Generally try to steer in the direction we need to go."

"Yeah," Mathias agrees. "I've never seen it list like this—you gotta be takin' more than a container stack. I've never seen it hang like this."

The Coast Guard will later conclude that *El Faro* must by now have been filling with water for some time, and possibly in more than one hold. The extra purchase afforded the wind by high container stacks also plays into how officers perceive the problem, since the ship didn't carry containers in Alaska, and thus they might in their minds exaggerate what percentage of list can be ascribed to wind, versus what could be the result of other factors.

Davidson's rough weather experience, the NTSB will later note, has been largely confined to deep-riding tankers or Ro-Ro freighters, which are less affected by wind heel than container ships. Otherwise he might be aware that, even on a container ship, a sixty- to eighty-knot wind blowing against the ship's side will only lean the vessel over by eight degrees or so—and *El Faro* does not have the wind on her beam, which means that the sail effect should be a lot less, implying in turn that something else is affecting stability. This possible overemphasis on wind effect informs the captain's next comment.

"Yeah, you got a lot of sail area," he says.

"It's like whiteout out there," Mathias remarks, looking at the windows.

"Yeah, just all this spray and rain, you get lightning," Davidson says, and a few minutes later to Hamm: "Put your rudder left ten, we're gonna steer up into it a little bit more." Right now they are still steering fifty degrees.

The ship's barometer now reads 950 millibars. Pressure at Joaquin's center at that hour stands at 948, only two millibars lower. This indicates the ship is now close to the eye of the storm.

"We're on the back side of it . . . only gonna get better from here," Davidson says to Mathias, still clinging to his notion that the hurricane is doing what the forecasts predicted, sliding out of range northwest of *El Faro*. The extent to which the captain repeats himself on this subject and others: on the similarity between these storm waves and normal conditions in Alaska, on getting permission from Tote to take the Old Bahama Channel north; must in part be a function of the responsibility he feels to keep the crew informed of his decisions and reassured as to their good sense.

But it also seems like the behavior of someone torn between what he hopes will happen and what he fears will occur—trying to believe that Joaquin is indeed moving away, that the vessel is fine even in these conditions; that his preparations will suffice to avert the End of Days.

Shultz is watching the inclinometer, a simple device, similar to a curved carpenter's level, that hangs above the bridge windows. "Yeah, eighteen-degree list on," he remarks.

"Waitin' for that wind to shift," Davidson says. If the wind shifts to the west, it will indicate that *El Faro* has finally punched her way south of the hurricane—

At 5:43 the bridge telephone rings.

"Bridge, Captain." Davidson listens for a few minutes: "We got a pro-o-o-blem . . . . Three-hold? . . . Okay. I'll send the mate down."

"Watch your step," he tells Shultz. "Go down to three-hold. Probably just water . . ."

"Suspected leak?" Shultz says.

"I would tend to concur."

". . . 'specially the scuttle."

It's the first acknowledgment by anyone on the bridge that *El Faro*'s list is not due only to wind pushing against the containers, tilting the ship; that the sea is somehow getting into her hull and sapping her stability. When the bridge telephone rings again, Shultz picks it up; the engineers are getting the bilge pumps running to pull water out of 3-hold.

The captain takes the phone and suggests transferring water from the starboard ballast tank to the port, to help compensate for the list.

Then Shultz picks up a walkie-talkie and goes below to check.

11

The ballast and bilge-pump system is nowhere near the oil pumps. It's located on the engine room's lowest level, all the way forward, against the bulkhead separating machinery from 3-hold. Apart from the pumps themselves—man-size metal insects with suckers poking in different directions—it's a bewildering puzzle of manifolds, junctions, and valves, painted in different colors; when some valves are closed off and others opened, the pumps will move water from port ramp tank to starboard ramp tank (or the other way around) or will suck it from the ship's bilges and shoot it out of an outlet in the hull's side. The oiler, Shawn

Thomas, knows the system well and most of the time does this kind of work alone; given the urgency now, one of the officers, maybe the senior third engineer, Holland, whose standard responsibilities include tanks and ballast, comes along to help.

Though the VDR gives no indication, it's near certain someone took a gander through one of the two watertight doors between the engine room and the aft section of 3-hold that are normally hooked open to allow cooler air in; this is why one of the engineers would be first to discover the water in the hold. He would have shut and dogged the door immediately. The temperature in the engine room would have started creeping upward at once.

The bilge pump's job is straightforward: pull water from the lowest part of *El Faro*, between the bottom plates and the ballast, fuel, and fructose tanks, and through the rose boxes—big steel colanders, located at the bottom of metal wells, that filter out the kind of junk that accumulates in bilges. The water then flows through the pump and out the discharge pipe to the ocean. In this ship, as in others of her age, the rose boxes tend to clog with rust from all the steel decaying around, but this time apparently the bilge pump draws fine and hundreds of gallons a minute are pulled from 3-hold and dumped back into the Atlantic. Now the engineers, sweating, open the valve on the suction pipe leading from the starboard ramp tank; they crack the discharge valve on the pipe leading to the port tank, and the pump whines, sucking water from starboard to port, right to left, transferring weight from downhill to uphill, which must help correct the list.

At the control console a lube-oil pressure alarm sounds again. The chief engineer picks up the telephone and calls the bridge. He and the captain both know that, even if the pumps can gain on the water in 3-hold, and even if shifting weight to the port ramp tank helps in the long run, they have no "long run" right now, both processes will take time, and the way the oil pumps are acting they don't have time to wait; something must be done *now* to get rid of the list that causes the pump to suck air.

Pusatere listens intently as Davidson says, "Okay—what I'm gonna do—I'm gonna turn the ship and get the wind . . . on the starboard side, give us a port list, and, um, see if we'll have a better look at it." "It" means the scuttle, but both men also realize that during the time the ship changes direction and heads into the wind; during the time the water in the hold takes to change sides, the ship will straighten up and the lack of tilt will give the lubricating system a breather.

The captain asks for more speed: "More rpm available?" The ship, laboring into the growing swells, is still going half her normal speed, because of the energy it takes to fight the storm.

12

As *El Faro*, rolling badly to starboard, starts to wrestle her way to port— pitching harder now as her bow starts to smash more directly into the dragon wind and the maelstrom of waves themselves—Shultz makes his way down to 3rd Deck, enters the engine-room main level, makes his way around the boilers, through a storeroom, and opens the heavy steel door to 3-hold. Water runs against the coaming in front of him, around the Rolocs and chains of the ranked trailers. The mate steps into the water. Closing the door behind him he inches forward and to the right, holding on to lashings, trailer to trailer, and, when he gets to the outermost starboard trailer looks forward and sees water gushing from overhead, out of the starboard scuttle leading to 2nd Deck, a pulsing Niagara down the steel side-shell that makes it impossible to climb the ladder and shut the hatch from below. His pant legs must be soaked to the knees, seawater is pooling deeply on that side of the ship.

He climbs back up to 2nd Deck, to a watertight door in the after bulkhead of the house, and finds seawater rampaging also on the deck in front of him. Dogging the door, he leaves the shelter of the companionway and boiler casing and sloshes out onto 2nd Deck, around the house, all the way starboard. The water's up to his knees here, too; he hangs on to something, another trailer, lashings, on the starboard edge of 3-hold. In the long space between trailers and the side shell he sees waves flooding through the side-shell ports, washing over the scuttle, which yawns open when the waves clear it for an instant, its hatch thrown back. He retraces his steps to the breezeway door and keys the transmit button on his walkie-talkie.

"Ya got water against the side . . . just enough to pour over the edge of the scuttle . . . about knee-deep water, rolls right over."

The captain tells him they're turning the ship to port to pull water away from the scuttle. He asks the mate if he's alone, if he needs help. "I'm by myself," Shultz replies.

"Don't move," Davidson says, "stay right there, don't move."

"Standing by."

The ship, pitching harder now, is turning slowly against the wind. Water starts to swirl and rush from the starboard side to port, making surf against the trailers, the chained automobiles. For a couple of minutes, maybe more, as the water shifts in *El Faro*'s holds, the ship is roughly on an even keel, and oil must be pumping normally. Jeff Mathias shows up on 2nd Deck and finds Shultz staring forward as seawater in 3-hold starts to eddy toward his left.

"I got Jeff Mathias with me here," Shultz radios the bridge, his words partially drowned in wind. "We're ready to go . . . starboard scuttle." Shultz and Mathias confer, yelling over the noise. Mathias volunteers to venture out onto the deck and shut the scuttle.

"The worst area's already dried out," Shultz yells into the walkie-talkie.

"All right, Chief Mate. You got a lifeline on him or anything? Is there any chance of him going over?"

"I think it's okay."

El Faro has completed her turn to port, chopping and pitching, water on 2nd Deck now cascading massively toward that side. Her heading is almost due north, 350 degrees. Slowly, soggily, she is leaning more and more heavily to port. After a few minutes she is listing in that direction at just as deep an angle as she did before to starboard.

Mathias, one arm crooked around trailers, lashings, anything he can find as the sea plucks at his legs, starts making his way along the starboard side of the house to the starboard scuttle. By the time he gets there, that side of the deck is almost free of water, as Davidson anticipated. The cover on the scuttle is still thrown back; the opening gapes, black and dripping. Mathias moves quickly, heaves the cover up and over, closing the hatch. He turns the locking wheel clockwise as hard and fast as it will go, then hurries back to the house.

"Okay, Captain, it's done," Shultz yells into the walkie-talkie.
"It's done."

It is one minute before six in the morning of October 1.

13

Just before 6:00 a.m. Danielle Randolph appears at the bridge companionway.

"Hi, how are you, Captain?" she says brightly.

"How are you?" Davidson replies. He sounds happy to see her, but his question, like hers, is ritual. Both officers know how they are, and it's not so hot. Davidson, as always, puts a bright face on the situation: "A scuttle popped open and there's a little bit of water in three-hold. They're pumping it out now."

The bridge telephone rings. The chief engineer now asks the captain to reverse his earlier move and turn the ship back to starboard, bringing the wind on the port side again to resume the starboard list. Apparently the list to port causes worse problems than a tilt the other way.

Once again, it's not clear if any of the engineers, who have probably never seen the sump housing opened, are aware either of the ten-inch vertical gap between the sump's bottom and the mouth of the oil intake pipe, or of the twenty-two-inch horizontal distance by which the flared mouth is offset to starboard of the sump's center. Oil lines coil back and forth under the deck plates, so it's hard to figure out just by looking at them where the lubricant is going. It's not certain, either, if the engine-room crew can immediately consult the pump's specs and diagrams to troubleshoot the issue. Tote has not provided the ship with a manual to guide engineers through this or similar problems.

What is pretty certain is that, either by studying general diagrams or through a basic understanding of how intake pipes are always set higher to avoid sucking in dregs collected in the lowest parts of a sump, Pusatere and his crew have a good idea of what must be going on. They understand that, with a strong list, any vertical gap between intake and sump bottom will shallow the pool of available oil; and that a pipe offset to one side means that a list the other way will slosh the oil even farther away from the intake, compounding the problem. Since the intake pipe is set to starboard, they need to turn the ship back in that direction, put waves and wind to port again, to regain a starboard list.

Offset oil: A cross-section view shows how a list to one side (left, or port) pulls oil away from an intake pipe set twenty-two inches to starboard, and ten inches above, the sump's center line. If the oil pump sucks air, it will stop the engine. Though the sump could contain 2,020 gallons, it only held 1,225 on October 1, 2015.

"Bring it back, roll back over to starboard," Davidson tells the helmsman. "Keep her right twenty."

"Rudder right twenty," says Hamm.

Shultz comes back from 2nd Deck, confirms the scuttle is secured. He volunteers to return to the cargo holds.

Davidson agrees. "We need eyes and ears down there."

One of the radars has crapped out. Randolph bends over the set, adjusting, rebooting. Soon the screen glows with the image of the islands the ship has left behind. She plots the ship's position off San Salvador.

The wind, changing angles as *El Faro* turns slowly to starboard, rips something else loose.

"There goes the lawn furniture," Randolph says.

"Let's hope that's all." It's the first time Davidson's words have betrayed any glumness.

Randolph quickly offers, "If you don't need me, you want me to stay with you?"

"Please," Davidson replies.

"It's just," he continues, "it's just the—" But he's interrupted by the walkie-talkie's call-up tone. Shultz has gone down to the engine room and is checking in from there, and Davidson asks him to tell the engineers to reverse the ballast procedure, fill the starboard ramp tank now to help with the general aim of bringing the ship's tilt back to starboard.

The chief mate confirms, "Port to starboard ramp tank."

"I'm not liking this list," Davidson tells the bridge at large.

And at that moment the world changes.

The ongoing pulse of engines deep below, the sempiternal tremble of deck and joinery that is the sign, tactile as much as auditory, that *El Faro*'s heart is beating, her engines driving her and all her people in the direction they're supposed to go in, begins to falter.

Slows in rhythm.

Fades, at last, to nothing.

In the alien, deadly silence that follows, the shriek of Joaquin against the windows, against the hull, grows to deafening volume by contrast.

"I think we just lost the plant," Davidson says.

Fatal tilt: *El Faro*, seen from the stern, lists twenty-five degrees to port in this computer-generated image. At such an angle, individual lashings on a container would start to snap, and loose containers would add strain to their neighbors' lashings in a perilous domino effect.

PART VI

THE ASSASSIN STORM

You turn again, but the storm adjusts. . . . Because this storm isn't something that blew in from far away, something that has nothing to do with you.

—Haruki Murakami

Of course Joaquin is not sentient. Of course this storm has not chosen *El Faro* and her people out of some animistic perversion, some sick need to destroy and kill a worthy vessel and a crew of thirty-three decent, hardworking humans; professionals, family people connected to a wide web of wives, children, parents, friends; all as innocent as people can be who go to sea knowing the dangers they face, the hubris all mariners in some way commit by betting they can always, successfully, pit wits and talent against something so vast.

Melville writes in *Moby-Dick*, a book that's all about man's hubris on great waters, "For ever and for ever, to the crack of doom, the sea will insult and murder [man], and pulverize the stateliest, stiffest frigate he can make; nevertheless . . . man has lost that sense of the full awfulness of the sea which aboriginally belongs to it."

Yet to anyone tracking Joaquin and *El Faro* together over the last two days, a sense of awfulness must come; for the storm's aura of ill intent seems only to deepen. By six in the morning of October 1 the hurricane—still drunk on overheated ocean, still trashing wind shear, still following the upper-level airflow—has been zeroing in on *El Faro*'s track for forty-eight hours straight. When the ship's engine shuts down, Joaquin's center is a mere twenty-five miles to the southeast; the opposite direction from that which Davidson expects, as if the storm were deliberately trying to lunge under his guard. *El Faro*, disabled and helpless, lies almost within the eye, inside its circle of strongest winds.

Joaquin is now approaching Category 4 status, winds averaging 115 knots, gusting to 130—close to 150 mph. Most humans in such winds would be blown off anything they clung to, and what they clung to would be ripped off sea or ship or earth and hurled after them. The waves routinely reach heights of twenty, sometimes thirty feet; occasionally, a wave will reach close to fifty feet, the height of a five-story building, a dark mass of water streaked like a rib-eye steak, only instead of fat veining the liquid flanks, these are white tendons of watery fury stretched by the massive energy of wind; and the wave tops are impossible to see, for that same wind is shearing off the waves' summits and using them to rocket some matter that is neither sea nor air but an abrasive mix of spume and salt water, a slurried ganache of surf that will rip clothes from the body and drown the very breath in your throat. On *El Faro*, even as what momentum she has left keeps her heading, temporarily, close to the wind, spume abrades every unsheltered surface, and waves must now consistently blast over Main Deck, crashing against the container stacks, the breezeway, and bottom of the house.

Second Deck has become part of the sea, a surging tumult of black water and phosphorescent eddies.

And Joaquin is not done. A mid- to upper-level trough over the eastern United States is starting to deepen, interfering with the southwest-tending airflow from the mid-Atlantic ridge that has dominated the hurricane's motion till now; so that Joaquin, having found the ship, having pulled her into its tightest, most violent band of winds, now starts to slow, for all the world like an assassin who, having tricked its victim into a blind alley, now moves around him, readying for the kill.

Pinched between trough and guiding winds, the eye of Joaquin circles the stricken ship.

2

"So . . . is there any chance of gettin' [the engine] back online?"

Davidson is on the phone again, talking to the engine room. He is in full emergency-management mode, a short, bristle-haired bundle of talk and energy, fielding telephone calls from the engineers, walkie-talkie transmissions from the chief mate, dealing with the helmsman, conferring with Randolph. *El Faro* still coasts along—a thirty-thousand-ton ship doesn't stop simply because her propeller quits turning, the momentum on her will sustain movement for several minutes more. But momentum is not enough for the rudder to bite, for the ship to go where pointed, she will not turn right to an easterly course, allowing the wind to blast her port side and reestablish a starboard list. Apparently it would require the full force of *El Faro*'s plant to push the ship against the wind and waves toward the right; the list to port creates extra drag on that side and makes a rightward turn yet harder.

She falls off the wind to port, and the wind pushes harder and harder against her starboard side. From now on her list leftward will continue, and deepen, making it that much more difficult to reestablish suction in the oil pump.

Even now the ship is leaning to port more than ever, probably somewhere around fifteen degrees.

Earlier Shultz mentioned an eighteen-degree list, which was probably a combined list and roll, but even fifteen degrees is a lot, it doesn't sound like much but imagine the floor of your house that much off true, to the extent that one foot set against the slope is four inches higher than the other; Earth's very gravity feels different, everything rolls or tumbles in that direction, you have to compensate with each movement, walk uphill against the incline, you can't set your coffee mug down without its sliding off the table. Bear in mind also that your house isn't rolling, pitching, or hitting swells about as subtly as a Mack truck driving into a wall.

Davidson hangs up. "They'll bring everything back up online," he announces.

It's 6:16 in the morning. The sun won't rise for almost an hour but even if it were day, what manner of light could pierce this apocalypse of rain and surf now blasting the bridge windows? Despite the eerie, unaccustomed absence of engine sounds everyone must speak loudly against the berserk howl of wind outside. The smash of driven water seems even more mind-numbing than before.

Water, probably from thrown spray, has been coming through the engine-room vents. Davidson gets back on the phone to the engineers. He wants to know if the starboard ramp tank has been filled back up to seek rightward tilt. The senior third engineer, Holland, confirms the ballast and bilge pumps are all running. Shultz is in the engine room, on walkie-talkie, and Davidson asks him for another update on the ballast; the captain seems more concerned with ballast than with water in the holds, perhaps he's unaware of the relatively insignificant effect filling a ramp tank will have. (Here, too, the ship's conversions, which took out several ballast tanks that the crew could have juggled to more effectively rebalance the ship, might have had an effect not only in reducing ballasting options, but in engendering faulty assumptions in the skipper's mind.) The captain asks Randolph to go below and wake Riehm up, and she asks for permission to detour to her cabin and change into work clothes.

Hamm points out water starting to drip into the bridge.

"Don't worry about it," the captain says.

When Randolph gets back, he asks her to start programming the two automated distress systems. The covert SSAS function will send an automated distress signal with GPS position attached. GMDSS is a SAT-C distress text message to which Randolph manually appends the ship's position; it has yes/no options for the type of emergency and where to send "Help!" emails. The second mate is unsure which to choose: "All I got is 'flooding,' or we can do, um, 'disabled and adrift.'"

"I would do a bunch of them," Davidson advises.

The engine room calls again. "That's good news," Davidson tells whomever he's talking to below, and, turning to Randolph: "They're gonna get that boiler back up online any second. . . . They're gettin' lube-oil pressure up."*

The radar goes out again but it's not important; rpms are showing on the indicator, the engine's running again, and Davidson tells Hamm, "All right Frank, you got some turns right now," meaning the prop is starting to spin. A slight tremble must arise as the turbine works again. But it's all too brief. The engine stops almost immediately.

"That's a small victory right there," Davidson remarks hopefully.

Hamm grunts, still holding the wheel to starboard. He has been hunched at the steering station now for more than an hour. "You okay, Frank?" the captain asks him.

---

* Though *El Faro*'s boilers have problems that might be aggravated by high seas, this is the only reference to boilers, versus repeated citing of oil pressure, as the reason for the engine cutting out. Probably Davidson, who is obviously under stress, conflated "boiler" with "plant."

"You're gettin' a leg workout," Randolph teases the AB. "Feelin' those thi-i-ighs burn?"

Waves smash in rapid succession against the house.

"That's why I don't go out there," Davidson comments.

And Randolph makes coffee.

"Cream and sugar?" she asks Hamm. "Do your thing," he says.

The second mate laughs. "Sugar is fine with the captain, right?"

"Give me Splenda," Hamm says, "not the regular sugar."

"Might be a little bumpy," Randolph says, "but coffee . . . yep."

At 6:55 Davidson picks up the satellite phone and punches in a set of digits posted over the bridge controls: it's the cell phone number of John Lawrence, the safety manager at Tote. Lawrence is in Atlanta, attending the safety convention. The call goes to voice mail.

"All the wind on the starboard side here," Davidson tells the recording. His voice is calm, though underneath his words an underlying tension is audible. "Now a scuttle was left open or popped open or whatever so we got some flooding down in 3-hold—a significant amount. Getting a pretty good list. Umm . . . everybody's safe now, we're not gonna abandon ship . . . we are in dire straits right now."

"How long we s'posed to be in this storm?" Hamm asks after the captain hangs up.

"Should get better all the time," the captain says brightly, and repeats what is sounding more and more like a mantra, or a wish that might come true by virtue of repetition: "Right now we're on the back side of it."

A series of metallic objects crashes into the house outside. After the noise subsides, Davidson picks up the sat-phone again to call Tote offices. At first he apparently gets a recording, and recites pretty much the same message he left earlier, except that he calls what happened a "navigational incident." Then, it appears, the call is automatically transferred to a call center the company has contracted with to handle off-schedule messages; a call center Davidson had problems with a year earlier.* It takes a while for someone to answer and when the call goes

---

* This call center apparently bungled communication at least once before, when it did not relay a message from Davidson in early September 2015, reporting a minor oil spill. Tote is aware of the problem, according to Jim Fisker-Andersen, but the same center is on call on October 1.

through, the woman on the other end sounds like a typical call-center operator, clueless and programmatic.

"Okay, sir."

"Are you connecting me through to a QI?" (QI is office-speak for "qualified individual.") Davidson sounds less calm, even aggressive: Is it possible he recognizes the voice on the other end from his call last year?

"That's what I'm getting right now," the operator replies politely, "is, seeing who is, uh, on call, I'm gonna get you right to them gimme one second sir, I'm gonna put you on a quick hold so one moment please.

"Okay sir," the operator continues shortly afterward, "I just need your name please." Davidson supplies it. The operator asks for his rank, and the captain supplies that. She then asks for the ship's name.

"*El Faro*," Davidson says impatiently.

"Spell that? E, l, . . ."

"O-o-o-h man, the clo—the clock is ticking, can I please *speak with a QI*!" The tension in the captain's voice is out in the open. But he must give in to the ritual, using the NATO phonetic alphabet: "*El Faro*! Echo, Lima, space, Foxtrot, Alpha, Romeo, Oscar! *El Faro*!"

The operator asks for, and Davidson supplies, his phone numbers. She then continues, "Got it sir, again I'm gonna get you reached right now, one moment please—" and puts him on hold once more. While he's on hold, Davidson addresses Shultz on the walkie-talkie, calling, "And mate, what do you see down there? What do you see?"

A different voice comes on the sat phone. "Hi, good morning, my name is Sharita, just give me a moment I'm gonna try to connect you now okay? Mister Davidson?"

"Okay."

"One moment please. Hi—"

"Oh, God."

"Thank you for waiting—"

"Oh God!"

"Just really briefly, what is the problem you're having?"

It takes several agonizing minutes for the operator to connect him to Lawrence's voice mail, and the safety manager is still unavailable so Davidson has to leave another message: but this time around Lawrence spots the voice mail and calls back almost immediately.

Davidson sketches out what has happened, mentioning a ten- to fifteen-degree list that he ascribes in good part to wind, waves that are "ten to twelve feet over [something inaudible]," adding that because of the lack of lube-oil pressure the engine is down; they are pumping out water but not gaining ground so far. "I just wanted to give you a heads-up before I push that [automated distress call] button," he explains. "We are gonna stay with the ship—no one's panicking. . . . Our safest bet is to stay with the ship during this particular time. The weather is ferocious out there. . . .

"I wanna push that SSAS button," he finishes. ". . . Just wanted to give you that courtesy so you wouldn't be blindsided by it—everybody's safe right now, we're in survival mode now."

The storm waves at *El Faro*'s position have grown well beyond twelve feet, according to weather data assembled later. They are probably closer to twenty on average, sometimes thirty; unless Davidson means twelve feet *over* 2nd Deck or Main, he underestimates their size. The list, too, most likely exceeds "ten to fifteen degrees"; the mate's estimate was eighteen degrees an hour ago. The captain's habit of resolutely looking on the bright side—despite the occasional, clashing mention of "survival" and "dire straits"—not to mention his drive to extend every courtesy to his employer, is so strong and evident that Lawrence, hanging up, doesn't get the sense *El Faro* is in immediate danger. Then again, like everyone else at Tote, he has not been tracking Joaquin and doesn't realize *El Faro* now rides near the very center of the storm.

Davidson turns to Randolph. "All right, Second Mate, send that message."

Randolph pushes the button. A strident alarm sounds as the SAT-C terminal responds to its own distress signal.

"Wake everybody up!" Davidson yells almost angrily. "Wake 'em up. . . . We're gonna be good, we're gonna make it right here."

3

All the mates are now awake, and all or most of the engineering officers as well, but in the unlicensed-personnel quarters three decks below the bridge a good portion of the crew have been asleep, or trying to sleep. They'd be looking for that last shut-eye before their alarms go off, since the day men and the eight-to-twelve watch, assuming they want a regular breakfast, need to be in the mess no later than seven thirty to eat before showing up for work fifteen minutes before shift as tradition dictates. They hunker down in a bunk that has canted more than fifteen degrees to port; a bunk that, even if you narrow it with life jackets, rolls and pitches and bucks around more and more as the night wears on. Davidson earlier twice referred to "getting everybody up," but it seems he was talking about alerting Tote and the Coast Guard, not his own crew. Perhaps this has something to do with his obsessive optimism; getting all the crew up and ready to abandon ship would be a final admission that everything has gone horribly wrong.*

To be fair, though, there's not much the crew could do anyway, save pick up life jacket and survival suit and hump them to their muster station, as they have done before in drills. Most of the muster stations are port and starboard on the "embarkation deck," otherwise known as the engineers' quarters, the level to which the lifeboats would be lowered for the crew to board. More important, it's also where the life rafts are stored. Everyone would have to stand or squat in the corridors at that level since it's far too rough to wait on the deck outside.

Coast Guard hearings later will reveal that the lifeboat drill on *El Faro* might have been skipped, or at least skimped on, several voyages running. Former members of the Polish riding crew will testify that they've never attended a drill aboard. It's another indication of the complacency that *El Faro*'s normally calm run to and from Puerto Rico has engendered among her crew. In any case, if there's one thing that's obvious to anyone with seafaring experience, it's that *El Faro*'s antiquated lifeboats will be useless in a storm like this. SOLAS regulations require only that lifeboats be able to launch at angles of fifteen

---

* That Davidson has not already mustered the crew, at least as a precaution given *El Faro*'s situation, is probably yet another result of the captain's stubbornly optimistic view of their prospects. A preliminary wake-up call and orders to report with lifesaving gear to the mess, if not yet to lifeboat stations, would seem reasonable, not to say responsible, given the situation. Both the Coast Guard and the NTSB will fault Davidson for not alerting his crew at this point or even earlier, when flooding was first detected; this would have given everybody more time to grab survival suits and prepare for a possible "abandon ship" command.

degrees or under, and *El Faro* at this point—especially given the added component of wave-induced roll—is certainly listing much more than that. And even if the boats could be launched in such waves, even if they managed to get clear of the ship without being smashed like rotten pumpkins against her sides, the massive blows of sea and wind combined would capsize or swamp the open craft within minutes, if not seconds.

The four twenty-five-man inflatable life rafts strapped next to the boats are the ticket out.

Jack Jackson will be awake. He's on watch at eight but more than likely he hasn't slept at all. Earlier he vowed to get his Gumby suit ready for action, he even talked about personal emergency beacons, and his awareness of where the ship is heading must have made sleep difficult if not impossible. Larry Davis is not on watch till noon, but he, too, was on the bridge when it became clear where the ship was going, and might have lain awake afterward.

The most obvious place to hang out, for those worrying about the ship's course or even those who can't sleep for other reasons, would probably be the crew's mess, where they could go not just for coffee and a bite but also to talk with others and find some atavistic comfort, some sense of hearth and shelter from the elements, in a place that most of the time is alive with hot drinks, food, and conversation, even if right now you have to hang on to the metal tables to stay upright. At this hour they can always count on talking with Lonnie Jordan, Ted Quammie, or Lashawn Rivera, as the galley crew does its level best to fix some sort of breakfast; in these waves, it's a little like trying to serve food on horseback. Maybe one of them has the Gordon Lightfoot song "The Wreck of the *Edmund Fitzgerald*" running through his head, in particular the lines "When suppertime came, the old cook came on deck sayin' / Fellas, it's too rough to feed ya"; though given how that song ends, no one willingly entertains this earworm right now. Jordan has to make sure plenty of coffee is available anyway, and the makings of a DIY meal of cereal, toast, jam. He might just be able to fix scrambled eggs, but a western omelet? Not a chance.

Some of the older, more experienced crew—Carey Hatch, the oiler; Lightfoot, the bosun; Mariette Wright, the AB—might have been woken up early by what felt to them like an event against nature, the stilling of *El Faro*'s plant. Silent engines are for quiet harbors. A steamship without engines has switched from agency, direction, and power to helplessness and passivity. She will lie parallel to the swells, in a position of maximum vulnerability to their roll and crash, and that roll and crash, combined with the silent engines, stir unease. The crew might not phrase it that way, but they're aware in their gut of how unnatural, and perilous, such a state must be in a storm; it may be that they're waiting, at best for someone to tell them what's going on, at worst for the first call to muster.

Instead, those who are up likely sit around a table together, holding on to coffee and Pop-Tarts so they don't slide to the deck, just feeling the ship move and shudder as she drifts sideways now, side-slammed by the wind; listening hard for the slowly strengthening, trembling beat that would mean the engines have started up again; feeling for the change in motion as *El Faro* pulls out of her sideways drift and faces the storm again as a fighting ship. Maybe one or three of them have followed Jackson's example and staggered back to their cabins to fetch life vests and Gumby suits. Waiting for the rest of the day crew, the electrician, the Polish riding gang, to straggle in—or not, since it's more than likely the ship's increasingly violent and passive motion has caused seasickness, especially among the Poles, who are not professional seamen. Seasickness is usually good for a few not-unsympathetic cracks, anything to break the tension of waiting.

4

Seawater spritzing from the ventilation ducts makes footing more hazardous than usual in the engine room, but so far does not affect the ship's electronics; ample power is still being supplied by the two generators, which, though powered by steam, like the main engine, are independently lubricated. Presumably Shawn Thomas keeps an eye on the control console while the engineering officers gather around the three pressure points at which the situation could be rectified: first, the bilge pump, which is valiantly chugging but not making headway against water in the holds. Mathias, true to his can-do, cranberry-farmer background, is trying to figure out a way to rig a separate, air-powered pump that will suck out more water through a different access hatch.

The second pressure point would be the valves controlling flow from the lube-oil gravity tank. Under Chief Pusatere the engine room has gone through multiple troubleshooting drills, but it's highly unlikely anyone posited a background condition of fifteen degrees of list—a list that is now getting much worse. The low-frequency boom of storm waves resonates throughout the light-dark space between machines. Tension digs deep lines in the faces and eyes of the engineers, and more shadow collects there now.

Later, tests conducted by the Coast Guard will show that *El Faro*'s sump-oil level at departure—24.6 inches—when paired with an eighteen-degree list would cause the mouth of the oil-pump intake pipe to break entirely free of the oil's surface and suck dry. If the oil was at the lower operating range of seventeen inches, the pump would suck air when the ship listed fifteen degrees. What has probably been happening is that hard rolls inevitably worsened the list to over fifteen degrees, causing air sporadically to enter the system and choke off oil flow. Now as the list deepens, the oil intake pipe is continuously dry.

If the sump held the recommended level of oil, twenty-seven inches, the oil would most likely keep flowing, even at a list of eighteen degrees.

The third pressure point is the ten-ton reserve oil tank, whose outflow pipe is too narrow to refill the sump, but which can be used to prime the oil pumps and get rid of any air trapped inside prior to starting them again.

Pusatere calls the bridge, looking for a status update, and Davidson tells him, talk to the chief mate, who has been in the holds and seen the water rising firsthand. Pusatere tells Shultz the bilge alarm in 2A-hold, the next forward from 3-hold, has just gone off, indicating this hold is also filling with water. No one has time to speculate about it on the bridge, but logically there could only be two reasons for this: either the gates between the different holds are allowing water through, probably because of faulty seals or because they weren't closed properly; or else there's another leak somewhere else. One source, Pusatere thinks, might be the firefighting system, whose main intake pipe allows water into the hull for use in fire hoses.

"The cars that are floating in three-hold?" Davidson asks Shultz once he has hung up, on the bridge.

"There are cars," Shultz agrees. "They're subs."

Davidson laughs, then asks if any of them were near the main fire pipe.

"I saw cars bobbing around."

"Think they coulda come through there?"

"Yeah, there's a fire main in the aft end, water could have . . ."

Davidson calls the engine room again. "Can you isolate the fire main from down in the, uh, engine room? . . . 'Cause that may be the root cause of the water comin' in. . . . Isolate it from your side, so there's no free communication from the sea."

5

On the bridge nothing much has changed except that the storm now lashes the starboard windows harder and the deck is tilting even more the other way, to port, as *El Faro* drifts on, her great length now lined up with the vast and deepening troughs of Joaquin's rollers. Hamm, at the wheel, is trying to tweak the ship's heading. More spray must be getting into the wheelhouse: white noise from frying electronics fills the area. Davidson tells the chief mate to shut down some of the electricity panels so water won't short them out.

Shultz mentions possible difficulties with pumping more than one hold—if the ballast pump sucks air, he suggests, it, too, could wind up shutting down.

Suddenly Davidson's reserves of optimism are sucking as dry as the lube-oil pump. "Don't think it's gettin' any better," he says, of the list most likely; maybe of everything else that has gone so badly wrong.

Randolph has been doing the second mate's job: navigating, staring at the working radar screen, the GPS repeater. "We're drifting southwest," she tells the captain now.

Mathias calls from the engine room with a general question about how things are going ("It's lookin' pretty nasty," Davidson says); and a more specific query about the down-flooding angle, the angle of heel at which ventilation intakes on 2nd Deck, normally well above any conceivable wave action, will be underwater, at which point the engine room will start to flood. It's not just a technical question: if the engine room starts to flood, the ship will sink. It's more like Mathias is asking how long *El Faro* has to live.

"Um, that I don't have an answer for ya," the captain says.[*]

Mathias suggests digging out information in the chief engineer's office, which nobody has time to do right now; and even if they tried they would be unsuccessful, since Tote's sparse stability guidelines include no information about downflooding angles, or even where flooding might occur.[†]

Clearly the list is going from bad to worse, and the rate at which it's getting worse is speeding up. Although Davidson tells Mathias, "We still got reserve buoyancy and stability," the next thing he says is "All right, we're gonna ring the general alarm here and get everybody up. . . . We're definitely not in good shape here.

"Just make a round on two-deck and see what you can see," he tells Shultz. "This isn't gettin' any better." Then, ever solicitous of his crew: "You all right?"

"Yeah," Shultz says. "I'm not sure I wanna go on second deck. I'll open a door down there and look out . . . chest-deep water."

The chief mate fights his way down the stairs, which must now be tilting like a fun-house corridor. Davidson calls him up almost immediately on the walkie-talkie.

"Hey, chief mate. This is just a heads-up. I'm gonna ring the general alarm. Get ya muster while you're down there. Muster all, mate." Then Davidson rings the engine room with the same message: "We're not gonna abandon ship or anything just yet, all right? We're gonna stay with it.

"Yeah, all is fine," Davidson continues, with a flash of his old opti-

---

[*] Later analysis will conclude that downflooding will start at an angle of heel of twenty-seven degrees, possibly much less if one factors in the probability of leaks or other wastage in the vents, not to mention seas reaching twenty-five to thirty feet and higher.

[†] It transpires during hearings that the CargoMax program on *El Faro*'s computers includes an emergency stability-calculating function that might answer this question and others; but it also appears no one on board knows of its existence, let alone how to use it. In any case, given the near-impossibility of knowing for sure how much water *El Faro* has taken in, it's hard to see how useful the function could be at this stage.

mism, ". . . but let everybody know I'm gonna ring the general alarm."
Then he turns to the second mate and shouts, "Ring it!"

A high-frequency ringing erupts throughout the bridge—throughout
the ship. A familiar sound at noon, when it's always tested; the sound
of danger, fear, a damn serious situation at any other time, and especially when the ship is tilting in this way, so obviously sick, jerking like
someone hurt, while what can be seen and heard through portholes and
windows speaks of something insane outside, crazy dangerous, wind and
sea gone into a whole other state, sick with senseless fury. Adrenaline
surges, pulse spikes. The stomach, if not already upset by the ship's
rolling, cramps with tension. Anyone still asleep will be jackknifing
out of his or her bunk at this point, halfway ejected to port if his bunk
is to starboard, ears numb from the alarm, stumbling against the list
and foul movement, groping for the light switch, throwing on pants
and T-shirt, fumbling out the life jacket, survival suit. In the corridors
people are yelling. The first reflex of most mariners, after grabbing life
vest and Gumby, is to pound on their buddies' doors, make sure they're
up. The second is to get to the muster station: embarkation deck, which
is the engineers' level, two flights up from the mess, one from the crew's
quarters. Moving as fast as possible on a deck that feels like it's lusting
to become vertical bulkhead, a wall; hanging on to railings with one
hand, Gumby with the other, trying not to be knocked on your ass when
the ship rolls hard—it takes time to put on a survival suit, you have to
lay it flat on the deck and drag it on one leg at a time, like pulling on
farmer johns made of thick rubber, no easy task; might as well get to
muster station first and await orders?

Shultz is on the embarkation deck yelling at everybody to muster
on the starboard side. Muster station for half the crew is normally to
port, but that side is close to the water and the deck there is regularly
being cleared by waves.

Davidson's voice crackles from the chief mate's walkie-talkie. "Yeah,
what I'd like to make sure, everybody has their immersion suits and,
uh—get a good head count."

On the bridge a mid-frequency beeping sounds insistently; it will
never quit. Randolph is looking out a window; from somewhere there's
enough light to see the deck through the storm waves now washing the

containers or looming mountainous against the canted windows. "All right, I got containers in the water!" she yells.

"All right," Davidson yells back. "All right, let's go ahead and ring it—ring the 'abandon ship.'"

For the first time in her life the second mate does what no mariner ever wants to do: she smacks the brightly colored button that signifies the ship is lost. A shrill bell, different from the general alarm, starts to clang, seven times in a row, then another seven—and keeps on clanging.

"Tell 'em we're goin' in!" Davidson calls.

"Can I get my vest?" Randolph asks the captain.

"Yup," Davidson says. "Bring mine up, too, and one for Frank."

"I need two," Hamm says—is the big AB actually *joking* in this?

"Bow is down," the captain remarks; and *El Faro* begins to die.

6

Spare life jackets are usually stored in the bridge lockers. It's not clear if they are missing for some reason or if Davidson and Randolph, in the great tension of the moment, simply forget. What is clear is this: Second Mate Randolph, Captain Davidson, and Able Seaman Hamm, while the ship is being evacuated, don't waste a second doubting that their job is to stay on *El Faro*'s bridge till the rest of the crew has been taken care of.

Randolph edges fast down the companionway, pushing herself off the port wall of the staircase to stay somewhat level, to her cabin on the next deck. One deck below that, Shultz is likely counting off crew members as they wrestle their way out the door on the house's starboard side; a door the sailors have probably struggled to hook open against the brute shove of 120 mph wind and rashers of seawater slashing in, climbing their way now up an ever-more slanted and soaked deck, breath rasping in their throats, ears ringing with the storm's noise, which is mind-blowing, stunning in and of itself; it sounds like women screaming at the volume of a jet engine, howling high from the pain of torture, and maybe above that the high-pitched shrieking of the sadistic, ululating Furies who stretch the women on a wrack of storm.

Some of the crew, Jack Jackson for example, might already have their suits on, but for those who haven't had time to don them, dragging themselves up while carrying the heavy suits is increasingly difficult.

For the engine-room crew the task is that much harder. Before evacuating, the chief will push the "trip" button on the console that shuts off boiler fires, it's part of the discipline in an emergency. If an engineer can get that far, he'll try to turn a safety valve that dumps steam from the boilers as well, but the valve is not as easy to reach as the trip button and, as one ex-engineer on *El Faro* puts it, "Once you go to 'abandon ship' you're just trying to get out." Getting out involves negotiating metal decks that are canted and slick; water now is most likely starting to pour from vent outlets into the machinery spaces, making steam where it touches hot surfaces. With luck none of the steam pipes hanging from old and rusted brackets have been dislodged and burst by the ship's increasingly violent rolls; it's hard enough navigating catwalks that are halfway to horizontal, then two flights of steel steps to Main Deck (or up the escape stairway aft to 2nd Deck) and another three to the embarkation deck—up, and up, with your heart in your mouth, you do not want to be trapped below when this happens—and finally climbing out of the engineering spaces through the starboard door of the embarkation deck to the wacked-out howling of Joaquin. Mitch Kuflik, at least, can be glad of his youth and fitness as he negotiates what must feel more like an obstacle course than a ship.

Davidson's voice comes loud through Shultz's walkie-talkie. "All right, Chief Mate—Chief Mate."

"Go ahead, Captain," Shultz replies.

"Yeah, yeah"—Davidson is yelling—"get into your rafts! Throw all your rafts in the water."

"Throw the rafts into the water," Shultz yells back, "roger."

"Everybody get off, get off the ship," the captain calls. "Stay together."

The rafts are unstrapped. The starboard side of *El Faro*'s hull is probably not all the way horizontal yet but it's not far off, which means the decks cant not far off the vertical. Standard operating procedure is to lift the rafts over the rail, holding on to a lanyard that once tugged will both inflate the raft and keep it tied to the ship; which is fine for calm weather, or even rough weather, but this is not rough weather, this is madness. Some waves, towering near fifty feet high, explode foaming over the ship, it feels like you are being eaten by a monster and a raft is just not made for this, two people must work together to manhandle it over the railing and the railing is suddenly much higher and because of the list and surging foam the deck is near-impossible to find footing on.

El Faro is sinking lower in the water. The waves, even the average twenty-, thirty-footers, wash over the ship's length now; the port side has long gone underwater, and surf washes up toward the bridge on that side and even over the starboard side, where most of the crew now crowds. The waves start to overwhelm the decks, wash among the sailors, great walls of whipped water and death reach for them; maybe one of the rafts, rolled with some difficulty over the rail and having barely had enough time to inflate, is torn away from its tether and disappears behind one of those water mountains. Maybe people jump after it on their own, in Gumbies or not in Gumbies—or crowd around the next raft, this time waiting for the ship to sink lower so they can board directly as she goes down.

Many of the containers are certainly loose by now, crowding into their neighbors, breaking the lashings of other containers, ripping open their corrugated sides as they fall into each other, against the house, against the hull. The wind, blowing over 120 mph, takes these goods intended for Walmart, Walgreens, Juanito's Hardware Store, the people of Puerto Rico, as they spill into the tempest—cans of paint, pallets of detergent, chairs, toasters, rice, Jet Skis, ballpoints, deodorant sticks, swing sets, alternators—the wind blasts them into the water and, also, from those boxes that tumbled and busted open on the vessel's side, blasts them back against *El Faro* in a so-called piñata effect, which turns disposable razors, boxes of screwdrivers, and bottles of Karo syrup into shrapnel that will cut like a shiv into any human standing in the way.

The two rafts on *El Faro*'s lower, port side are underwater; their hydrostatic release inflates them automatically when submerged. They might get clear of the collapsing superstructure, might survive the piñata effect, but they are too far away for the crew to reach, assuming they can even see the rafts. You can swim in a Gumby suit but not fast, and unoccupied rafts, even with the water-filled baffles underneath that are meant to prevent this, will be snatched up by such a wind and pitched into oblivion.

El Faro is leaning ever farther; the surf on her upper side must be powerful enough to wash what's left of the crew off embarkation deck, and if that's the case they would try to simultaneously inflate, hang on to, and board the last raft as the wind tackles them off-balance and the breakers roar and surge now over them, maybe ripping some people away, or grabbing the raft or taking all of them who clutch the raft's tether and boarding lines. Hanging on to a raft in this hurricane feels like—no, it *is* like hanging on to a parachute deployed, more than likely the wind just takes this raft, too, and makes it fly—it is ripped from the hands of anyone hanging on as brutally and finally as if they were trying to hang on to a speeding train.

Those without Gumby suits will try to swim, and they will be buried, with merciful speed, as waves now the size of ships topple onto them and they cannot find their way out in the liquid dark, or even know which way is up when the blackness takes them.

Those who managed to pull a survival suit on will assume they'll float off and maybe survive, because in water this warm they can live for days. And if the suit has been fastened correctly, it should keep them on the surface. The trouble is, "surface" is the term for a clear interface between water and air, and no such interface exists here with combers between twenty and fifty feet rolling and collapsing on top of you. And even on the waves' summits, or in a brief calm between them, the mix of water and air whipped off by such winds is not something you can breathe; every time you draw breath you are taking in not oxygen but an emulsion of surf and wind, something that's half-Atlantic and half–Force 11 and all Joaquin; it will fill your lungs and drown you almost as quickly as if you sank five fathoms under.

Drowning slowly is no fun, at least at first. Saltwater drowning is different from dying in fresh water because the sea's water is hypertonic, meaning that for a given volume it contains more particulates and less water than the fluid inside lung cells, which means that water will be sucked out of the cells, through osmosis, to reestablish balance. This makes the blood thicker; thickened blood, being much harder to pump, overloads the circulatory system and causes cardiac arrest within eight minutes.

Drowning fast, when the person drowning cannot hold his or her breath any longer, means going from voluntary breath-holding, or apnea, to involuntary, otherwise known as lack of oxygen due to inhaling water.

In most people the process takes less than two minutes and is marked at first by panic and agony. The blood is so full of carbon dioxide that the brain doesn't work right and figures breathing water is no worse than holding your breath, whereupon the mouth gulps down water against the swimmer's will. In some people a phenomenon known as laryngospasm shuts down the windpipe, and the person passes out without ingesting any more water. In most, water floods the lungs. Blackness closes in, and the swimmer loses consciousness.

But the cliché of seeing one's life pass before one's eyes, apparently, is not so far-fetched. As the brain shuts down, it releases endorphins, allowing the illusion of a serene, out-of-body state. The survivor of a ship sunk in the late nineteenth century in a hurricane off Sri Lanka (then Ceylon) wrote this of the experience: "Gradually the pain seemed to ease up. I appeared to be in a pleasant dream. . . . Before losing consciousness, the pain had completely disappeared and the sensation was actually pleasant." * The writer, a Scottish doctor, floated to the surface while unconscious and lived to tell the tale.

7

El Faro is capsizing now.† Michael Davidson is still on the bridge, and so is the able seaman on duty, Frank Hamm. The deck is approaching vertical. The voyage data recorder is still running. It is time to let these men speak entirely for themselves:

HAMM: "Cap."
DAVIDSON: "What? . . . Come on, Frank. Gotta move. We gotta move. You gotta get up. You gotta snap out of it—and we gotta get out."

---

* Cited in *The Perfect Storm*, by Sebastian Junger.

† Later the Coast Guard will criticize Davidson for not using the satellite phone to send a final Mayday message, a measure his training would demand and that would be crucial for survival, at least in normal circumstances; but these are not "normal" circumstances, and common sense indicates that on a capsizing ship, where every muscle is straining merely to stay in one place, let alone move, it might have been impossible to reach the equipment. And it would have made no practical difference to *El Faro*'s crew.

HAMM: "Okay."

DAVIDSON: "Come up."

HAMM: "Okay. . . . Help me."

DAVIDSON (yelling): "You gotta get to safety, ya gotta get to safety, Frank!"

HAMM: "Cap. Captain!"

DAVIDSON: ". . . Ya all right?"

The sound of a loud electronic pulsing alarm starts up, repeating about two pulses per second. The pulsing alarm, along with the previous ringing, continues to the end of the recording.

HAMM: "Captain! . . . Help me."

DAVIDSON: "Frank? . . . Don't panic. Don't panic. Work your way up here."

HAMM: "I can't."

DAVIDSON: "Frank."

HAMM: "Help me!"

DAVIDSON: "You're okay. Come on. . . . Don't freeze up, Frank! Come on."

HAMM: "Cap! Are you—?"

DAVIDSON: "Where are the life preservers on the bridge? . . . Yeah! Go ahead and grab one . . . follow me."

HAMM: "I can't."

DAVIDSON: "Yes, you can."

HAMM: "My feet are slipping. . . . Goin' down!"

DAVIDSON: "You're not goin' down. Come on."

HAMM: "I need a ladder."

DAVIDSON: "We don't have a ladder, Frank."

HAMM: "A line!"

DAVIDSON: "I don't have a line, Frank."

HAMM: "You gonna leave me."

DAVIDSON: "I'm not leavin' you, let's go!"

HAMM (shouting): . . . "I need someone to . . . help me. You gonna help me?"

DAVIDSON: "I'm the only one here, Frank."

HAMM: "I can't. I can't! I'm gone."

DAVIDSON: "No, you're not."
HAMM: "Just help me."
DAVIDSON: "Frank! Let's go."

A low-frequency rumble builds until the end of the recording.

DAVIDSON: "Frank . . . it's time to come this way."

A yelling starts, and is cut off by the termination of the recording.

8

And so *El Faro* capsizes. She's lying almost entirely submerged on her port side. Her wheelhouse is underwater, though the starboard bridge wing probably pokes out of a trough now and again. The starboard running light, well insulated against the elements, still bravely shines its green into inferno. Most of her crew have been washed away, lacerated, crushed into the sea, drowned. Given the difficulty of climbing out of a ship that's on her side, or close, one or two people, particularly among the engineering staff, might not have made it to the embarkation deck doors in time and will either have drowned inside the house or are trapped in air pockets.

Water pours through all twenty-two vents, filling the engine room and cargo spaces at the rate of tens of thousands of gallons, hundreds of tons a minute. The waves have been pounding the containers, over and over, like hill-sized sledgehammers, and these blows, combined with the pull of gravity dragging the boxes sideways, and the pile-on effect from containers that busted loose before, have caused the ship's deck load to break free entirely. Now the boxes, cracked open or whole, are rolling in and out of troughs in the hull's lee like ice cubes in a cocktail shaker, crushing between their steel sides and macerated contents anything or anybody still floating on that side of the ship.

Paradoxically, with the weight of containers gone, the water that has filled most of *El Faro*'s holds, together with the weight of cars and trailers in her nether compartments, lowers the ship's center of gravity once more.

The waves are bigger than ever, regularly rolling over forty feet; the ship, though, rides with her starboard side at surface level, barely afloat, if you can call a temporary presence among this range of moving, wind-savaged mountains "afloat." The waves and wind have little to push against, and slowly, painfully, the great weight in her gut levers the ship upright, raising the right side of the house out of the sea. The water streaming off decks and companionways is immediately torn away by wind, though wind pressure, in a ghostly replay of the sailing effect that started the ship's earlier list, also works against the side, slows this righting.

Or it could be that the weight of water in the ship's holds, moving in the opposite direction on the buoyancy scale, reaches the sinking threshold while the vessel is still canted over so that she starts to drop sideways at first, slowly righting herself as she goes down until, ironically, she is riding the way she was designed to, bottom down, wheelhouse on top, but underwater now. The tumult of storm loosens its grip on the last man-made protuberances: a davit, a broken raft lanyard, a still-tethered lifeboat. Or, if the ship rights herself first, the mast on the wheelhouse roof and whatever else survives there stands against the wind for a few seconds, until the deep quiet and pressure of underwater envelops the entire ship, leaving nothing but the flotsam of *El Faro*'s broken world to be chewed and raged upon and gloated over by her assassin.

Calculations of sinking rates based on other shipwrecks, most notably that of RMS *Titanic*, indicate that a ship *El Faro*'s size going down on a relatively even keel would reach speeds, more perpendicular than vertical, of between 35 and 50 mph. She probably starts her long dive in reverse, down by the stern, since her deck cargo has gone and the weight of engines and ballast aft is pulling her that way: backing out of the living world, turning now in the opposite direction of her last, northwest heading, sinking three vertical feet for every horizontal foot, plunging southwestward into the caverns of the sea.

The exact depth underneath *El Faro* at her final surface position, forty-six nautical miles southeast of San Salvador, is 15,400 feet: 2.92 miles.

What little light Joaquin's thunderheads let through, filtered by ocean water, quickly dims to nothing as the ship goes down. At fifteen feet reds disappear; yellows are gone at forty-five feet, and greens at seventy-five. Although somewhere high above Joaquin's thunderheads the sun is rising, almost no light shines at the surface, and by the time the ship reaches two hundred feet she is in total darkness.

The pressure of water increases by one atmosphere, 14.7 pounds, every thirty-three feet. Air pockets inside the house, squeezed by rapidly increasing pressure, find chinks in accommodation spaces and companionways, and a thousand globules burble madly upward from every corner of the ship through the encroaching depths. Eventually, in fealty to the laws of physics, the pressurized gas jimmies open whatever panels or bulkheads kept it contained, and if someone is still alive in there he might be knocked unconscious by the blowout. If the bulkheads hold, he could breathe and survive for some time since the trapped air would be pressurized, as in a scuba tank, to the same number of atmospheres as the surrounding water. The deepest a human has ever dived without protection is just over a thousand feet, and so he might continue to breathe as his ship sank deeper and deeper, until the monstrous pressure, acting on the different densities of liquid and air inside his organs, tore them apart; but it won't happen that way.

It won't happen that way because El Faro's engine room contains two four-story-high boilers holding fireboxes of commensurate size that until a few minutes ago were generating steam at a pressure of 850 psi each, heated to 900°F, holding that steam hermetically sealed inside a jungle gym of pipes, valves, and machinery. Pusatere and his officers, once the "abandon ship" was sounded, killed the fires and probably tried to release the steam, but they'd only have had seconds to do so before the list got so bad that they couldn't operate anymore down there, and anyway they had to look to their own survival and get out, so the process could not have been completed.

The Atlantic water is warm. At almost 90°F its warmth is what allowed Joaquin to become the monster it has turned into; but in a process that's the opposite of its atmospheric equivalent, the deeper you go, the less sun can warm it, so the water chills down fast with depth. Anyway, even at ninety degrees it would be killingly cold by contrast with nine-hundred-degree steam pipes. Once water gets inside the insulation and feels up the metal of the boilers' shells, thermal stress created between the rapidly moving molecules in hot areas, versus the slower molecules in spaces touched by seawater, causes the steel to crack. It's as if some of the various forces that have both powered and affected *El Faro* so far—heated vapor, cooled water, imbalances in stress and temperature—have finally burst through the structures that, by separating them, allowed them usefully to turn, unifying and fusing their elements in one final, cataclysmic event. One boiler probably explodes first, as powerfully as a bomb, setting off the boiler beside it.

The exploding steam and blown water and chunks of boiler debris blast their way into the path of least resistance, the casing through which the engine's exhaust system vertically extends. The shock wave blows the smokestack clean off, along with everything else left on the wheelhouse roof, mast and radar scanner and GPS antennas. But it doesn't stop there, the blast is too big and needs more room; it explodes in the joins between structural members and deck plates and lifts the entire top two decks, the navigating officers' quarters and ship's office, as well as the wheelhouse and bridge wings; peels them all off as if they were a pop-top in the paws of Godzilla, tosses them aside, setting them on their own downward wobble to the bottom.

Any last pockets of air left in the accommodation are blown out like burst balloons, and if any crew members have survived in there, the shock wave would kill them at once.

The explosion is strong enough to send waves of sound bouncing through the Atlantic, echoing along thermal planes of water defining the SOFAR channel (for "sound fixing and ranging") between 1,200 and 3,900 feet deep, to be recorded as a series of thuds and screeches by hydrophone arrays the US Navy set up to listen for enemy subs.

At 40 mph, even if her vector is diagonal, it would take *El Faro* less than eight minutes to reach the ocean floor.

She hits bottom stern first, roughly a mile to the southwest of where she started to sink. Her rudder and prop assembly, the heel of her flat transom, drive deep into dozens of feet of silt composed of dead fish and amoebas, plankton and minerals, jellyfish and whale bone, seaweed and jetsam, broken ships, dead pirates; all accumulated there over centuries, over millennia.

The landing crumples the transom. As the rest of the ship slams into the bottom, the hull cracks in several places. The biggest crack opens at frame 200, just aft of the engine room, three feet wide at its broadest point, and runs up the hull's side and right across the Main Deck. In that area a boiler explosion might have had strong effect; or the crack could be due to the stresses of hitting the ocean floor. Channels running through bottom silt outward from the crack indicate a sudden outflow of water such as might be expected from impact.

But that crack, or the others, might also have existed before hitting bottom; started where the hull began to fail while *El Faro* was still alive and moving toward Puerto Rico, allowing the first ingress of water that ultimately killed her, a microscopic thread of entropy that extended as the hull pounded and twisted in the clutches of the hurricane.

A great cloud of silt explodes around the ship as she settles. The stern sinks deeper. The hull's forward part presses less deeply, fourteen feet into soft bottom. Bits of ship and cargo, sinking at slower rates, continue to patter down onto the surrounding seabed. The wheelhouse and navigating officers' deck land right side up eleven hundred yards to the north-northeast of the hull. The stack hits nine hundred yards away in the same direction; the mast—including the voyage data recorder, or black box, housed in a heavy-duty fiberglass cartridge fastened to one of the mast's supporting beams—six hundred and fifty yards off. All but two of the 391 containers have disappeared, most sunk, some floating off to go down later. The two remaining boxes rest askew on the forward half of Main Deck. A single trailer hangs like a broken tooth, three-quarters of the way out of the forward loading ramp on 2nd Deck.

Bunker seeps from the ship's ruptured fuel tanks, and gasoline from smashed Chevrolets and Hondas. Lube oil drifts upward from the shattered engine.

Usually, at almost three miles down, and except for the almost inaudible noise of deep-dwelling shrimp, it is deathly silent. Now there is noise: the last pockets of air in *El Faro*'s structure seep away with a slight hiss, metal creaks as the ship settles further; but after a few hours, a few days, the wreck of *El Faro* subsides into the ambient dark, the killing pressure, and all is silent again forever.

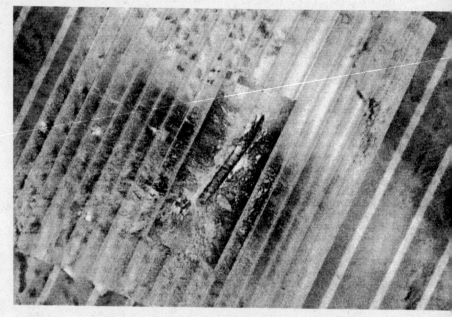

Resting place: The wreck of *El Faro* lies three miles down, almost intact, facing northeast, her last heading, in this composite image recorded by deep-sea sonar.

PART VII

AFTERMATH

You go on anyway, maybe because you know you have to go on, though you might not even remember why.

—Bernard Moitessier

1

Though the search-and-rescue duty officer who correlates *El Faro*'s position with that of Joaquin, connecting the dots of effect with those of probable cause, has a gut feeling the ship is in serious trouble, he and other Coast Guard officers following what is at that point merely an "incident," in the words of Coast Guard captain Jason Neubauer (who later will lead the investigation into the loss), have "a lot of denial" to overcome before accepting that a ship as large as *El Faro* can simply vanish like this.

Lawrence, the Tote safety officer, has told the Coast Guard that Tote has hired tugs through T&T Salvage to aid the stricken vessel, and at the time this seems a rational response. For a full day, Neubauer remembers, people speculate that the ship is alive but incommunicado, her antennas knocked off in the storm, making it impossible for her to respond to VHF calls, even from Hurricane Hunter aircraft flying high over her last known position.

There are issues with "last known position" though, among other problems that hinder search-and-rescue operations. The GMDSS message that Danielle Randolph programmed into the Inmarsat unit included the ship's GPS position. *El Faro* drifted after the second mate finished the programming, though only for a short while before she capsized. And given the scale of downflooding she probably sank between fifteen and forty-five minutes after that, so this difference cannot be great.

Coast Guard officers, however, don't know that. They must assume *El Faro* continues to drift, without power, blown probably to the southwest by the fury of a hurricane that still seems to have a mind of its own, still stalks the area where *El Faro* died.

The Coast Guard 7th District uses advanced models that pull in weather and ocean data and process them to calculate how far a vessel in trouble and lacking power might drift. But the overall search-and-rescue operations program (called, with the usual federal addiction to acronyms, SAROPS), which has just been updated, keeps crashing and proves largely ineffective. Luckily one of the officers on duty has experience figuring drift the traditional way, using tables that tell you how far a given strength of wind and waves will push a ship of a certain size and shape; wielding also, as Danielle Randolph did only hours ago, the charts, dividers, and parallel rulers of the traditional navigator's trade.

There's another glitch. Inmarsat distress messages format a ship's position—her latitude and longitude—in ambiguous fashion; the minutes and seconds of degree can be read as either minutes (sixty of them per degree) or decimals of a degree (one hundred per degree). If Randolph's position, which she wrote in minutes, is read in decimal format, a serious discrepancy will occur; and that's exactly what happens, the degrees being read as a digital percentage. As a result, all Coast Guard search-and-rescue operations use a last-known position (LKP, in federalese) that is over twenty nautical miles to the northeast of the actual latitude and longitude of *El Faro*'s sinking.

None of it will make any difference in the long run. No helicopters can fly search patterns inside the Category 4 hurricane that Joaquin is on October 2. One of the Jayhawks from Great Inagua does manage to fly in a direction away from the hurricane and, in the course of two genuinely heroic missions, pulls twelve seamen out of the water; it's the entire crew of *Minouche*, the 212-foot, Bolivia-registered, Haitian-crewed coaster that capsized and sank off Haiti during the evening of October 1.

A fishing boat also capsizes off Haiti's north coast between Petit-Trou-de-Nippes and Grand Boucan, but such boats rarely possess radios, and no one tries to rescue its crew. A Haitian fisherman in his thirties drowns.

Lack of nerve or effort is not one of the hindering factors in the Coast Guard's search for *El Faro*. The C-130 turboprop, tail number 1503, that performs the first close-quarters search into the storm on October 2 is a case in point. The pilot, Lieutenant-Commander Jeffery Hustace, is shocked by how powerful and defined are the different bands of wind and precipitation swirling around Joaquin's horizontal layer cake and tries to slalom through them from the north, without success. Islands that should show up on radar are masked by the bands of wind and rain. He decides on a different tactic, flying out of the hurricane and then back in from the south at near-barnstorming altitude, around two thousand feet over the LKP. It's the trickiest flying Hustace has ever performed; the C-130 is a big, slow, four-engine turboprop built for military use in all sorts of rough weather and terrains, but this one is bounced like a Ping-Pong ball, eight hundred feet up and down, by the extreme turbulence Joaquin generates; sometimes the huge plane free-falls to within a thousand feet of the surface. Flying so low, so dangerously, allows her crew to look up close and personal at the churned surface of the ocean. "They were giant rollers . . . fifty feet [high]," Hustace says later, "because of the wind, water was blowing off one wave to the next in solid sheets." The tortured foam, the somber chasms of waves reach greedily for the bucketing aircraft. Nothing else is visible. After seven and a half hours of white-knuckle flying the plane returns to base in Clearwater, Florida, where technicians find the turbulence has stripped out fasteners in one wing, causing fuel to leak. A second C-130 is dispatched to the area later in the day. It is not damaged but reports conditions so severe that all search operations are suspended for the rest of October 2.

On October 3 the Great Inagua Jayhawk that rescued the *Minouche* survivors flies north. The pilots, Lieutenants Joe Chevalier and Kevin Murphy, are charged with finding an EPIRB, possibly from *El Faro*, that is transmitting near Rum Cay. As they near the Cay the winds approach one hundred knots, and Chevalier has to tack into the storm, following radar to find gaps between lightning-cracked clouds and convective cells; gaps that the hurricane's circular rush often shuts down before they get there. Conditions are as bad as these pilots have ever seen. The normally clear-blue ocean, Chevalier says, has turned dark; near the islands the water has churned into a sick cloudy color. The white-scarfed rollers are so huge, the terrain-sensing system that under normal circumstances allows the chopper to hold automatically at a given height can't find a level, and Chevalier dares not fly lower than five hundred feet in case of downdrafts that could drop his aircraft into the drink like a shot of whiskey into a boilermaker. Homing in on the EPIRB's signal, they fly directly over its position, two miles southeast of Sandy Point on Rum Cay, looking for a survival suit or raft, but nothing is visible in the wrack below. Finally, low on fuel, they return to Great Inagua.

The EPIRB is never located.*

Later that same day, a Jayhawk finds an *El Faro* life ring. Early on October 4, with conditions improving in the area, choppers out of Clearwater and Great Inagua locate fields of debris and oil not far from *El Faro*'s last reported position.

On the morning of October 4, *El Faro*'s sister ship *El Yunque* is heading south from Jacksonville on her regularly scheduled route. If things had gone differently, if *El Faro* had taken the Old Bahama Channel, traded cargoes in San Juan, and headed north again, *El Yunque* would be looking to contact *El Faro* on VHF today as they crossed paths. Somewhat ironically, given what Davidson did not do, *El Yunque* has hugged the Florida coast to avoid the trailing edges of Joaquin, then jinked east through the Northwest Providence Channel. She's now closing in on a position that the ship's captain, Earl Loftfield, has figured out from wind and current data should be the most likely site of *El Faro*'s wreck. The sea is calmer now. "Normal working overtime for the deck gang [during the transit] will be as lookouts," her captain tells Tote headquarters. "NO PLANS for search pattern. However motor-lifeboat is ready for good fortune."

At ten thirty that day, not far from the LKP, *El Yunque*'s lookouts spot an "apparent point of origin for plume of oil rising and creating a slick. . . . At this position," Loftfield's transmission reads, "oil was black on the water and air smelled strongly of same. We found the slick after

---

* Later, Coast Guard investigators will determine that this signal did not come from the single beacon registered in *El Faro*'s name, and they'll suggest it came from the *Emerald Express*. However, a video shot by a crew member on the *Emerald Express* after the ship went aground shows her EPIRB still in place, unactivated. The *Minouche* was far too distant for her beacon to be washed to Rum Cay. It is possible that one of *El Faro*'s crew included a personal EPIRB in his or her preparations: in the voyage data recording, Jack Jackson refers to two men possessing EPIRBs, and it's possible he himself had bought a unit for kayaking near New Orleans.

traveling through a debris field for 25 miles, at times having as many as 50 simultaneous sightings."

At 4:35 p.m. on October 4, the crew of the Coast Guard Jayhawk that spotted a floating Gumby suit twenty-two nautical miles east of the ship's last position lowers a rescue swimmer into the swells; thrashing his way over, he finds the suit holds a lifeless body. After three nights and four days exposed to warm seawater and powerful winds, the corpse is so decomposed that the swimmer cannot even tell if it's a man or a woman. While he's checking the suit, the on-scene search coordinator, operating from the cutter *Northland*, relays a message from a Navy P-8 sub-hunting jet that has spotted another immersion suit, twenty minutes of chopper-flying time from this one. He asks the Jayhawk to investigate. The swimmer attaches a miniature transponder to the body and is wound up into the helicopter. The Jayhawk cannot locate another Gumby, only a piece of floating orange plastic, flopping back and forth in the swells in such a manner as to resemble a waving arm. The chopper goes back to retrieve the first Gumby, but cannot find it; the transponder, meanwhile, has gone silent.

The dead mariner in the survival suit, the only one of *El Faro*'s crew to be found, sinks to rejoin his, or her, shipmates.

On Tuesday the sixth, in San Juan, *El Yunque*'s crew assembles in the ship's mess. The captain summarizes what is said at the meeting: "Significance of what we have witnessed is acknowledged. The Pain. The Rage. The Knowing. The Work. Our safety through situational awareness and the stifling of afflictive emotions."*

A Coast Guard statement reads, "From October 4 to October 7 another 42 sorties were conducted. Debris confirmed to be from *El Faro* confirmed that the ship had sunk. No survivors or additional bodies were discovered."

At 0715 EST on October 7, 2015, after covering almost two hundred thousand square miles of ocean, the search for *El Faro* and her crew officially ends.

---

* The statement also includes a "cautionary mention of predators ashore wanting to exploit the grieving and the possibility of 'hearing the truth you've spoken twisted by knaves to make a trap for fools.'" The caution, and the Kipling quote, presumably are a reference to media coverage.

On the same day *El Yunque*, now heading back north to Florida, spots and recovers a second life ring marked EL FARO. In Jacksonville she unloads, and reloads, as her sister ship did only nine days before and, still dutifully hewing to schedule, heads for Puerto Rico again, this time bearing a bouquet of roses that the wives of the Polish riding gang have requested be dropped over *El Faro*'s grave. As *El Yunque* crosses the site she transmits this message back to Tote: "Crew gathered on the bow. Moonless night. Sea was flat. Eternity over the rail. With each of 33 strikes of the ship's bell a flower was dropped in the water. Our ritual is complete. The mark on our souls will endure—is supposed to endure—forever.

"Lightning began far in the distance two points [twenty-two degrees] to port and continued throughout the watch. A meteor burned bright, arcing towards the lightning. . . . We sailors see what we see and have our judgments about what's indicated."*

2

By the time the search for *El Faro* ends on October 7, Joaquin, having moved eastward under the influence of the continental high-pressure ridge, has skirted Bermuda, become embedded in a mid-latitude westerly airflow, and traveled northeast into colder waters off Newfoundland. These suck away its power, degrade it into a tropical storm.

Finally, on October 9, it subsides into a weak, "post-tropical" low. Now a mere swirl of rain and gale, it ambles past the Azores, swipes at Lisbon, then heads back out to sea. And there, finally, Joaquin dies—like

---

* On October 7, President Barack Obama issued a statement about *El Faro*'s loss. "The captain and crew of the *El Faro* were Americans and Poles, men and women, experienced mariners and young seamen," Obama said. "They were beloved sons and daughters and loving husbands and fathers. They were dedicated engineers, technicians, and a cook. And these thirty-three sailors were united by a bond that has linked our merchant mariners for more than two centuries—a love of the sea. As their ship battled the storm, they were no doubt working as they lived—together, as one crew," the president continued. "This tragedy also reminds us that most of the goods and products we rely on every day still move by sea. As Americans, our economic prosperity and quality of life depend upon men and women who serve aboard ships like the *El Faro*."

a mortally wounded animal seeking shelter in its home den—in the Atlantic waters off the Canary Islands where it first became a storm.

3

Tote's officers are conscientious and attentive to the families of *El Faro's* crew. They release a statement: "We have no doubt these are the darkest days of Tote's years as an organization and indeed the darkest days in the memory of most seafarers. A legacy of this painful event must be an understanding that serves all who go to sea."

The company flies family members to Jacksonville, arranges tribute ceremonies, helps sponsor a memorial under the Dames Point Bridge, within sight of the Blount Island dock: it's a stylized lighthouse of reddish metal engraved with the crew's names, flanked on one side by a series of thirty-three bollards (short metal stumps over which mooring lines are looped), each dedicated to a crew member. The company also funds monetary settlements for family members. But some of the families, dissatisfied with the sums, sue the corporation in court, claiming that the poor physical condition of *El Faro* proved negligence on Tote's part.

Tote files for protection under an 1851 maritime law limiting liability for shipowners; a federal judge, agreeing Tote is covered by the law, sets a $15 million cap on total liabilities. Tote eventually settles with all the crew members' families, for sums reportedly averaging $500,000.

In late October of 2015 the US Navy's oceangoing tug *Apache*, carrying a team of Coast Guard and National Transportation Safety Board experts, arrives at the area where *El Faro* disappeared. The experts drop hydrophones into the swells, listening for the locating beacon the voyage data recorder is supposed to transmit for a month after sinking, but the depths are silent. Then they lower into the sea and start to tow a yellow kite-shaped rig called Orion, housing a side-scan sonar—a mechanism that, "flying" at depth, sends out serial pings on both sides of its path that bounce off undersea targets back to receptors, which then plot a picture of the topography based on how long the pings took to return. At 1:36 p.m., during the fifth of a planned series of thirteen passes,

Orion picks up an object of *El Faro*'s size and shape sitting upright on the ocean floor three miles down. It is two miles from the position the SSAS system automatically plugged into its distress message—the message Danielle Randolph sent out twenty-seven minutes before the voyage data recorder went dead.

The team drops a subsea robot, or ROV (for "remotely operated vehicle")—this one bearing the awkward name of CURVE 21—in the wreck's vicinity. CURVE is an unmanned submersible that resembles a yellow generator the size of a compact car. It carries lights, video cameras, and mechanical arms. In *Apache*'s control room, a pilot stares at the video picture transmitted up a cable from the ROV and carefully tweaks a joystick to steer the sub's propellers. Hazed by silt and deep-sea organisms, the picture shows a great blue hull, and on the shattered transom the words EL FARO SAN JUAN PR.

CURVE 21 moves down the vessel's side, floats easily over the deck of what was once the engineers' cabins, for the two upper decks have disappeared. Deep-sea plankton snow across camera lenses. Virtually every square yard of *El Faro* has been cracked, broken, twisted, abraded by Joaquin's fury and the violence visited on the ship as she sank. Lines, lanyards, a pilot ladder, hang forlornly off the outer decks, presumably where the crew tried to keep the inflating rafts close enough to a surging hull that they could slide down the ropes with some hope of making it into a raft.

When the bridge and the navigating officers' deck are located to the northeast, surrounded by torn bulkheads from various cabins, CURVE's cameras peer into the windows, the open door of the navigating area; but the openings are black, light does not seem to penetrate—if you stare hard enough at the footage, though, you begin to suspect movement in that blackness, the mind plays tricks when you're aware that they are in there, not alive but people all the same, ghosts of the imagination who only a few weeks ago were moving, laughing, drinking coffee: Frank and Danielle, Larry and Captain Mike, Jack and Jeff, Jeremie and Joe, Lashawn and Jackie, Mitch and Dylan, Rich and Carey, all the rest . . .

With the single exception of the lost body in the survival suit, no physical traces of the crew are located at the wreck site or anywhere else, then or ever.

On two subsequent expeditions, in April and August of 2016, *Apache* locates the VDR, a cylinder painted bright yellow and half-buried in silt, still attached to a supporting beam of the bridge-top mast. CURVE's mechanical arms, working through clouds of silt, tug at the specially designed metal loops fastening the device and detach, lift, and place the cylinder inside the ROV's sample basket for the three-mile ride back to the surface.

4

The Coast Guard/NTSB hearings last a total of six weeks in 2016 and 2017. They are mind-bogglingly thorough, delving into aspects of *El Faro*'s "accident voyage" as arcane as the relative battery life of different data recorders, the design of Roloc boxes, and the academic backgrounds of boiler engineers. During those six weeks many dozens of expert witnesses are called. "Parties of interest" in the hearings include Tote, ABS, and Michael Davidson's widow, Theresa. Mrs. Davidson settles early with the company; her lawyer, William Bennett, while emphasizing Michael Davidson's competence in questions to witnesses during the Coast Guard/NTSB hearings, confers frequently with Tote's legal team and generally avoids asking hard questions of the company. During testimony, according to family members who attended all the hearings, Bennett seems to take Tote's side by casting doubt on a former captain's statement suggesting he was fired by Tote for reporting safety issues.

Coast Guard traveling inspectors attending a standard ABS audit of *El Yunque* in February 2016 find such severe corrosion in the Main Deck vents that they can poke holes in the metal with a hammer; continuing evidence, the inspectors believe, that such conditions were prevalent on her sister ship. The traveling inspectors are informed that they must report to the sector's commander, Captain Jeffrey L. Dixon, after the first day of the audit. The chief inspector accordingly fires up his cell phone and calls Dixon, who orders him to cease the inspection on grounds that he is exceeding the parameters of the ABS audit. In April 2017, Captain Dixon voluntarily retires from his command and from the Coast Guard. Two weeks later he joins Tote Services Inc. as vice president for marine operations.

The Coast Guard Marine Board of Investigation analyzes the recordings and evidence from the hearings and releases its findings on October 13, 2017. Principal blame for the tragedy is ascribed to the captain's faulty decision making, followed by Tote's poor maintenance of and support for a superannuated and badly flawed ship. Crew fatigue, weather-forecasting problems, and failures in inspection practices and the Alternate Compliance Program are also cited.

Although six of the first twelve conclusions drawn in the Coast Guard's final report directly implicate Tote in the most significant circumstances of the sinking, the Coast Guard—because of a lack of statutory authority, according to one officer—only files four enforcement findings, two of which have to do with relatively picayune reporting issues. The other two concern crew-fatigue violations and failure to include the Polish riding gang in lifeboat drills.

Following the hearings, Tote takes a number of remedial actions, which include changing emergency call centers, fitting its ships with a second EPIRB, and training officers in best use of the CargoMax program.

The National Transportation Safety Board's report, issued December 12, 2017, mostly replicates the Coast Guard's, except that it identifies the breach of firefighting pipes as a major contributing factor, which the Coast Guard does not. It also emphasizes the impact of poor bridge-resource management. Specifically, in the final hearing in Washington, DC, on December 12, 2017, NTSB's chairman—against the strong objections of the board's sole female member—amends the report to criticize *El Faro*'s junior officers for not doing more to convince their captain to alter course. Deficiencies in ABS inspectors' training and Tote's safety management plan are noted. The board also suggests that all US-flag vessels be required to carry fully enclosed lifeboats.

NTSB does not have the power to pass judgment, write rules, or mete out punishment.

Total penalties assessed on Tote and all affiliate companies, according to the Coast Guard's chief investigator, Captain Jason Neubauer, cannot exceed $80,000.

5

Glen Jackson, a retired fisheries and wildlife officer for the state of Louisiana, still lives in New Orleans, although the sights and sounds of the city where he and Jack once roamed on a Norton motorbike seem bittersweet to him now. He spends most of his waking hours diligently researching every aspect of *El Faro*'s loss—speaking to investigators, other family members, various maritime experts—in order fully to understand what happened to his brother. While careful not to jump to conclusions, he notes that the Coast Guard's report following *El Faro*'s loss includes many of the same recommendations made, but not implemented, after the loss of the *Marine Electric* in 1983, in particular, an overhaul of the marine inspection program. The shipping industry, he believes, killed the impetus for reform. "Money talks," he comments wryly, "what can I say?"

Kurt Bruer still ships out, though not on Tote vessels. He is doing relief work—one-off jobs on different ships, the requirements of which show up at the modern, heavily air-conditioned SIU hall in Jacksonville, on the electronic job board hung a few dozen yards from one of the three *El Faro* life rings recovered after the ship went down. Working relief allows him to spend extra time with his wife and son, and if he had the choice, Bruer says firmly, he'd stay ashore and never again go to sea, where the memories of Larry Davis and the rest of what he calls his *El Faro* family inevitably await him. "But I couldn't make this kind of money if I worked shoreside," he says. "I couldn't make the mortgage on my house. Money is the only thing keeping me going to sea."

Piotr Krause's wife, Anna, found it too hard emotionally to stay in the Gdynia apartment she and her husband bought together when they first married. She now lives just outside the seaport, which she says she still loves. The gray horizon of the Baltic Sea is visible from her bedroom window. Sometimes, when she has a hard decision to make, she goes for a walk on the nearby beach and tries to imagine what Piotr would advise her to do. At night as their son Viktor, now three years old, sleeps peacefully in the next room, she writes, "Behind the windows is a strong wind, which will always give me anxiety. The wind always brings me back to that place in the dark, empty ocean, to my husband."

But outside her bedroom window ships continue to unload and load, even as the wind howls louder. Their green, red, white navigation lights pass slowly between the city's residential towers and disappear into the night, into the darkness of the Baltic, the Atlantic to the west. Almost all these ships are newer than *El Faro*, and tonight no major storm is forecast. Many of the ships will be tracked by state-of-the-art systems and routed by home office via the safest course to destination. Some of them, perhaps, will have better equipment and hew to more stringent operating regulations thanks to lessons learned from *El Faro*'s loss. But their crews know that, inevitably and despite all the technology, one day conditions will worsen, trouble will come that they cannot be routed out of, parts of their equipment, no matter how modern and "foolproof," will fail, and then some other equipment will go and they will be confronted by the terrifying power of the sea to sweep man's strongest and finest works to oblivion. And when that day comes they will have to draw on their reserves of skill and courage, as the men and women of *El Faro* did, as everyone who goes to sea someday must, and hope it will be enough to see them through.

AFTERWORD

In autumn of 2018, a little over three years after *El Faro* sank, I meet with Jeff Mathias's wife, Jenn, in the Blueberry Muffin, a coffee shop located in a strip mall in Kingston, Massachusetts.

It's a fine day in New England's harvest season, and down the road, toward Plymouth, a hard sun hones the pinkish shine of cranberries floating on the bogs, deepening by contrast the reds and oranges of surrounding maples.

Almost three years ago I began researching a book on the sinking of the SS *El Faro*, and the start of my research took place here, at the Blueberry Muffin, talking to Jenn Mathias; and now, as then, I have to ask her questions to which there can be no adequate response, such as how is she doing, and how are her kids, and Jeff's parents; how are they all coping, three years on, with the loss of their husband, father, son, who was chief engineer in charge of conversion work on a giant ship that should never have sunk, in a hurricane that for a long time wasn't even supposed to happen?

Jenn is an attractive former schoolteacher in her early forties, with light brown hair cut in bangs, and hazel eyes; she wears Jeff's wedding ring on a thin chain around her neck and speaks calmly, as she eats an omelet, on subjects that would make most people want to roll around the floor and wail.

"You get up in the morning, you put on your clothes, you smile, you laugh," she says, "you have kids to raise. But inside you're a mess."

And yet, in early 2017, just sixteen months after the accident, Jenn took her children to sea, on a cruise liner. "Jeff never wanted to go on a cruise; he said, 'I do this for a living.' But," Jenn continues, "I don't want my children to live in fear of the ocean, or of ships." The children enjoyed the trip.

Jenn and her three children—Hayden, age ten, Heidi, eight, and Caleb, six—attend regular family-counseling sessions. And Jenn is part of another group of people who have lost spouses or partners, all of whom understand that, as Jenn puts it, "It sucks, it really sucks. Some people, unless you live with it, don't get it—but the group gets what it's like not to have a partner."

Every year on July 24 she and her kids drive to Jeff's favorite place, a cottage his grandfather built in Myles Standish State Forest, in Plymouth. There they eat lemon cake, which was Jeff's favorite dessert, to celebrate his birthday.

A few weeks before our meeting, on October 1, 2018, the third anniversary of *El Faro*'s loss, Jenn and her family flew to Florida for a commemorative brunch at the headquarters of Jeff's union, the American Maritime Officers (AMO). They also attended the ceremonies taking place at Dames Point, in Jacksonville, where Tote Inc., the company that owned *El Faro*, had erected a miniature copper-colored lighthouse in honor of the sunken ship, whose name means "lighthouse" in Spanish. Tote also paid for thirty-three full-size mooring bollards at Dames Point, one for each of the crew, opposite the secure port area where *El Faro* used to dock every two weeks to take on cargo for Puerto Rico.

Laurie Bobillot, the mother of *El Faro*'s second mate, Danielle Randolph, did not attend either ceremony. "The anniversary was tough," she tells me over the phone from her home in Denmark, Wisconsin. "It doesn't feel like three years, it feels just as raw to me today; and it gets harder and harder day by day, as time goes by. I mean," she continues, "how many times do I reach for the phone to call Danielle and then say, 'Oh, wait a minute, I can't'—or, 'I've got to ask Danielle where she put—oh, shit.' . . . There are good days and bad days. I try to keep my composure."

Kurt Bruer, who lives in Jacksonville, attended the Dames Point ceremony, which this year was organized by the Coast Guard chaplain and featured an address from Pastor Robert Green, the stepfather of *El Faro*'s cook, Lashawn Rivera. Each of the thirty-three bollards holds a plaque with the name of one of the crew inscribed, and Kurt bought a bouquet of flowers to lay on Danielle's bollard, as well as one for his friend Larry Davis, who was an able seaman on *El Faro*.

But Kurt, who was traumatized by the loss of Larry and Jackie "Pop" Jones (another AB), and the rest of his former shipmates on *El Faro*, has had more trouble coping with the loss than some other members of what they call "the *El Faro* family." After volunteering advice to the National Transportation Safety Board and the US Coast Guard on improving working conditions at sea, he resumed shipping out, this time on ships owned by Crowley Maritime. While working as AB on a Crowley tanker, the *Lone Star State*, two years after *El Faro*'s sinking, he got into a heated argument with another mariner, who pulled a knife and stabbed Kurt multiple times in the abdomen. Once medevaced, once ashore, once on the mend and embroiled in a lawsuit over the stabbing, Kurt fell into a deepening spiral of depression, debt, and worst of all, separation from his wife and from Christian, his four-year-old son. He lost his house and, because of the ongoing divorce, only saw his child six times last year. "The shrink says I have PTSD, from survivor's guilt. I miss my boy," he continues, folding that into his other losses, "I miss my buddies, Larry, Pop, the other guys."

Pastor Green, for his part, helped mark Lashawn's loss by lobbying Jacksonville city hall to have October 1 officially commemorated in Jacksonville. This year the city's leaders acceded to his requests, proclaiming October 1, 2018, "*El Faro* 33 Memorial Day" in the ship's home port.

Possibly the most substantive commemorative effort came from Rochelle Hamm, the wife of Frank Hamm, who, together with Captain Davidson, was the last crew member standing watch on *El Faro*'s bridge as the ship, battered by massive waves and winds approaching 150 mph, capsized and sank. Rochelle was outraged by the fact that *El Faro*'s officers had not been prevented from, or even cautioned about, leaving port with a storm looming. She got in touch with the office of Florida's US senator Bill Nelson and with his help began lobbying for what she called the Hamm Act, which she originally hoped might achieve the kind of stringent oversight that would prevent any American ship from sailing in harm's way ever again.

The original idea foundered in a web of complexities surrounding who might hold power to prevent a ship's captain or owner from making independent decisions about a vessel's safety. Still, a version of Rochelle's initiative was sheepdogged through the Senate by Nelson, and through the House by Representative Duncan Hunter of California, then chairman of the subcommittee in charge of maritime affairs, and later, when Hunter was stripped of his chairmanship for misuse of campaign funds, by other members of that committee.

After passing the House, and after modification and eventual passage in the Senate, the Hamm Alert Act—now cosponsored by Alaska senator Dan Sullivan, and tucked deep inside another piece of legislation called the Save Our Seas Act of 2018, aimed at "amending the Marine Debris Act to promote international action to reduce marine debris, and other purposes"—was signed into law by President Donald Trump on October 18, 2018.

At the signing ceremony for the Save Our Seas Act, Trump wanted to talk about celebrities. "And we're having lunch with Jim Brown, one of the great football players of all time and a great guy, and Kanye West. He's coming in—they're coming in for lunch. And after that, we're doing some additional interesting things." The president also fielded questions about Hurricane Michael, which was rampaging through the Southeast at the time. ("It was the fastest hurricane anybody has seen. It just was speedy.") And after that, Trump wanted to talk about marine debris:

"Every year, over eight million tons of garbage is dumped into our beautiful oceans by many countries of the world. That includes China, that includes Japan, and that includes many, many countries. . . . And we're charged with removing it, which is a very unfair situation. It comes from other countries very far away. . . . It's a very unfair situation.

"As president," he went on, "I will continue to do everything I can to stop other nations from making our oceans into their landfills. That's why I'm pleased—very pleased, I must say—to put my signature on this important legislation."

Trump did not mention any part of the Hamm Alert Act, which Rochelle had worked so hard for. Most likely, given his much-documented management style, he had no idea it was included, in the middle of the overall Save Our Seas bill, under Title II, Sections 201 through 219.

One might assume that, had the president known about it, and taking into account his penchant for suppressing regulation of private enterprise—given his general deregulatory directive number 13771, and the May 2018 "Request for Information" (RFI) that called for lessening, not increasing, regulation of the merchant marine—Trump might have balked at signing it.

Or maybe not.

Because Title II of the Save Our Seas Act—which "may be cited," trumpets the boilerplate, "[as] The Hamm Alert Maritime Safety Act of 2018"—does not do very much.

The part (Section 217) that most directly and concretely addresses Rochelle Hamm's concerns establishes, as a pilot program, an 800-number tip line on which any mariner can anonymously report a dangerous situation affecting his or her ship. Also, Section 208 requires that shipowners provide some form of emergency beacon (or EPIRB) for every person on board; a rule that, even if enacted before the sinking, would not have done much to help *El Faro*'s crew, but could be useful in less dire predicaments.

The Hamm Alert Act also provides for increased safety training for Coast Guard section commanders, more training for USCG personnel on steam engine inspections, and advanced training on oversight of non–Coast Guard inspection societies such as the American Bureau of Shipping (ABS). Additionally, a Coast Guard office specializing in such oversight is to be set up by December 2020, and an audit of non–Coast Guard inspection groups was to be completed within 180 days of the act's passage.

The rest of the act specifically avoids concrete action and calls instead for examination of, or negotiations concerning, possible steps to take. For example, the Coast Guard is called upon to provide a briefing on a review of four issues that had a direct bearing on *El Faro*'s loss, among them the policy regarding major conversions, which in 2006, due to Tote's lobbying, resulted in the ship's conversion to carry containers being labeled a "minor" change, thus allowing Tote to forgo the expense of replacing her antiquated lifeboats. The other issues are: safety aspects of vents and hull openings and fire dampers, stability standards, and "lifesaving equipment, including survival suits and life jackets."

Altogether, the Hamm Alert Maritime Safety Act of 2018 uses terminology for talk, as opposed to action—specifically, the words *briefing*, *report*, *negotiation*, *audit*, *review*, and *assessment*—fifty-four times. In a text running 321 lines, that comes out to roughly once every six lines.

None of the concrete actions that might prevent recurrence of an *El Faro*-type tragedy are to be found in the bill. These would include installing modern, fully enclosed, chute-launched lifeboats; requiring clear and accessible manuals on cargo lashing, and on engine maintenance and lubrication, in heavy weather; mandating immediate inspection of, and if necessary repair of, all vents and fire dampers on American ships; instituting a clear and risk-free mechanism for querying dangerous decisions taken by a superior at sea, as well as a way to immediately register disagreement without fear of consequences; and requiring that all navigational equipment, including weather instruments, be functional before leaving harbor. Of the list just cited, only two, regarding vents and fire dampers and satellite weather systems, are mentioned at all, let alone acted upon.

A solid effort to resolve *El Faro*-type issues would also require vastly upgrading, or scrapping altogether, the Alternate Compliance Program (ACP), a program, lobbied for by American shipowners, under which non–Coast Guard societies, such as the American Bureau of Shipping, inspected older US ships according to more lenient standards. The ABS notoriously passed *El Faro* before she sank, despite a number of defects—some of which, the Coast Guard found, contributed to her loss.

Whether campaign contributions from Tote's parent company, Saltchuk, to all four chairpersons and ranking members of the Senate and House subcommittees dealing with merchant marine affairs played a part in the relatively toothless nature of the Hamm Alert Act must remain a matter for speculation.

Still, even if it has nothing to do with immediate actions, or even plans, some powerful language distinguishes the Hamm Alert section of the Save Our Seas Act. It reiterates what everyone associated with the *El Faro* tragedy has already learned the hard way:

"Safety issues are not limited to the *El Faro*," the preamble reads. "For 2017, over 21,000 deficiencies were issued to United States commercial vessels and more than 2,500 U.S. vessels were issued 'no-sail' requirements.

"The maritime industry, particularly the men and women of the United States merchant marine, play a vital and important role to [*sic*] the national security and economy of our country, and a strong safety regime is necessary to ensure the vitality of the industry and the protection of current and future mariners, and to honor lost mariners."

Several members of the *El Faro* family, who did not want to be named either because they are still sailing and fear being blackballed by shipowners, or because they're bound by a gag order associated with a Tote settlement, expressed dissatisfaction with the act. "A Band-Aid," one said. "It's because of the freakin' [shipowners'] money." "They need to get rid of the ACP. They've screwed up so many times." "Legislatively," a third said, "I expected nothing, so anything that survives the final wording is a plus. However, the main issue of enclosed lifeboats is not addressed. I am more angry now than I was a year ago."

Robert Frump, the Pulitzer Prize–winning reporter who investigated the last great US merchant marine tragedy before *El Faro*, the sinking of the *Marine Electric* in 1983—a loss that had several key points in common with *El Faro*'s—is more sanguine.

"I think the outcome depends on the funding," he says. "If they fund and follow up, this truly could be major. Tactically, it [would] have a real impact because the travelers [the Coast Guard traveling inspectors, who carry out the non-ACP inspections] have a free hand and can crack down. And they are inclined to crack down hard not just on the Jones Act fleet but the military sealift fleet as well, which is ABS-driven for the most part. . . . If they do fund a tripling of the travelers, that will help ABS fly straight. . . . Will it happen? I'm hopeful. But there is of course always the bright new shiny thing that may attract Coast Guard budgets."

Frump points out that, even after *El Faro*'s loss, ABS gave a pass to *El Yunque* although she was plagued by a number of the same problems as her sister ship *El Faro*. At the same time, a total of thirteen older American ships were scrapped as a result of concerns arising from the *El Faro* disaster.

And yet. The SS *Matsonia*, an older sister ship of *El Faro* and *El Yunque*'s, still plies a regular route between Oakland, California, and Honolulu; at the time this edition went to press in late February 2019, she had just docked in Oakland, according to the satellite vessel tracker www.vesselfinder.com. Photographs taken on that date show *Matsonia* still carries open lifeboats, apparently identical to *El Faro*'s, snugged into davits like her sister ships', on the port and starboard sides of the accommodation decks.

Soon after docking, according to the Coast Guard, on February 21, 2019, crew members noticed a fuel-oil sheen spreading from the ship's starboard side; divers subsequently found the ship's hull had cracked on that side, fifteen feet below the waterline, just forward of the fuel tanks. *Matsonia*, like *El Faro*, was lengthened from her original 700 feet; if the process happened at the same place as on *El Faro*, the fracture might well have occurred at or near the point the hull was cut to permit the lengthening.

Whatever effect policy might have on the shipping trade, it can only do so much to palliate the pain of the survivors, who continue to live their lives, protect their families, and honor the memory of *El Faro*'s crew with, in every case I have come across, a courage and grace that leave this writer awed, and humbled, and turning often for inspiration to their stories, such as this one from Able Seaman Jack Jackson's brother Glen:

"My family, being military, moved to New Orleans when my father got orders for Vietnam—in front of the house we lived in was a mature elm tree. My brother and I . . . when a summer storm was approaching, we would climb into the upper reaches of that tree and feel the limbs sway, not unlike being up in the rigging of a sailing ship, and laugh and holler in the pure exhilaration of being witness to Nature's power. I am constantly waiting for him to call me on Tuesday to check in and for me to remind him to buy a Powerball ticket so he could stop going to sea—should he want to. Maybe, as the old saying goes, no one is dead as long as someone remembers them. I hope, for all of us, that is a true statement."

ACKNOWLEDGMENTS

I was immeasurably helped in the preparation of this book by *El Faro*'s extended family, both immediate relatives and close friends and shipmates. Except for those who requested anonymity, their many names are cited in these pages; but I would particularly like to mention Laurie Randolph Bobillot, Glen Jackson, Eddie Pittman, Pastor Robert Green, Jenn Mathias, Frank and Lillian Pusatere, Evan Bradley, and Kurt Bruer. The generous and courageous help of *El Faro*'s family made it possible to put together an accurate picture of the last voyage of the ship and her crew, and in doing so provide a testimonial to the skills, bravery, and integrity of the men and women who sailed on *El Faro*. I would also like to thank Dr. James Delgado, Farley Chase, Chief Robert Young, Alana Miller, Joel Lorquet of the US embassy in Haiti, Professor Rob O'Leary, Rodney Dickson, Virginia Warner, Sarah Goldberg, Dan Cuddy, Kyle Kabel, and Wing Pepper. I have used the assistance and information these people so generously provided to draw as exact and balanced a portrait of *El Faro*'s loss as possible; any mistakes that slipped through are mine and mine alone.

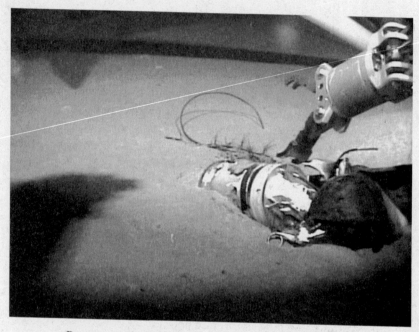

Deep rescue: The CURVE 21 submersible managed to retrieve the ship's voyage data recorder from the wreckage field, fifteen thousand feet under the surface of the Atlantic, in August 2016. NTSB engineers spent eleven hundred hours retrieving the audio.

NOTE ON SOURCES

Many months' worth of hearings, separate interviews, and working-group investigations took place during 2016 and 2017, conducted by the Coast Guard and National Transportation Safety Board; these resulted in thousands of pages of evidence, testimony from scores of expert witnesses, graphs, photos, and charts, together with more than five hundred pages of transcribed VDR recordings, all of which can be consulted online. Together they provide the most complete factual background possible of the *El Faro* tragedy.

I also interviewed dozens of former *El Faro* mariners and family members of those who died aboard, some of whose names are mentioned in the book's pages, or the acknowledgments. Many others helped anonymously.

In addition, research in meteorology was greatly assisted by Dr. Jeff Masters, of Weather Underground; in engineering by Captain Brad Lima, of the Massachusetts Maritime Academy; in navigation and ship-handling by Captain John Nicoll; in the background of Coast Guard investigations by Captain Jason Neubauer; in details of the Jacksonville hearings by Tricia Booker, Bob Snell, Anne Schindler of FirstCoast News, and Sebastian Kitchen of the *Florida Times-Union*. Other, less personable sources include the various volumes of Nathaniel Bowditch's *American Practical Navigator*; the official Navy *Watch Officer's Guide*, by Admiral James Stavridis and Captain Robert Girrier; *Introduction to Marine Engineering*, by D. A. Taylor; *Cargo Work for Maritime Operations*, by D. J. House; and *Business Notes for Shipmasters*, by John F. Kemp and Peter Young.

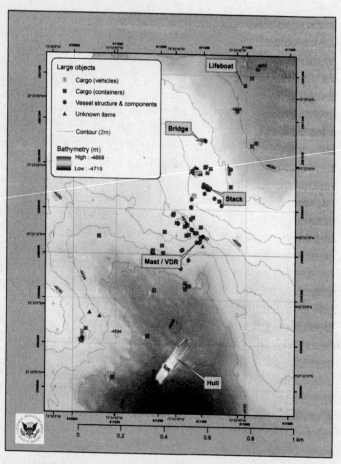

Wreckage field: Probably blown off by the explosion of *El Faro's* boilers, the two upper decks of the house lie eleven hundred yards from the hull, while the mast and VDR lie six hundred and fifty yards away, both along the line of the ship's final descent.

INDEX

ABOUT THE AUTHOR

George Michelsen Foy is the author of *Finding North: How Navigation Makes Us Human* and *Zero Decibels: The Quest for Absolute Silence*, and several critically acclaimed novels. He was a recipient of a National Endowment for the Arts fellowship in fiction, and his articles, reviews, and stories have been published by *Rolling Stone*, the *Boston Globe*, *Harper's*, the *New York Times*, and *Men's Journal*, among others. A former commercial fisherman, and a watch-keeping officer on British tramp coasters, he holds a 100-ton captain's license from the US Coast Guard. Foy teaches creative writing at New York University, and with his family divides his time between coastal Massachusetts and New York.